Life Journeys toward Wholeness:

Wellness, Transformation, Spiritual Maturity

HAKYUNG CHO-KIM PH.D.

All Scripture quotations not otherwise identified are from the New Revised Standard Version Bible Copyright © 1989, Division of Christian Education of the National Council of the Churches of Christ in the United States of America. Used by permission.

Scripture quotations designated as THE MESSAGE are from The Message, copyright © 2002, Eugene H. Peterson. Used by permission of NavPress Publishing Group.

Library Congress Cataloging-in-Publication Data
Hakyung Cho-Kim,
Life Journeys toward Wholeness: Wellness, Transformation, Spiritual Journey

ISBN –13:978-0692246771
ISBN –10:0692246770

1. Christian living. 2. Wholeness. 3. Wellness (Healing).
4. Transformation. 5. Spiritual Growth. 5. Discipleship/Church

DEDICATION

To
Judith R. Brideau,
My Soul Friend

For
The life-giving love
Of
Donating her kidney

BOOKS WRITTEN BY HAKYUNG CHO-KIM:

The Way of Life (in Korean only)

A Family System's Approach to the Small Membership Church

The Spiritual Gifts (in both Korean and English)

Christian Mentoring in Triads as a Model for Making Disciples
(In both Korean and English)

God of Active Verbs, A to Z (Available from the Amazon.com/books)

ACKNOWLEDGEMENTS

To

M. Robert Mulholland Jr. who challenged me with spiritual formation;

Andrew Purves who taught me the Christian meaning of compassion;

Jim Fleming who challenged me with his deep knowledge of the Bible;

Don Richard Riso who mentored me with the wisdom of Enneagram;

E. Gene Rooney who inspired me with values of metaphors and parables;

My family and fellow sojourners in my life journey toward wholeness;

God's nurturing communities, which I served

And

Karen Davies for her creative editorial works for this book.

CONTENTS

INTRODUCTION

WHY I WROTE THIS BOOK

I have been in leadership positions in the Mainline Protestant Church for the past 35 years as a lay leader and an ordained clergy. As an ordained minister I have served as the pastor of six local congregations and the Conference staff for three regional judicatories (Pennsylvania, Indiana, and New England) of The United Methodist Church. Now I am retired from the 25-years of active ministry.

I have observed powerlessly the human pains and sufferings from the brokenness or fragmentation in human beings, the dysfunctions in families, churches, and work places, as well as the government. Many of us are suffering from natural disasters, poverty, terminal illness, psychosomatic syndromes, post-traumatic disorders, sex, drug and chemical addictions, inner conflicts, severe neurosis, personality disorders, break-up of families, dividing spirit within the church, and our apathy and indifference toward the poor and the orphans of the society. And there are many tensions between different regions in the globe as well as the threats of nuclear and biological warfare.

I heard that Mahatma Gandhi explained why he did not become a Christian by saying: "I love your Christ, but I don't like Christians." I know many other seekers have been turned away from becoming Christians because they see Christian hypocrisy and in-congruency. From the Christians they expect to see forgiveness, acceptance, and *agape* love in the church and our living out the Christ-like presence in the loveless and unjust world.

We Christians are criticized for our divisive, self-righteous, and exclusive attitudes in the Church and our work places. How can we witness the good news that God can save human beings from our bondage, heal our brokenness and diseases, free us from our false selves, and bring life out of our deadness, when we have lost our identity as the salt of the earth and the light of the world? Why are we not relevant Christians by demonstrating the liberation and freedom in Jesus Christ? Why are we living as though Christ has never risen from death? Why are we not *on the spiritual journey* toward wholeness: wellness, transformation, and spiritual maturity? Against this background a few critical voices have continued to emphasize that the main cause of our distressed conditions, individual and social—is lack of Christian discipleship (It means following Jesus Christ as the Lord and Savior).

George Barna, a Christian social researcher, laments about the sad state of the church in general. He said, "Most non-Christians don't read the Bible, so they judge Christianity by the lives of the Christians they see [and read about]. The problem is that millions of Christians don't live like Christians—and that's partially because they don't know what they believe and therefore cannot apply appropriate scriptural values [principles] to their lives." (Barna, *Barna Addresses Four Top Ministry Issues of Church Leader,* Barna Research Online, www.barna.org, September 25, 2000)

Carl Thomas, a Christian syndicated columnist and social commentator, calls Christians to look at the quality of our discipleship instead of directing our indignation to the moral decay of the post-modern world. Barna quotes Thomas: "The problem in our culture…isn't the abortionists. It isn't the pornographers or drug dealers or criminals. It is the undisciplined, undiscipled, disobedient, biblically ignorant church of Jesus Christ." (Barna, *Growing True Disciples,* 62)

14

In addition to the above constructive voices, the following examples below (illustrations 1 to 4), made me quest for answers to "Why some Christians are not living spiritually as the "disciples" of Christ?" "Why some Christians behave like "immature" children?" "What are the factors that stop us from growing toward spiritual maturity?" "Why are we not transformed so that we may be conformed to the image of Christ?" "What is the Church for?" The quest for answers ultimately led me to write this book, *Life's Journey toward Wholeness: Wellness, Transformation, and Spiritual Maturity.*

ILLUSTRATION 1

On a Sunday morning, I preached a sermon on "Why do people come to this church?" when I was serving a 'declining church' in Pennsylvania. I thought it was a hopeful, spirit-filled worship. As I was greeting at the door after the service, I shook the hand of an old member of the church. And I asked him with a smile, "Did you get anything out of the sermon?" He answered, "Nope." I protested, "Why not?" He answered, "Because I turned off my hearing-aids during the service."

ILLUSTRATION 2

Another occasion, I preached on "the Parable of a Good Samaritan," at a 'conservative church' in Indiana. I felt that my words were not received well. In fact, I sensed that my spoken words were hitting the walls of the sanctuary and echoing back to me. I experienced a feeling of sadness that welled up inside my soul. After preaching my sermon, I could not lead the hymn-singing after my sermon. So I went down to the alter rail and wept bitterly. A couple of people came to me after the service and said, "Is everything alright with you at home?" They had no idea why I wept. Later, I remembered, how "Jesus wept" for Jerusalem (Luke 19:41) as he looked at the Temple and foresaw her destruction by the Roman Empire. This actually happened at 70 AD.

ILLUSTRATION 3

When I was a church consultant, I was assigned to a rural church in a verge of break up due to a severe conflict within the congregation. My initial research on the congregation showed that there had been three pastors appointed during the previous five years due to two major factions. When I arrived on a Sunday morning at 9:00 AM, many people were leaving the church after attending the Sunday school without attending the worship service. At 11:00 AM a new group of people came for the worship service. I interviewed twenty members of the church in the afternoon. From these interviews I gleaned that the Chair of the Trustee led the 'Sunday school group', while his sister, the Choir Director, led the 'Sunday worship group'.

For the past five years the church repeated a pattern. If the brother's group supported a new pastor, the sister's group would be against the pastor and got rid of him or her. And if the sister's group supported the next pastor, then, the brother's group would do everything possible to get rid of him or her. So, the three pastors became victims of this typical dysfunctional church caused by two 'antagonists' in the church. I asked both of them what was the root cause(s) of their divisiveness in the beginning, and both could not remember the "why." They simply shrugged and said, "I don't remember, because it happened very long time ago." It is so sad that they brought their family's dysfunctional problem to the church family causing the congregational dysfunction.

ILLUSTRATION 4

I met my friend's grandfather, David, who came for a spiritual direction. He was in his early 70's and a fine looking gentleman. He told me his story. Although he was a PK (preacher's kid) and his son and grand-son were pastors of large membership churches, he was away from the church for many decades. He worked very hard in his work and lived his life according to the worldly ways of 'bitter competition and selfish greed and ambition.' When he retired from the investment business, he was a successful, rich man, and yet he felt a big void inside of his heart. He recognized his "restless heart" and asked me for counseling.

As I listened to his story, I was reminded of the church at Laodicea in the Book of *Revelation*. The Angel of the Lord is speaking to the people of the Church:

> "For you say, "I am rich, and have prospered, and I need nothing. You do not realize that you are wretched, pitiable, poor, blind, and naked. Therefore I counsel you to buy from me gold refined by fire so that you may be rich; and white robes to clothe you and to keep the shame of your naked-ness from being seen; and salve to anoint your eyes so that you may see. I reprove and discipline those whom I love. Be earnest, therefore, and repent" (Revelation 3:17-19).

I suggested that he go fishing for a daylong silent retreat. And I gave him a piece of paper containing scriptural verses to prayerfully reflect on them. David took my advice and went fishing by himself to be alone. Later, he told me his experience of the retreat.

In the quite, peaceful surrounding he read the scripture verses and began to reflect on his life. And he began to ask himself a series of questions:

17

"How do I want to be remembered by my loved ones?"

"If my friends and family remembered only one thing about me after I died, what would they say?"

"What kind of legacy am I leaving behind?"

"If I could change one thing in my life right now, what would that be?"

"Then, I lay down on the grass and listen to chirping of crickets and cicadas and

I felt a gentle breeze and a warm sunlight. And suddenly, I felt a deep quite peace.

That God-moment was like an eternity. The God of 'steadfast love' touched my soul. I realized that I have been living a meaningless, hopeless life, and mostly godless life. The prayerful reflection on scriptural verses given by you made me realize the truth that the present life on earth is transient, unpredictable, and brief, and that I have been living for a false hope based on an illusion. Then, I repented (*metanoia,* meaning a change mind) and decided to turn around from the old life of a self-made man [person] to a God-made man [person]."

The following Sunday David went to worship at a church in his hometown. Then, he got actively involved in the church's ministries of nurturing, outreaching, and worshipping/witnessing. That was a new beginning of his spiritual journey toward spiritual maturity. In his regular quite time alone with God, he began to notice the mysterious presence of God. The experiences made him appreciate the wonder of life here on earth more than ever before, he also fears death less and less, and hopes for the eternal home more and more. He sits alone sometimes, and now and then he enters that moment of being united with God who reminded David of God's self-sacrificing love, forgiveness, and acceptance. Like David, we are grateful for the good news: "To all who receive him [Christ], who believed in his name, he gave *power* to become children of God" (John 1:12). From the above illustrations (1-4) we realize that the "biological" ages have little to do with the "spiritual maturity" and that all believers are in different stages of becoming God's "mature" children and the "healthy" disciples of Jesus Christ for the sake of others.

My **vision** is:

Christians "hidden with Christ in God" are living toward both personal wholeness (holiness) and societal transformation by incarnating God's just-love by participating in Christ's ministry of compassion toward those who are suffering in this perilous world.

We, as disciples of Christ, are his agents or instruments in the ministry of reconciliation between God and humanity through our authentic expressions of faith, hope, and love, propelled by the divine compassion.

Because we are endowed with the God's amazing grace, the resurrection power, and the spiritual gifts, we can move forward in our *life's journeys toward wholeness*:

- By holistic healing of our whole being (the body-mind-spirit);

- By transforming personality to discover the true self and to begin a new life "hidden with Christ in God";

- By growing toward the spiritual maturity as the children of God and by following the Jesus Christ's teaching and examples as his faithful disciples;

- By living ever more fully into our objective life in Christ and by becoming participants of his ministry of compassion in the hurting world.

This book, *Life's Journeys toward Wholeness: Wellness, Transformation, Spiritual Maturity,* is a sequel to my previous book, *God of Active Verbs, A to Z.* My writing these books is to share the love of God to others as Kurt Kaiser proclaims:

19

"Once we experience it [God's love], we want to pass it on.

I want my world to know [that] the Lord of Love has come to me.

I want to pass it on. Once you've experienced it,

You want to spread his love to everyone." (The United Methodist Hymnal, #572)

WHAT IS YOUR LIFE?

The Time Magazine's cover story (August 5, 2013 Issue) was about the epic event of the Detroit's bankruptcy: "IS YOUR CITY NEXT?" The article was warning that there would be more cities like Detroit facing a similar economic crisis.

In addition to an economic uncertainty and an insecure future, contemporary culture is leaning more and more toward the materialistic, technocratic, godless worldviews. Most of us are feeling the urgency that humanity is at an important milestone.

In spite of a seeming improvement in technology and knowledge, the constants that have not seen improvements, are human moral virtues and ethical values. We are faced with many real-life issues where our understanding of human nature and personhood is critical in making godly decisions in bioethics, genetic technologies, cloning, the sanctity of life, abortion, and issues of caring for persons at the end of life.

During the last century we have witnessed enormous strides in science, medicine, and computer technology. But, real understanding and healing of the human psyche or the soul have not advanced much. With our enormous technological power, there is increased potential for destruction of planet earth. Now is the time that we must gain genuine self-knowledge that can lead us to discover the true self from the ego-inflated personality (the false self). Then, human beings will learn to live together in peace and harmony; we will not strip the earth of its resources; we will not fear those who are unlike us; we will prove that love is stronger power than hatred.

With these challenging pictures of the contemporary life, it would be a wise thing for us to consider one of God's questions: "What is your life?" (James 4:14)

Our reflections on this question are very timely, because it can guide us, inspire us, stimulate us, annoy us, upset us, or bless us. St. James, the brother of Jesus, penned one of God's messages to human beings:

"Come now, you who say, 'Today or tomorrow we will go to such and such a town and spend a year there, doing business and making money.'

'Yet you do not even know what tomorrow will bring. What is your life?

> You are the mist that appears for a little while, and then vanishes. Instead you ought to say, 'If the Lord wishes, we will live and do this or that.' As it is, you boast in your arrogance; all such boasting is evil. Anyone, then, who knows the right thing to do and fails to do it, commits sin" (James 4: 13-17).

The text inspires us to live according to God's way that leads to the blessed life of our loving union with God through much learning and growing from the spiritual birth to our loving union with God in the heavenly places.

Karen Salmansohn in her book, *How to Be Happy*, expresses this truth that we are here on earth to grow by learning life's lessons, in a delightful way.

> "As soon as you were born into this world, you were whacked (spanked)...You were only 3.5 seconds old and you learned a first big life lesson about pain. You learned the first lesson that even when you're good, you can get whacked. Without

apology… Without explanation… It's not until later that you finally learn that pain back in Life Lesson #1 was for your benefit…You were being taught to breath, invited to suck down a yummy oxygen/nitrogen cocktail. That painful whack was necessary for your growth…Of course, had you been told this at that time, you still would not have understood with your naïve lil' baby mind. And so it goes for much of the pain in your life. Often you need to evolve a bit more before you can understand a bit more." (Salmansohn, *How to Be Happy*, pp. 2-21)

"What is your life?" The question is important because it determines how we ought to live our lives in a perilous world. St. James reminds us that the human life devoid of God is meaningless. Human beings know instinctively that human life on earth is meaningless without faith, hope, and love (*agape*). We are mortal, but many people live as if they are unaware of this human condition. I heard someone say, "Life is short and uncertain, therefore, eat your desert first."

Ever since our physical birth and spiritual birth, everyday we learn and grow toward becoming more whole persons as we draw one day closer to death. It seems like a tragedy because humans are immortal and death is unavoidable. But it is more tragic to live as if we can plan and determine our destinies as though we live forever.

In his seminar Dr. Anthony Campolo shared a sociological study in which fifty people over the age of ninety-five were asked *one* question: "If you could live your life over again, what would you do differently?" It was an open-ended question, and a multiplicity of answers came from these eldest of senior citizens. However, three answers constantly re-emerged and dominated the results of the study. These three answers were:

1. If I had it to do over again, I would reflect more;

2. If I had it to do over again, I would risk more;

3. If I had it to do over again, I would do more things that would live on after I am dead.

As these folks late in life had gained the perspective of eternity, we all should learn from their wisdom, so that we do not have any regrets when our times are up.

In our understanding of growing and maturing we often use the imagery of a journey. Here we are *not* talking about the organic metaphors of growing seeds where growth and maturity are the expansion of an organic structure in size and complexity through a continuous series of transformations. These changes and their sequence are more or less programmed within the seeds from the beginning. Rather we are talking about the process of our life journeys that begin with our conversion (spiritual birth) and move towards the *goal* of our life's journeys: our loving union with God and our being conformed to the image of Christ for others.

"What is your life?" The question challenges us to change our thinking, feeling, and our doing/willing. When we are filled with the Spirit of the living God, our eyes see the world differently with many colors of the rainbow and our ears are fine-tuned to hear the ever-loving voice of "God of active verbs" saying, "You are my Beloved."

The truth of Psalm 8:3-5 is that we celebrate not only God's majesty but also our undeniable significance before God.

"When I look at your heavens, the work of your fingers,
the moon and the stars that you have established;
what are human beings that you are mindful of them?
mortals that you care for them?

Yet you have made them a little lower than God,
and crowned them with glory and honor."

We must recognize that we are neither molecules nor gods. Our approach to life must be grounded in the realization of God's immeasurable grace toward us and our response of a radical trust toward God. The degrees of our trust in God is measured by how much we love God by loving our neighbors as ourselves and obey his will by praying without ceasing, "If the Lord wishes, we will live and do this or that... Not my will, but your will be done. Amen."

WHAT IS WHOLENESS?

The words *wholeness* and *holiness* come from the same root *holy*. It is derived from the
Anglo Saxon term *halig*, meaning "health or wellness." Our word *whole* comes from the Anglo Saxon word *hal*, meaning "completeness, unity (oneness), or integration, symbolized by a circle." Therefore "wholeness" means healing (from dis-ease), wellness (from balance and harmony), completeness (from incompleteness), unity (from division), holiness (from ungodliness), integration (from fragmentation), transformation (from false self), salvation (from condemnation), and loving union with God (from enmity with God). Any degree of wholeness we attain here on earth will be relative rather than ultimate. The nurturing power of the Holy Spirit keeps us moving *toward* a higher level of wholeness (holiness) until we may reach the ultimate goal of "becoming participants of the divine nature." It also means a destination--the Promised Palace or the Holy City or the Heavenly Father's Home. As faithful disciples of Christ, we understand that we are *not there yet*, but we are *already* on the journey toward wholeness in Christ who invites us, "Come and follow me!"

St. Paul's theology of grace has a dramatic impact on the Protestant movement led by Martin Luther. After reading Luther's writings John Calvin had a conversion experience more than 500 years ago. Calvin was a brilliant young man who intended to be a Roman Catholic priest but broke away from Roman Catholicism and he left France and settled in Switzerland as an exile. The 27-year old Calvin wrote one of the greatest theological works ever written, *The Institutes of the Christian Religion.* He emphasized the *sovereignty* of God and wrote that "God is Lord over all!" This belief in God's sovereignty has shaped Christian thought through the centuries, and it had a dramatic impact on the Protestant movement since 16th Century.

John Calvin believed that *knowledge of self* required *knowledge of God.* Since he did not have excessive optimism concerning the human condition, John got his *Presbyterian* theology of grace from St. Paul who wrote: "For *by grace* you have been saved through faith and this is not your own doing; it is the gift of God" (Ephesians 2:8).

John and Charles Wesley were Christian disciples and theologians of the 18th century. John (1703-1791) and Charles (1707-1791) were concerned about lack of Christian Discipleship that is required for living in Christ through the Spirit with integrity and congruency. They launched a movement of renewal (known as the Methodist or Evangelical revival) that breathed new life into their beloved Church of England. They revitalized the life of the church in their time. Their insights are of potentially equal value for us today.

According to Wesley Chilcote, "The living faith the Wesley brothers (John and Charles) rediscovered was both rooted in and oriented toward the love of God...God's love, in its multiple dimensions, is the only proper foundation for discipleship in Christ...For the Christian, Jesus Christ is the central reference point in that ongoing process, the gospel of which is for us to be changed by God into more loving, more Christ-like people...For the Wesleyan Christian, in this dynamic process of knowing and living the faith, the Bible provides the authoritative Word of God for both faith and practice…They tended to see matters of faith from a *both* personal *and* social salvation…God's self revelation in Scripture is balanced by tradition, reason and experience…The truth we encounter in the Word is attested to in the received faith tradition, ordered by our God-given ability to think and reflect, and practiced in our ongoing experience of Christ's Spirit in our lives." (Chilcote, *Recapturing the Wesleys' Vision*, pp. 15-17)

The most distinctive characteristics of the Wesleyan theology are connecting faith and works: a reformation theology of salvation (justification by grace through faith) and a Roman Catholic theology of salvation (sanctification is a process toward holy living or perfection in love). It means if our faith is genuine, then other people will be able to see it lived out in loving ways: "In Christ Jesus neither circumcision nor un-circumcision counts for anything; the only thing that counts is faith working through love (Galatians 5:6). John Wesley used the above phrase, "faith working through love", and was able to connect faith and love working together for salvation. Therefore, salvation in Christ involves both justifying grace and the sanctifying grace (see Appendix V).

Max Lucado expresses it so well when he writes: "God loves you just the way you are, but he refuses to leave you that way. He wants you to be just like Jesus." (Lucado, *Just Like Jesus*, p. 3)

ATTRIBUTES OF A WHOLE PERSON

Cecil G. Osborn provides us with a set of goals that he tried to achieve. He writes:

"I could never reach fully. Yet, one must be lured toward spiritual and emotional maturity by goals high enough

to be challenging, knowing at the same time that failure to reach them all does not condemn one...God's love
and grace are conferred, but growth [to maturity] is
achieved by our efforts with the empowering power of
the Holy Spirit." (Osborn, *The Art of Becoming a whole
person*, pp. 14-15)

All religions, except for Christianity, attempt resolution for the
conflict within the human soul—some religions by human efforts
(works) and others by asceticism. But, Christian faith alone insists that
God comes to save us from human bondage and dilemma. In Jesus,
God became man, in him "all the fullness of the Deity lives in bodily
form" (Colossians 2:9). He is the one who reconciles us with God (2
Corinthians 5:19). What God did for us objectively in Christ becomes a
subjective reality. Through the Holy Spirit, the "Christ for us" becomes
the "Christ in us" (Galatians 2:20; 4:19, Colossians 1:27). Thank God
that it is not we ought to save ourselves, but it is God who comes to save
us and it is God who dwells in us to sanctify us (make us whole).

Appendix I summarizes how we begin the journey of faith by responding to the God of love. The love relationships with God and others
we seek to keep cannot be established by human effort. Our loving
actions must spring out from within through the God's grace and our
faithful responses to *God's loving actions.*

First, we experience God who reveals himself to humanity in three
different ways as the Creator, the Redeemer, and the Sustainer. These
experiences result in our appropriate responses to each of God's loving
actions;

Second, the deeper experience of God's loving actions awakens our
souls and empowers us to be on a life journey toward wholeness;

Third, our constant yielding to the Spirit's guidance and leading,
helps us become participants of the divine nature.

WHAT IS THE HUMAN NATURE?

Before we move into a holistic approach to personal wellness (heal-ing/wellness of the physical, the psychological, and spiritual dimensions), we need to understand the traditional Christian view of human nature or personhood. It is imperative also to be aware of "what contemporary science saying about the human person." Listen to the evolutionary biologist Richard Dawkin's outlandish statement:

> "We are machines built by DNA whose purpose is to make more copies of the same DNA... This is exactly what we are for... We are machines for propagating DNA, and the propagation of DNA is a self-sustaining process. It is every living object's sole reason for living."
> (Green and Palmer, *In Search of the Soul*, p.7)

Dawkins insists that the purpose of human lives--individually and collectively--has been reduced to accommodating those impulses arising at the level of our molecular biology. (Ibid. p.11)

Neuroscientists also, speak of human life in terms of embodiment as physical persons. Since 2002 their focus has been on the nature of the relationship of mind and brain by using functional magnetic resonance imaging (fMRI).

> Green and Palmer warns neuroscientists and molecular biologists: "They do this on account of the complex and subtle dependencies of our thought processes on the state and functioning of our brains...These experimental data have generally led scientists away from belief in nonmaterial entity of the soul, as a way of explaining the human self." (Ibid. pp.16-17)

28

It means the demise of the idea of a human soul. Green and Palmer propose the following issues to be considered in the debate on the reality of a human soul. (Ibid. pp. 23-32)

Are we (only) animals?

Are we of sacred worth?

Do I have choice?

What does it means to be saved?

What about life after death?

According to Green and Palmer the traditional Christian faith is firmly founded in *substance dualism*: the relation of body (*soma*) and soul (*psyche*/mind). Historically, Christians have been broadly divided into two extreme camps: more or less reductive materialists and more or less radical dualists. They further clarify the different views:

"Dispersed between two poles are other categories within which the debate among Christians tends to be localized:

- Reductive materialists (The constitution view of person) with scientific worldview would say: 'Your joys and free will are in fact no more than the behavior of a vast assembly of nerve cells and their associated molecules…We are animals.'

- Radical dualists would say: 'The soul acts apart from bodily processes, and the body is nothing more than a temporary and disposable holding tank for the soul.'

- Nonreductive physicalists (a type of Monism) would say: 'The phenomenological experiences that we label are not reducible to brain activity and represent essential aspect or capacities of the self, rather than a substantial, ontological entity such as a soul.'

Their idea is grounded in physicalism of the scientific worldview that denies the Christian view of <u>dualism</u>.

- <u>Holistic dualists</u> would say: "The soul and the body are highly interactive; they enter into deep causal connection and functional dependencies with each other. The soul is *immaterial substance* different from the body to which it is related. It allows for the possibility that the soul (mind) may exist independent of the body with which it is currently functionally integrated or in a disembodied state altogether."

With these multiple voices, now let us turn to the traditional Christian view of human nature: <u>Substance Dualism</u> (body-soul). There are two kinds of substance dualism: *Cartesian* <u>dualism</u> explicates the philosophy of Rene Descartes who <u>replaced</u> *soul* with *mind* and <u>Aristotelian/ Thomistic Dualism</u> explicates the theology of Thomas Aquinas' Body/ Soul. (Ibid. p.20-21)

<u>Cartesian Dualism</u> considers the mind is substance externally related by causal relation to the body, a corporeal substance that is merely *physical machine*. It involves dualism of two separable substances—mind and body. According to the Cartesian dualism, the mind as a substance is an *ego* that contains the capacities for mental functioning. For modern Cartesians, the mind is a substance and the body is a property-thing. Their relationship is an external causal relationship.

By contrast <u>Thomistic Substantive Dualism</u> focuses on the *soul,* not the *mind.* The <u>mind</u> (*nous*) is a faculty of the <u>soul</u> (*psyche*), but the soul goes beyond mental functioning (thinking, feeling, and doing) and serves as the integrative ground and developer of the body (*soma*). The soul is <u>immaterial substance</u> and it animates and makes the <u>body</u> *alive.* The *body constantly affects the psyche,* and the body is nothing (except a corpse) without its living reality of the <u>soul</u> (*psyche*). The <u>soul</u>

30

is never in un-embodied state (not even in the Jesus' Resurrection), and the body that lacks soul lacks life. Thomistic dualists identify a person with the soul and they believe that there is life after death and the soul continuously exists in an *intermediate state* [like angelic beings] until the soul receives a *new resurrection body* at the general Resurrection. It is consistent with "functional" holism but not with "ontological" holism because the latter insists that disembodiment of the soul is not possible.

In conclusion, the traditional Christian view of human nature or personhood is Thomistic Substance Dualism. A Christian substance dualist would say, the soul--I, self, mind—is an *immaterial substance* different from the body to which it is related. And the soul is an immaterial entity that could, in principle, survive death and ground personal identity in the afterlife. The soul survives our physical death and exists in the intermediate state, waiting for the final Resurrection (Rev. 20:5-6).

The Thomist Dualist view of a human person is consistent with the traditional Christian faith and it resists the prevailing winds of secularity, scientism, and physicalism. With this understanding of human nature we could make conscientious debates on many bioethical issues—abortion, cloning, embryo research, euthanasia, physician-assisted suicide, and care of persons at the end of life.

In search of the meaning and purpose in our life's journeys we must ask: "How do we become the people we were born to be?

PART ONE

A Holistic Approach toward
Healing and Wellness

CHAPTER 1

HEALING AND WELLNESS IN THE PHYSICAL DIMENSION

THE HEALING POWER OF THE BODY

About forty years ago, I was an owner-pharmacist in Pittsburgh, PA. In the beginning, the business was very slow, so I used to come out of the prescription counter and interact with my customers by answering questions about their medications and recommending over-the-counter (OTC) drugs according to their self-diagnosis.

One day, a regular customer came into my pharmacy and I could tell from the way she was walking that she was in a great pain. She came to ask me to recommend a pain medicine for her. I noticed that her one shoes had a big hole with her pinky toe sticking out in 45-degree angle. I ask her to sit down on a chair and take off her shoes very carefully. I could tell that her toe was out of joint, but she was afraid to go to the emergency room of a nearby hospital. With her permission I touched the inflamed pinky toe. I felt that it was begging me: "Help me. Put me back into joint." I began to touch it gently and then pull it very quickly and put it back into joint. She screamed, but she had an immediate release from her pain. I taped her foot and sent her home. A few days later, she came to the store with a big smile with many words of thanks. She did not need a pain pill. She needed the *corrective* measure of putting the toe back into joint. Then, the amazing healing power of the body took over and she became well again.

Since we are interested in the wellness of the body, a shift in attitude toward the body will take us a long way. As the Psalmist says, "For it was you who formed my inward parts; you knit me together in my mother's womb. I praise you, for I am fearfully and wonderfully made..." (Psalm 139:13-14).

The body does not require the intercession of our brains to make it breath, to keep the heart breathing, and to blink our eyes automatically. Many functions of the body are self-regulating.

Mirka Knaster presents amazing facts of healthy body parts that are working 24/7 without stopping:

- The eye weighs quarter of an ounce. The muscles operating its lenses move up to hundred thousand times a day so that we can focus on all the varied objects that attract our attention. We would have to walk fifty miles every day just to give our leg muscles the equivalent amount of exercise. Each optic nerve is composed of about 1.25 million individual fibers.

- In the nine ounces of red marrow in our bones, red blood cells are created at the rate of approximately two million every second to replace an equal number destroyed.

- The brain has ten million nerve cells and each has a potential of twenty-five thousand interconnections with other nerve cells.

- The nose can detect up to ten thousand different odors, yet our sense of smell, located in the upper part of the nasal cavity, is no more than two patches of membrane containing several million receptors.

- The inner lining of the stomach is a mucous membrane into which holds up to thirty-five million tiny glands that secrete gastric juice to break down proteins and carbohydrates.

- In the three hundred million air sacs (alveoli) of the lungs, carbon dioxide is

- exchanged for oxygen in one-third to three quarters of a second depending on whether we're at rest or engaged in exercise.

- The kidneys filter five hundred gallons of blood daily.

- The heart, no bigger than a fist, pumps blood day and night through a network of blood vessels calculated to be sixty thousand miles long. When a person is at rest, the heart pumps at sixty-six gallons an hour. Over a lifetime of seventy years, that amounts to nearly sixty million gallons of blood. When a world-class athlete is at the height of exertion, the rate increases six-fold. Remarkably, the heart carries out this feat with no more power than that of two tiny electric motors of size found in many toys. It beats a hundred thousand times a day without rest our entire lives.

- The liver alone, sometimes referred to as the body's chemical factor, is able to perform more than five hundred different functions, including the production of more than a thousand different enzymes essential for food digestion and healthy metabolism.

"Let us consider how beautifully the body is organized. Each part of a cell—the average human body consists of about fifty trillion cells—and each cell as a whole performs a special function. Each tissue, in turn, is specialized to accomplish characteristic tasks. Each organ and each system are experts in particular operations for the benefit of the body as a whole. Everything is intricately integrated. Whenever something happens in one part of the body to disturb the existing condition, other parts compensate to restore the original condition—they adjust to maintain a steady state, or *homeostasis*." (Knaster, *Discovering the Body's Wisdom*, pp. 44-45)

In Psalm 139, the Psalmist (King David) reflects on the way in which God has intricately created him when he was an unformed substance. With him, we too marvel at the skill of God in fashioning the details of our beings in the secret place of the womb. David sees the person who gives thanks and praise to God as the same person who was skillfully woven together in the womb (vv.13-18) and as the same person who is known by God inside and out (vv. 1-6). It is not solely that God painstakingly and intricately created David in the womb; it is also that the person who was being created in the womb is the same person who is writing the Psalm.

Wellness of the body can be defined as a positive state of being healthy, more than just not being sick. Physical wellness (health) involves the health of our physical beings. It means taking responsibility (not abusing the body) for our physical wellness with vitality and excellence of the body:

• By responding to manifestations of warning symptoms, such as vital signs and pains, by getting medical professional help to get corrective measures of health;

- By practicing preventative measures of health with regular check-ups and good health habits;

- By learning about your prescription drugs, including their indications, side effects, and their interactions with other prescription drugs, over-the-counter (OTC) drugs, and with food;

- By identifying existing or potential *health factors*, so that one can take corrective and preventive actions;

- By eating a well balanced diet (energy intake and energy expenditure relationship);

- By eating Healthy food and supplements (vitamins and minerals);

- By doing the right kinds of exercise and getting restful sleep.

PREVENTATIVE PHYSICAL HEALTH

Today's medical technology is doing excellent work in *corrective* health care. We, as individuals, must take our responsibility of *preventative* health care more seriously to reduce the high cost of health care in the U.S. According to the U.S. Surgeon General's Office, reducing stress and excessive life-style risks could prevent more than two-thirds of all illness and death before age 65.

It is more cost-effective to deal with <u>preventative physical health</u> before there is brokenness, imbalance, or disharmony in the body. There are many *health factors* adversely affecting our well-being. Some factors that we can't completely control are heredity, the environment (pollutants and toxic materials), accidents, natural disaster, war, and personal violence. But, other factors that we can control are diet (food and supplements), exercise, rest, positive attitude, healthy habits, and stress control.

Since many diseases are caused by environmental contaminants and by disease-causing microorganisms, one of the most important things that we can do for our physical health is reduce our outside exposures and proactively develop the body's inner strength, such as serenity and the body's immune system.

SERENITY (INNER PEACE)

Rev. Reinhold Niebuhr offered following prayer for his friend's obituary. A portion of this prayer is widely used by many self-help groups, such as the Alcoholic's Anonymous (AA). It's called the *Serenity Prayer*:

> "God, grant me the *serenity* to accept the things I cannot change; *courage* to change the things I can; and *wisdom* to know the difference. Living one day at a time; enjoying one moment at a time; accepting hardships as the pathway to peace; taking as Christ did, this sinful world as it is, not as I would have it; trusting that You will make all things right if I surrender to Your Will; that I may be reasonably happy in this life and supremely happy with You forever in the next. Amen."

The author of the "serenity prayer" used to seek a *saved* society, not just individual salvation. So he as the pastor of a small congregation in Detroit in 1920's, became a very frustrated cynic because he believed that the church had lost its influence upon the society of auto industry

40

built upon the drive of power and greed. We find following diary entry in his notebook:

"I am afraid that the individualistic traditions of Protestantism, and perhaps also the strong Pauline strain in Protestant theology, have obscured the social implications of Jesus' gospel... It seems to me that we better admit our failure in the church's relationships to society, particularly to the facts of modern industry." (Reinhold Niebuhr, *Leaves from the Notebook of a Tamed Cynic*, pp.151-152)

After fifteen years in the pastoral ministry preaching the *social gospel*, he left Detroit and went to teach at the Union Seminary as a professor for the rest of his life. When we read the above prayer written by Reinhold Niebuhr, we can see a true disciple of Christ with humility and humanity. The whole prayer teaches us that an individual must have the inner peace to accept the things one cannot change, but one must exercise the courage to change those factors that one can. That is a right and wise things to do so that each of us may have a reasonably stress-free, healthy life in this sinful world and supremely happy with God forever in the heavenly place.

PREVENTATIVE CARE

The preventative physical care involves:

Diet is eating sensible *amounts* of healthy foods to improve our health and control weight. There are "good foods" and "bad foods" for each person with a different "body type" or "blood type" or "temperament." It is remarkable that our body remembers the genetic message of our ancestors' diets, habits, and life styles. Many of their traits are still affecting our body or blood types including the health of our vital organs, such as our heart, our stomach vision and our brain. Knowing these predispositions helps us to choose the right kinds of food and to find an *individualized* diet solution to achieve our ideal weight because each diet works well with *only* a certain type of people.

Exercise promotes healthy heart, lungs, kidney, pancreas and other vital organs and muscles. The right kind and amount of exercise help control weight and stress by making us live a healthy and happy life.

Resting sleep of 7 to 8 hours of sleep each night is good for health. It is also vital to have good time management skills. Recreation needs to be an important part of rejuvenation.

Attitude of a positive outlook can be the first step toward lasting wellness. Its effect on recovery of illness has been well documented.

Bad habits of smoking, drug/alcohol abuse, and free-sex are life-style risks. Avoiding them can help prevent serious brokenness in physical, mental, relational, vocational, and moral dimensions of the total human being.

PRESCRIPTION DRUG USE

It is very important for us to know our prescription drugs so that we can avoid following issues:

- Drug dependency—Certain pain medications are habit-forming and may cause drug addiction.

- Drug side effects—Consult your pharmacist when you pick up your prescriptions at the pharmacy: Ask about medicines you are taking.

- Unexpected drug-drug interactions and drug-food interactions—Consult your pharmacist by bringing a list of your medicines and OTC drugs, which you are taking. Ask about any drug interactions and their symptoms.

- Taking too many medicines---Follow the directions on the label for their safe use. Sometimes, you may get same prescriptions from different specialists. Also you may have duplicate prescription bottles, one with a brand name on the label and another with generic name on it. As the result, you may end up double-dosing yourself.

- Do not stop taking a maintaining drug without consulting your doctor.

A CASE STUDY OF INFLAMMATORY DISEASES

According to Dr. Floyd H. Chilton, a physician scientist in the field of inflammatory diseases for the past forty years, warns that we are faced with the "secret epidemic" rise in these diseases occurring in the "affluent" countries. (Chilton, *Win the War Within,* p. 24)

Dr. Chilton identifies three categories of inflammatory disease:

1. Diseases <u>known</u> to be caused by "overactive" inflammation:

2. They are asthma, allergies, rheumatoid arthritis, atopic dermatitis, gout, lupus, inflammatory bowel disease (IBD), Crohn's disease, psoriasis, and scleroderma.

3. Diseases <u>thought</u> to be caused by overactive inflammation: They are atherosclerosis (hardening of arteries), diabetes, chronic

kidney failure, chronic hepatitis, chronic thyroid disease, chronic pancreatitis, osteoarthritis, chronic bronchitis and emphysema.

4. Diseases in which overactive inflammation is <u>suspected</u>: They are Alzheimer's, dementia and cancer.

In his book, *Win the War Within*, Dr. Chilton writes:

"From the above list we can agree that at best these illnesses compromise our quality of life; at worst, they can be painful, debilitating, and fatal…Seventy million Americans suffer from arthritis—one in every three adults. More than 20 million Americans suffer every year from allergies. More than 100 percent increase in the prevalence of hay fever. There were 18.2 million people in the United States with diabetes in 2002, killing two hundred thousand each year, and the number is growing. Cardiovascular disease is the number one killer of Americans. About 64 million Americans have it in some form, killing a million people in 2001, and the number is increasing. One million Americans are suffering from IBD. And the numbers have been growing." (Chilton, pp. 30-36)

Increasingly, chronic inflammation is being suggested as the common link between all chronic illnesses. Dr. Woodson Merrell is in agreement with Dr. Chilton and he writes:

"Chronic inflammation occurs when the inflammatory machinery doesn't get turned off. This is the abnormal process central to such common illnesses as coronary artery, disease, diabetes, arthritis, Crohn's disease and ulcerative colitis, obesity, Alzheimer's, Parkinson's, and chronic fatigue." (Merrell, *Power Up*, p.68)

Dr. Chilton rightly concludes:

"Each one of these diseases, taken individually, represents a serious health problem in this country. When taken together, as a category of inflammatory diseases, this can only be seen as a pandemic. I don't think I'm overstating the problem when I say that inflammatory diseases affect as many as *half* of the population in this country." (Chilton, pp. 4-5)

Fortunately, Dr. Chilton offers some hope to the inflammation sufferer by providing a well-documented approach (the Chilton Diet) to limit the devastation of the destructive and painful effects of out-of-control inflammation on our physical wellness. Throughout the book, Dr. Chilton "emphasizes outcome and preventive medicine in the field of nutrition, reminding us of the ultimate quest of medical practice: not only to diagnose and treat, but to predict negative outcomes, and to avoid them whenever possible." (Ibid. p. xv)

THE BODY'S DEFENSE MECHANISM

The body's immune system fights against invading bacteria, viruses, parasites and carcinogens. According to Dr. Chilton, Arachidonic acid (AA) that we eat as vegetable oils produces inflammatory messengers, such as prostaglandins and leukotrienes. They play a crucial role in the inflammatory process. Upon receiving their warning signal, your body sends out its army of white blood cells made in the marrow of your bones. This white blood cell army is made up of B-lymphocytes, neutrophils, Macrophages, and T lymphocytes (T cells).

There are many types of inflammatory messengers, but prostaglandins and leukotrienes are mainly responsible for many of the signs and symptoms (swelling, redness, and pain) we traditionally associate with inflammation. How can something so central and important cause inflammation diseases in such epidemic numbers? We used to think that a disease happens when some vital organ or system in the body stops working. In contrast, an inflammatory disease is not caused by a malfunction in the system works. The system, in fact, is over working—it's just firing of inflammatory messengers too frequently. The internal dial in our bodies, set to trigger this vital defense reaction, is permanently set on a constant "red alert."

Inflammatory disease is, in practice, the opposite of AIDS and other immunodeficiency disorders. In those diseases, the messengers are sleeping at the desk. In contrast, arthritis, asthma, and other inflammatory diseases occur when that pendulum swings the other way. The body considers that it is defending itself.

THE IMMUNE SYSTEM AND INFLAMMATION

All inflammatory diseases occur due to an overactive immune system that fails to turn off the inflammation mechanism at the appropriate time. The inflammation mechanism is a part of the complex immune system that fights against infection from bacteria, viruses, or fungus to heal itself. But when the inflammation mechanism fails to turn off, inflammation becomes long lasting and widespread. This, then, alters metabolism and damages blood vessels, bones, and other body tissues, bringing on a variety of chronic illnesses.

Dr. Chilton confidently states that his dietary program can provide a model for the food choices so that we are using food to help us to protect our bodies against inflammatory diseases, not as an instrument of harm.

According to Dr. Chilton "allergy is the smoking gun behind many inflammatory diseases, including asthma, and many skin diseases. An allergic reaction happens when your body's immune system becomes so hypersensitive that it breaks out the big guns in response to the most harmless invader." (Chilton, p. 39)

He defines autoimmunity: "Autoimmune disorders, like rheumatoid arthritis and lupus, make up another major category of chronic inflammatory disease. In these disorders, your body becomes allergic to its own tissues, responding to them as though they were hostile trespassers. Friendly fire is the metaphor that I most often use to describe these disorders." (Ibid. p. 39)

The rational behind the Chilton Program is outlined below (Ibid. pp. 113-128):

1. By lowering the amount of arachidonic acid (AA) that we eat as vegetable oils, we decrease the amount of AA in our bloodstream;

2. By blocking the critical enzymes that convert AA to inflammatory messengers which bring inflammation;

3. By receiving carbohydrates with low-to-moderate value on the Glycemic Index;

4. By taking in a more balanced ratio of gammalinolenic acid (GLA) and eicosapentaenoic acid (EPA) and docosahexaenoic acid (DHA), both known as Omega-3 fatty acids, to block the production of inflammatory messengers.

I am more impressed with the "Chilton Food Program" than other food diet programs because it focuses on choosing the right carbohydrates that are low on the <u>Glycemic Index</u> and proteins and vegetables that are low on the <u>Inflammatory Index.</u> This regulates the blood sugar systems that both affect, and are affected by, the inflammatory messengers. It also focuses on wild fish (not farm-grown fish) and lean meats. Unlike the Atkins Diet, which also focuses on protein, poultry plays less of significant role in the Chilton Diet, and egg yolks play no role at all. Dr. Chilton is more specific about vegetables than the USDA Food Pyramid, and places the focus of his diet on non-starchy vegetables, like broccoli and lettuce. (Ibid. p. 139)

There are many possible theories to explain the pandemic of inflammatory diseases. Dr. Chilton considers the genetic theory, the pollution theory, the "disease of old age" theory, the hygiene hypothesis (we are too clean by using antibiotic soaps), food factors (food dyes, preservatives, and additives as well as the change in our diets) and fish factors (where we get the fish we eat: wild fish vs. farmed fish). His final diagnosis for the pandemic of inflammatory diseases is "Affluenza," foods of *affluence.* (Ibid. p.24)

A SOLUTION FOR INFLAMMATORY DISEASES (IBID. P. 234)

- Eat foods whose values add up to no more than 100 on the <u>Inflammatory Index</u> per day.

- Eat an average of at least 400mg a day of EPA (eicosapentaenoic acid). This equates to roughly four servings of Category 1 or 2 fish a week, or five servings of Category 3 fish. If you would prefer to supplement instead, take one capsule (typically 150 to 180mg) of EPA three times daily, with meals.

- Take an average of at least 650 to 950mg of GLA (gammalino-lenic acid)

- daily in supplement form, which means a capsule (typically about 210

- to 240mg) three times daily, with meals.

- Do not take the recommended dose of GLA without having EPA- either   through the fish you're eating or by supplementation in your diet.

- Choose carbohydrates with a low to moderate Glycemic Index value. In conclusion, it is highly recommended to bring overactive inflammation back into balance by following the Chilton Program (the diet, exercise, and weight control).

Dr. Chilton concludes: "You can regain the balance lost by these changes in our food supply and content, simply by changing what you eat. Then, the food you eat will be working to improve your health, instead of fueling your inflammatory disease." (Ibid. p.28)

THE EFFECTS OF STRESS ON OBESITY AND WEIGHT GAIN

Persistent high levels of stress can cause obesity and weight gain, and they in-turn cause low-grade whole-body inflammation; they also raise our risk of inflammatory diseases. Even on low levels of on-going stresses such as that from a demanding job, raising children or other family conflicts, financial worries or chronic health problems, can increase inflammation in the arteries. This damages in the inner lining of the blood vessels, promotes accumulation of cholesterol and increases the risk for clots--the cause of most heart attacks. Well known physical effects of stress are: increased blood sugar, more pain, impaired memory, and weight gain.

In obese or overweight people "fat produces protein-like messengers--C-reactive protein, tumor necrosis factor-alpha, and interleukin-6. Like the fatty acid messengers, the protein messengers also turn against the body's own immune system thus causing inflammation and chronic pain.

STRENGTHENING THE BODY'S DEFENSE MECHANISM

Dr. Andrew Weil reported: "While antimicrobial agents have been considered the "wonder drugs" of the 20th century, clinicians and researchers are now acutely aware that microbial resistance to drugs (antibiotics) has become a major clinical problem...The pharmaceutical industry is attempting to develop new agents that are less susceptible to current resistance mechanisms. Unfortunately, the microbial organisms appear to rapidly develop new resistance mechanisms...It means patients could die of infection... In fact, infectious-disease specialists throughout the world are now wringing their hands over the possibility of untreatable plagues of resistant organisms." (Weil, *Spontaneous Healing*, pp. 4-5)

Dr. Weil advocates for principles of the Chinese medicine. "Because they are not acting against germs (and do not therefore influence their evolution), rather they are strengthening the body's defense mechanism. They increase activity and efficiency of cells of the immune system, helping patients resist all kinds of infections, not just those caused by microorganisms.

Antibiotics are only effective against bacterial infections; they are of no use in viral infections, such as HIV infection. "The Eastern concept of strengthening internal defenses assumes that the body has a natural ability to resist and deal with agents of disease. If that assumption were more prominent in Western medicine, we would not now have an economic crisis in health care systems, because the preventative methods that take advantage of the body's natural healing abilities are far cheaper than the intensive interventions of technological medicine, as well as being safer and more effective over time." (Ibid. p. 6)

THE MIND- BODY- SPIRIT CONNECTION

Dr. Merrell warns us: "Lifestyle can magnify the inflammatory response—poor eating habits, high stress levels, and exposure to toxins (like tobacco smoke, air pollution, and heavy metals) can throw off the body's ability to maintain the balance between promoting and quelling inflammation, thereby creating a chronic state of life threatening inflammatory diseases." (*Merrell*, p. 68)

Dr. M. Scott Peck, a psychiatrist, affirms that there is "a force" that seems to operate routinely in most people to protect and to foster their mental health even under the most adverse conditions:

> "An increasing number of thinkers are beginning to suggest that almost all disorders are psychosomatic – that the psyche is somehow involved in the causation of the various failures that occur in the resistant system. But

the amazing thing is not these failures of the resistance system; it is that the resistance system works as well as it does. We can therefore say the same thing about physical diseases that we said about mental disorders." (Peck, *The Road Less Traveled.* p. 230)

He hints that the mysterious force is the amazing grace of God. He describes that his patients consist of those suffering from neuroses and character disorders. He defines the difference between them:

"The *neurotic* assumes too much responsibility; the person with a *character disorder* assumes not enough responsibility. When neurotics are in conflict with the world they automatically assume that they are at fault. When those with character disorders are in conflict with the world they automatically assume that the world is at fault." (Ibid. p.35)

We define *psychotic* as a person suffering from delusions and distortion in one's perception of reality. When the emotional disturbance is *less severe*, it is called a *neurotic* person. The psychotic individuals are disoriented; their perception of reality is *severely distorted*, while the neurotic persons are different in that their perception of reality is *unsound*. Because both psychotic and neurotic persons operate with illusions, their physical functioning is not grounded in reality. Thus, mental illness involves a physical implication. Since it is the human spirit that propels the person, the spirit is also involved in every emotional illness.

The next illustration is a poignant example of how anxiety, stress and depression can affect our total well being according to the mind- body-spirit connection. This connection works both ways: disintegration to brokenness; and integration to wellness.

52

ILLUSTRATION 5

Sandra and her husband, Richard, were happily married had a teenage boy. From the outside, they represented an American dream family. Richard was feeling a lot of pressure at work. His boss told him that afternoon: "We are going to cut back a few positions because of the bad economic situation. He suggested that Richard should get five more investment accounts for the company if he wants to keep his job as an investment advisor.

Richard was very upset and he went to a bar for a drink on his way home. Unfortunately, he had too many drinks and he had a car accident that night. His right knee was smashed badly and doctors had to put an iron bar inside of his right leg surgically. One month after the surgical procedure, he went back to the surgeon for a follow-up. He received the bad news that his knee was not healing because the metal bar they put into his right leg was a quarter inch too long! It was the beginning of many complications, which resulted in the amputation of his leg.

Richard lost his job. He began to drink even more and his behavior became unbearable: he showed bad tempers, screaming rage, verbal and physical abuse toward Sally and their son. Sandra always went to church on Sunday with her son. So she kindly asked whether or not he wanted to come along. He refused and then he spoke very badly about the church where he and Sally were married and their son was baptized. Richard was rude to the caring ministry team members who came to visit and then they began to avoid Richard because of his rude behaviors. He would say to Sandra: "They are all hypocrites! All they want is my money."

After hearing the bad news that Richard might lose his job, he displayed a *character disorder*. He wanted to handle his fear of losing his job by drinking alcohol. Because of his unfortunate car accident and the doctor's error, he ended up losing his one leg below the knee. He collected a good sum of money by suing the doctor for the malpractice. But, his drinking was out of control and his verbal and physical abuse toward Sandra and her son got worse and they ended up in a divorce. His defense was rationalization by blaming others-- his wife, his son, his boss, his church, and even his God. He became a very angry person thinking about no one but himself. He became very depressed. Richard finally reached out to a psychiatrist who prescribed antidepressant drugs, but their adverse effects caused him to become suicidal. Is there hope for Richard?

Many techniques and ways of stress reduction and anger management are being suggested. They work some degree. But, they are temporary solutions like using Band-Aids for a deep wound. A person's physical existence has a spiritual as well as mental existence. There is no mental disturbance that is not also a physical and spiritual disturbance. The mentally depressed person is physically depressed (no energy) as well as spiritually depressed.

A sad individual will regain one's faith and hope when the situation changes. A dejected individual will spring up again when the cause of one's condition is removed. A blue person will lighten up at the prospect of pleasure. Because these reversals happen at the conscious level, improvement may occur. But nothing evokes any response from depressed persons, because their inner conflicts happen at a deep, unconscious level.

PRAYER AND HEALING

A small but growing minority of physicians is starting to give a respectable nod to the power of prayer. In his article in "McCall's" magazine (April, 1996), Gurney Williams III introduced Dr. Dale A Matthews, M.D. who prays for his patients. He reported that of 212 studies examining the effects of religious commitment—including prayer—on such health-care outcomes as reduced blood pressure, depression, and anxiety, 160 of them, or 75 percent, demonstrated the value of faith. The National Institute published his report for Healthcare Research (NIHR), a private group in Rockville, MD. The NIHR works closely with the John Templeton Foundation, which was established to explore and encourage the link between science and religion.

A recent study of 232 patients by the Dartmouth Medical School in Lebanon, NH, showed that people who reported drawing strength and comfort from religion were three times as likely to be alive six months after open-heart surgery as those who found no solace in faith. Thirty-seven of the patients in a study by Thomas Oxman, M.D., described themselves as deeply religious. "Not one of them died." He said, "Now, guess what very religious people do. They pray."

According to Dr. Dave Hilton, M.D., several hundred studies reported in the medical literature support the theory that the immune system, controlling health, and disease, is regulated primarily by relationships, feelings, and beliefs. Many other investigations have shown that anger and resentment are powerful suppressors of the immune system and that one of its most powerful remedies is loving relationships and using the power of forgiveness.

Being an integral part of a faith community where people pray and support for one another and where there is a nurturing atmosphere of acceptance, love, caring, and forgiveness is an important part of promoting our personal health.

CHAPTER 2

HEALING AND WELLNESS IN THE PSYCHOLOGICAL DIMENSION

THE ENNEAGRAM, INTEGRATION OF PSYCHOLOGY AND SPIRITUALITY

For the past twenty years I have applied the Enneagram in my ministry as a pastor and a spiritual director. I learned that the Enneagram is much more than a personality typology. It is a powerful tool for personality transformation by providing direction, steps, and goals for inner healing and taming the inflated ego. I studied Don Richard Riso's two books, *Discovering Your Personality Type* (1992) and *Enneagram Transformations* (1993). Later, I attended workshops led by Don Riso and his teaching partner Russ Hudson and followed their published books, such as *The Wisdom of the Enneagram* (1999) and *The Understanding the Enneagram: the practical guide to the personality types* (2000).

Riso and Hudson have taught many students, like me, a new insight that "both psychological transformation [and integration] and spiritual transformation [and maturity] must not be separate processes toward wholeness. They guide us through a psycho-spiritual approach toward wholeness by insisting: "<u>without</u> spirituality, psychology cannot really free us or lead us to the deepest truths about ourselves, <u>without</u> psychology, spirituality can only lead to grandiosity, delusion, and an attempt to escape from reality." (Riso and Hudson, *The Wisdom of the Enneagram*, p.28)

This Chapter focuses on the psycho-spiritual approach toward wholeness by integrating two disciplines: the Riso-Hudson's Enneagram and Christian spirituality.

THE CORE OF THE HUMAN BEING

There is so much confusion in our use of three terms to designate the core of the human being: <u>the ego, the self, and the soul</u>. We easily can avoid using these terms or we use them as loosely interchangeable, as if each term referred to the same entity and meant approximately the same thing. Or we could consider ego, self, and soul as pointing to three quite separate and discrete entities.

Charles Gerkin, a Pastoral Theology Professor, in his book, *the Human Document* clarifies these three terms for us (Gerkin, *the Human Document*. pp.98-100):

- "The term *ego* is a psychological term best used to point to the core of individual human functioning at which the nexus of forces that shape human conflict come together and are mediated. *Ego* points to the center of the *self* when seen from the perspective of dynamic psychology. The *ego* is subject to the givens of conflicting forces within the individual person as well as the interjected forces coming from the primary relationship… The *ego* demands mediation and compromise."

- In the Freud's system, "the *ego* is the conscious aspect of the psyche that chooses between the base instincts [passion] of the *id* and the morality of the *superego*. A person with an "ego problem" is considered to be *self-centered*. He or she is thought of as boastful, selfish, and obnoxious.

- "The term *self* is the interpretive core of human being experience when viewed through the perspective and language of *object relations theory* (psychology). To use the designation *self* is to emphasize the line of experienced continuity and interpretive capacity." The *self* seeks meaning, while the *ego* seeks force."

- "The term *soul* is used as a theological term [unfortunately, the church no longer uses this term] that points to the self's central core subject to the ego's conflicting forces and to the ultimate origins of the *self* in God. The *soul* (theological term) is the gift of God bestowed upon the individual with the breath of life. It is thus the *self*, including its *ego* conflicts, as seen from an ultimate perspective—the perspective of the *self* as nurtured and sustained in the life of God."

- "All three terms--*ego, self, soul*--point toward the same entity, the *central core* of individual human life. They are separate entities, but in functional unity."

- "The life of the *soul* is thus seen as having largely to do with the *self*'s struggle with the conferred identity of the *self*'s historical social context and the claiming of that identity conferred upon the *self* by virtue of its participation in the coming Kingdom."

- "There is another term that has been used with increasing frequency in recent years with reference to a central core of the human individual: the term *identity*. "In psychological circles the term *identity* has become popular in response to the pluralistic and privatized social situation of contemporary life. *Identity* designates the self's effort to maintain some level of consistent attitude, vision, and response in what otherwise would be a situation of fragmentation."

- "Psychologist Erick Erikson's use of the term *identity* has more technical meaning, having to do with a certain configuration of characteristics of a private self with a sense of continuity and self-sameness through the changing circumstances and altering tasks of the human life cycle. *Identity*, for Erikson, points to a certain idiosyncratic way in which the individual *ego* performs its tasks of perceiving, valuing, reasoning, compromising, and choosing."

- *Identity* is both an individual human project and something conferred upon the individual by the significant figure in the person's life."

- "Theologian Jürgen Moltmann uses the term *identity* in a less psychologically technical sense than does Erikson. In Moltmann's concept of the paradoxical *identity* of the church and of the *self*, he does emphasize the conferred nature of *identity*. Both *identity* embedded in history and the *eschatological identity* is received: the one from the historical circumstances in which human life takes place and the other from the church's or the individual's participation in *the coming kingdom of God*."

- "Both Erickson and Moltmann emphasize the importance of context in relation to *identity*. Human historicity creates a certain "given-ness" of context. For better or worse that context will largely determine who we are. But, for Moltmann there is another context: the context of the coming into reality of the Kingdom. It is that context that holds forth the transforming possibility for human life, including life of the *self.*"

I hope that the readers appreciate this lengthy explanation of these terms and understand why it is so vital to reclaim the word *soul* in Christian's expression of the core of personhood. The founder of the Methodist Movement in 19th Century in England, John Wesley used to greet people by asking: "How is your soul?"

Wellness of the *psyche* (soul or mind) can be defined as the balanced state of "feeling, thinking, and doing" more than just not being neurotic. The goal of psychological wellness involves unity of Three Intelligence Centers called "the Triads."

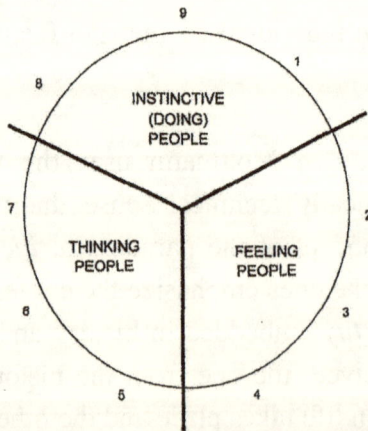

Figure 1. The Triads: Three Intelligence Center

THE TRIADIC SELF: INSTINCTIVE, FEELING, AND THINKING PERSON

The late Don Richard Riso and Russ Hudson taught their insights concerning the Triadic Self, *the Triads*:

> "If human beings were able to stay centered in their Essential unity, there would be no need for the Enneagram. But without working on ourselves, we cannot become centered. It is a universal perception of the great spiritual traditions that human nature is divided—against itself, and against the Divine. Our *lack* of unity is, in fact, more characteristic of our "normal" reality than our Essential unity...The Triads are important for transformational work because they specify where our chief imbalance lies. The Triads represent the three main clusters of issues and defenses of the ego-self, and they reveal the principal ways in which we contract our awareness and limit ourselves. This first grouping of the types refers to the three basic components of the human psyche: instinctive (doing), feeling, and thinking." (Riso and Hudson. *The Wisdom of Enneagram*, p. 49)

The Instinctive Triad is concerned with resistance and control of the environment. The instinctive persons have issues with aggression and repression. They seek <u>autonomy</u>. Underneath their ego defenses they carry a great deal of rage (anger). Their primary temptation is *power*-seeking.

The Feeling Triad is concerned with love of false self and self-image. The feeling persons have issues with identity and hostility resulting from their "narcissistic wounding." They seek <u>attention</u>. Underneath their ego defenses they carry a great deal of shame and guilt. Their primary temptation is *popularity*-seeking via sensationalism.

61

While the Instinctive Triad is about maintaining a felt sense of self and the Feeling Triad is about maintaining a personal identity, *the Thinking Triad* is concerned with finding a sense of inner guidance and support. The thinking persons have issues with insecurity and anxiety. They seek security. Underneath their ego defenses their underlying feeling is fear. Their primary temptation is *possession*-seeking. From above information we can identify and focus on three essential factors blocking the wellness in the psychological dimension. They are *anger (rage)* in the instinctive type persons; *shame* in the feeling type persons, and *fear* in the thinking type persons. The rest of this chapter will focus on healing of these three factors so that one may recover the original harmony of human Essence in the Triads: the Instinctive [Doing] Center, the Feeling Center, and the Thinking Center:

A. Healing Anger with Forgiveness for the wellness in the Instinctive /Doing Types;

B. Healing Shame with God's gift of Self-Worth for the wellness in the Feeling Types;

C. Healing Fears with Trusting God's Providence in the Thinking Types.

HEALING ANGER (RAGE) WITH FORGIVENESS

ILLUSTRATION 6

Thi Kim Phuc was a victim of the napalm strike in Vietnam. Many of us saw the Pulitzer-prize-winning photograph of a 9-year-old girl running naked because she had ripped off her burning clothes as she was running in the aftermath of a napalm attack.

A quarter century after the Vietnam War (1972), John Plummer, now a pastor of a United Methodist Church in a small town in Virginia, saw the picture with a short description. "Her picture was indelibly burned into my heart and soul and was to haunt me for many, many years. It was I who had sent the bombs into her village, Trang Bang. Each time he saw the picture, he wanted to tell Kim Phuc how sorry he was." In June 1996 Plummer happened to see a network news story that she was not only alive but also living in Toronto.

She had been operated on by San Francisco plastic surgeon, Dr. Mark Gorney, to remove the scar tissue that had hardened into a scaly crust. Her chin had been fused to her chest by scar tissue, and she was left with her left arm stuck to her rib cage. In an interview, she said: "It took a 14 month hospital stay... I was raised a Buddhist and I became a Christian in 1982."

When Palmer finally met Kim, he began to shake all over as wracking sobs were torn from his body. He also felt like he was going to scream at the revelation that not only he was responsible for Kim's burns but that he had also killed her two brothers. All he could say was: "I am sorry; I am so sorry; I am so deeply sorry..." At that point Plummer's friends surrounded and embraced him in a silent show of support.

Later Kim was asked how she felt when she met the pilot of the plane who destroyed her village and her family. She told them that she forgave him and that they cannot change the past, but she hopes that they both could work together to build the future. "She is, Plummer declared, "the closest thing to a saint I ever met." He told how she got down on her knees and prayed for him in the hotel lobby on that day. She now considers Plummer her brother and calls often to chat. There was unconditional forgiveness and reconciliation, allowing for healing for both of them.

THE SOURCE OF ANGER

There are a large number of people who approach every life situation defensively. They are quick to combat and seem to be continually in a stage of anger against some persons or some causes. These persons are always itching for a fight because they have build-up angry feelings. They are assertive people (Karen Horney's "moving against people") who insist or demand that they get what they want. This happens to many people who have experienced various kinds of childhood trauma. They think that if they just don't acknowledge what happened by ignoring it or numbing it, the traumatic memories will go away. But the hurt does not go away. The impact of the ignored trauma grows and grows, so does their anger toward those who hurt them when they were helpless and defenseless children. As the painful memories become unbearable, they have built-up of angry feelings.

Usually the persons dominated by anger or rage is not happy about their unhealthy condition. They do not want to make enemies or lose their capacity to operate effectively in life. They know that their aggressive behaviors continually cause them difficulty. The syndrome of unbalanced emotions growing out of anger can be noted in the breakup of the home, in international relations, in racial relations, in the varied aspects of interpersonal relations (in job and even in church), as well as the manifestation of *psychosomatic* disorders.

St. Paul, in writing to the early Church in Ephesus, gathers together in one sentence the characteristics of the angry person and invites his readers to put aside such behaviors. He knows how disruptive such feelings are in the life of the church and the individuals in it. He knows (as I do) because there was a time when he lived and was driven by these same angry feelings. If anger emerges, it is because it was already present—latent, contained, but very real.

64

But he also provides us with a prescription for "how to overcome anger (rage)."

> "Put away from you all bitterness and wrath and anger and wrangling and slander, together with all malice, and be kind to one another, tenderhearted, forgiving one another, as God in Christ has forgiven you" (Ephesians 4:31,32).

We can picture the mounting destructiveness of angry feelings. Coming out of bitterness, seething in wrath and welling up in anger, and finally bursting forth with the uncontrolled rage of the clamorous person in words that injure and cripple personalities—this, says St. Paul, is the way anger (rage) works. But the inner healing of persistent anger is possible by the way of forgiveness. The power of the forgiving spirit can transform the destructive energy of anger into a positive driving force for personal development and for standing for social justice and peace. This was demonstrated in the story of Thi Kim Phuc and John Plummer in the Illustration 6.

FORGIVING SOMEONE WHO HURTS US

Forgiveness is not possible in our own human strength of determination. Only those who have experienced God's unconditional forgiveness convince me that forgiveness is possible. It is an unmerited favor that we receive at the moment we put our trust in the redemptive work of Jesus Christ. We are forgiven by the grace of God, so that we are empowered to forgive those who hurt us when we were helpless, defenseless, powerless victims.

I have dedicated one chapter on the theme of <u>forgiveness</u> in my recent book, *God of Active Verbs, A to Z,* including my own experience and biblical/theological reflections. In my book I introduce the concept of "*Han,*" a Korean philosophical concept, as an emotion coming from "critical wound generated by unjust social, political, economic, and cultural repression or oppression." (Cho-Kim, pp. 67-68)

The Korean-American theologian Andrew Sung Park, enlightens the Western minds: "*Han* entrenches itself in the soul of victims of sin and crime. *Han* is demonstrated by diverse reactions such as those of the survivors of the Nazi holocaust, the Palestinians in occupied land in the Middle East, the racially discriminated against, battered wives, the molested, the abused, and the exploited. *Han* is a festering wound, a frustrated hope." (The Living Pulpit, <u>8</u>(4): 22-23, 1999)

Professor Park further explains: "Unresolved anger becomes *Han* because of its powerlessness and frustration and unresolved anger that may result in "*Sal,*" an ill-fated revenge. The person experiencing *Han* may negatively seek revenge and try to destroy the oppressor. In this case the *Han* is like the "black hole" of the universe. The sin of oppressors may cause *Han* of the oppressed. And the vicious cycle of unresolved anger ensues. However, when *Han* is resolved in justice-based unconditional forgiveness, *Han* can be the energy of sublimation as demonstrated by the life of Nelson Rolihlahla Mandela.

AN EXTRAORDINARY GIFT OF UNCONDITIONAL FORGIVENESS

I read the tribute to Mandela given by Rev. Peter Storey during the memorial gathering on December 10, 2013. He was the former prison Chaplain during Mandela's imprisonment. Nelson R. Mandela served twenty-seven years in prison for leading the political movement against the apartheid regime in South Africa. He writes: "We are so grateful that God made Nelson R. Mandela, purified him in suffering and gave him two divided land to help us become different—the kind of people we were meant to be. Mandela was keenly aware that his life was inextricably bound up with the lives of all his fellow human beings, especially his enemies. He would not bend an inch in his determination to win freedom for his people, and would not be humiliated by the cruelty of his prison guards, and yet he said to his comrades as soon as they arrived on Robben Island, "Chaps, these Afrikaners may be brutal. But they are human beings. We need to understand them and touch the human being inside them, and with them."

As I watched the broadcasting of the event, I was amazed by numbers of the world leaders gathered at the Mandela's memorial gathering. Some of them were enemies to each other. I was wondering how they would remember and honor a person whose legacy is forgiving his enemies and reconciling with the ones who persecuted him.

When Peter Storey was elected to lead the Methodist Church in South Africa, he received a letter of encouragement from Mandela who was in Prison on Robben Island. In it Mandela wrote: "The greatest glory in living is not never falling, but in rising every time you fall."

Richard Stengel, Time's managing editor, wrote Mandala's biography. In his interview with Mandela in his 90th birthday celebration, asked very poignant question: "When you walked onto Robben Island in 1964, you were emotional, headstrong, easily stung. But after 27 years in prison you emerged as a balanced and disciplined man. How did the man who emerged from prison differ from the willful young man who had entered it?" After much thoughts Mandela said: "I came out mature."

Stengel points out: "In many ways, Mandela's greatest legacy as President of South Africa is the way he chose to leave it after serving only one term. When he was elected in 1994, Mandela probably could have pressed to be President for life—and there were many who felt that in return for his 27 years in prison, that was the least South Africa could do... Mandela was determined to set a precedent for all who followed him, not only in South Africa but accross the rest of the continent...And he devoted the rest of his life as a 'peace-maker.' And he concludes his article (Time, July 21, 2008, p48): "There is nothing so rare—or so valuable—as a mature man."

Many of us feel guilty that we cannot forgive someone(s) who hurt us. In reality the guilty feelings are from our inner pain inflicted by the wounds. When our deep inner wounds are healed by experiencing God's unconditional forgiveness in our personal lives, the inner wounds are healed by God's grace, and the old painful feelings of persistent anger and resentment melt swiftly away as the sun removes the piled-up winter snow.

RECEIVING UNCONDITIONAL FORGIVENESS

James W. Kemp, in his book, "The Gospel According to Dr. Seuss," writes his reflections on Dr. Seuss's delightful children's stories. He admits that Dr. Seuss (His real name was Theodor S. Geisel) was his "favorite theologian." He said: "When I was a pastor, I found that I could find no better illustrations for biblical principles than I found in Dr. Seuss's stories." I have chosen his reflection on the story, "How the Grinch Stole Christmas!" because it brings relevance to my theme on transforming effects of receiving unconditional forgiveness. (Kemp, pp. 35-41, 77-81)

> "The Grinch is a bitter, grouchy, cave-dwelling crea-
> ture with a heart "two sizes too small" and he lives
> on snowy Mount Crumpet, a steep high mountain just

north of *Whoville*, home of the merry and warm-hearted *Whos*. His only companion is his unloved, but loyal <u>dog</u>, Max. From his perch high atop, the Grinch can hear the noisy Christmas festivities that take place in *Whoville*. Annoyed, he decides to stop Christmas from coming by stealing their presents, trees, and food for their Christmas feast. He crudely disguises himself as <u>Santa Claus</u> , and forces poor Max, disguised as a reindeer by tying an antler from a deer plaque on his wall, to drag a sleigh to *Whoville*, where he slides down the chimney and steals all of the *Whos'* Christmas presents, the <u>Christmas tree</u> , and the <u>log</u> of <u>fire</u> . He is briefly interrupted in his burglary by Cindy Lou, a little *Whos'* girl, but concocts a crafty lie to cover his escape from her home. The Grinch then takes his sleigh to the top of Mount Crumpet, and prepares to dump all of the presents into the abyss. As dawn breaks, he expects to hear the *Whos'* bitter and sorrowful cries, but is confused to hear them singing a joyous Christmas song instead. He puzzles for a moment until it dawns upon him that perhaps Christmas is more than presents and feasting: "Maybe Christmas, he thought, means a little bit more." The Grinch's shrunken heart suddenly grows three sizes larger. The transformed Grinch returns all of the *Whos'* presents and trimmings and is warmly invited to the *Whos'* feast, where he has the honor of carving the Roast Beast."

According to Merriam-Webster Dictionary, *grinch* is an "unpleasant person who spoils other people's fun or enjoyment." The Grinch in the story is an altogether miserable fellow. His whole motivation for trying to ruin, to steal Christmas, is to drag other people down to his level of misery and discontent. Because he is angry, he can't stand other people being happy.

We wonder what makes him so miserable and unhappy. The movie version of the story shows him as an alienated and rejected child by other kids.

James Kemp suggests three lessons we can glean from the story:

1. We can't pull ourselves up by dragging other people down—and we shouldn't allow others to do so;

2. In the movie version we can know how the Grinch became so miserable and angry. We see him very unpopular—an outcast. The other children ridicule him and bully him. It is in response to the pain of rejection and alienation that he flees to Mt. Crumpet to escape from his tormentors and wallows in his misery and bitterness. As he grew older, he became very angry person thinking about no one but himself.

3. We learn that an angry person can be changed by healing power of forgiveness. As dawn breaks on Christmas morning, he expects to hear the *Whos'* bitter and sorrowful cries, but Grinch is confused to hear them singing a joyous Christmas song in the town square.

The village people didn't care that everything was missing because they knew that material things are not the point of Christmas. And so the *Whos* formed a big circle and held hands, young and old, male and female, they joined together in song, celebrating life and love, family and friends.

When Grinch observed this unexpected scene, there was a new understanding that empowered the Grinch's undersized heart to grow three sizes. The change took place but not as a result of force or torture or punishment for the Grinch's crime of stealing Christmas. Coercion may successfully modify person's behavior, but it cannot transform a person's heart. A new insight, a new model, a new way of looking at things inspire change that rises up from within, and a new set of priorities.

Kemp concludes: "Instead of punishment, those humble *Whos* gave the Grinch a healthy dose of [forgiving] grace. And it was enough to change him forever."

WHAT FORGIVENESS DOES NOT MEAN?

Ray Pritchard in his book, "The Healing Power of Forgiveness," writes: "We can also find it helpful to know what forgiveness does not mean." (Prichard. p.156)

- Denying the evil that was done;

- Excusing sinful behavior;

- Pretending it never happened;

- Glossing over the pain you suffered;

- Removing all consequences for wrong behavior;

- Overlooking criminal behavior;

- Approving of evil;

- Condoning abuse;

- Acting as if the sin never happened;

- Letting others continually abuse you;

- Pretending you weren't hurt."

Forgiveness is not a magic trick we can force others to become our friend again. It's not a tool designed to manipulate others into confessing what they hurt us so greatly. He also provides a list of many different word pictures of forgiveness. Here are just two of them as the examples.

- "To forgive is to grant a full pardon to a condemned criminal.

- "When we forgive, we consciously, before God, cancel the debt. We discard the note." (Ibid. pp. 156-157)

FORGIVE AND FORGET VS. REMEMBER AND FORGIVE

As I grew in the Spirit, I became aware that the fundamental orientation of Christian life needs to be grounded in the truth that we are people who can get hurt easily, but also we are capable of committing horrifying sins, including the evil violence that crucified Jesus Christ on the cross. The good news is that we are forgiven sinners who are enabled by the Holy Spirit to forgive others as a way of life. The problem is that we refuse to accept the truth of our being sinners and of the divine solution of breaking the cycle of sin.

Clichés like "forgive and forget," get in the way of the deep understanding of forgiveness. This mandate is not only bad theological

72

advice, but is also without psychological or sociological merit. As Christians our biblical faith is grounded in *remembrance*. We are called to remember the pain and suffering of Jesus on the cross by the sacrament of *Holy Communion*. Forgiveness is not a magical act that wipes a slate clean. Our acts impact the world in ways that cannot be erased. Past traumas that have caused pain and suffering are only redemptive when, through faith, we live into a different future; we remember past horrors (traumas) so that <u>they are not repeated</u>. We are not to "forgive and forget," but rather to "remember and forgive."

The Holy Spirit helped me to <u>forgive</u> Chuck (my step-father) who molested me when I was a teen-ager by remembering that we all share our human nature. And we all stand in need of the grace and love of God who forgives. I simply forgave him as a person who shares our common sinful nature. I am certain that God forgave Chuck too when I forgave him. I could not tell Chuck that I have forgiven him in person because he died of a major stroke and he could not even remember what he did to me. I have learned to develop the spirit of forgiving others who hurt me, by writing my <u>hurts on the sand</u> and by engraving my <u>good benefits and blessings in my heart.</u>

I was uplifted by the following parable story written by unknown person:

> "Two friends were walking through the desert. During some point of the journey they had an argument and one friend slapped the other one's face. The one who got slapped was hurt emotionally, but without saying anything, wrote on the sand: 'Today, my best friend slapped my face.'
>
> They kept on walking, until they found an oasis, where they decided to take a bath. The one who had been

slapped by his best friend, got stuck in the mire and started drowning, but his friend saved him. After he recovered from the near drowning, he wrote on his pocket book: 'Today, my best friend saved my life.'

The friend who had slapped and saved his best friend asked him, 'after I slapped you, you wrote on the sand, but now, you write in your pocket book. "Why?" The other friend replied. 'When someone hurts me, I write it down on the sand where the wind [in Hebrew *ruach* means Spirit] of forgiving Spirit can take it away. But, when someone does something good to me, I write on my note book so that the wind will engrave it in my heart to remember and be grateful.'"

IS FORGIVENESS AN EVENT OR A PROCESS?

I think both are correct. It is an event because at one point we have to decide to forgive for it is good for our souls. It is a process because we decide to forgive someone in our head, but it takes longer to forgive someone in our heart. Meanwhile, we feel guilty that our painful feelings keep coming back. Our relationships remain damaged with awkward tensions.

It took me thirty-five years to confront my mother in a loving way in telling her that I had been angry with her for long time for not believing my story about the sexual abuse by my stepfather. She said, "Was it true? I am very sorry that I did not believe you." And I told her, "I forgive you." We shared our tears together. Then, we embraced each other for a long time. (Cho-Kim, p. 61)

74

HEALING SHAME (AND GUILT) WITH GOD-GIVEN SELF-WORTH

ILLUSTRATION 7

While I was at a clergy support group in my District, a pastor told the group about a young Korean woman without identification who was in a hospital because she attempted suicide by starving herself. As I was listening, I knew intuitively who that person might be. I had an urgent prompting to go to the hospital and see her.

I found her in a Psych Unit of the hospital. When I saw her being fed by IV, I believe that I was sent there through divine guidance. She was no longer "Jane Doe," because I provided her personal information to the hospital administration. As Mia became stronger daily, she told me her story about how she was found half dead on the street. I had known her since she came to the United States four years ago to study at a college in Pittsburgh. Her parents had stopped sending her the tuition money because of their financial bankruptcy in Korea. So she became a nanny for professional couple with two young children. The husband was a medical doctor and his wife was a graduate student in psychology.

When Mia successively completed a bachelor's degree in Computer Science, I was able to help her to get a full scholarship in a graduate degree program at the University of Pittsburgh. I became her mentor and we used to meet regularly while I was doing research at the same campus as a research professor. She had bad scar on her face from a house fire when she was very young. She had several corrective plastic surgeries in Korea. She was a very pleasant and kind person and good to two children (3 and 1 year old) in her charge. I remember one time she told me that the older child always asks her to "play horse" so that she can ride on Mia's back. I am not sure whether she was trying to tell me what was going on inside of that house. I should have asked more leading questions about her comment.

After I became an ordained United Methodist clergy (please refer to my story (found in Cho-Kim, pp. 101-102), I was appointed to a church far away from the city and we were disconnected from each other for a year. But, on that day the Spirit moved me to go visit this "un-identified woman" at the hospital.

Something bad must have happened to her! Because she had quit her job as a nanny and had taken an apartment. She told me that she had a mental health issue (I did not know that!) so she could not hold onto any decent job. Consequently, she could not afford to pay for her rent, utility bills, and food. She told me that she starved for three weeks and finally she went out to the street to seek help. People who found her called an ambulance.

My church friends raised money for recovering Mia to pay for the back rent and utility bills. When she was discharged from the hospital, she was not able to sustain herself. So, I made an arrangement through her best friend in Los Angeles to take care of her until she was strong enough to return to Korea.

What drove her to attempt a suicide? I believe that it was her feeling of *shame* that drove her to *depression* and *suicide attempt*. I wonder whether I could have done more for her. Later, I heard from her friend in Los Angeles that she was doing much better in Korea.

THE SOURCE OF SHAME AND/OR GUILT

Shame comes from the presence of violence in the form of sexual abuse, physical abuse, and verbal abuse, particularly in early childhood. The abuse usually violates the common sense and reasoning. If a child simply breaks a household item by mistake, and was punished harshly and unreasonably, that child's sense of fairness and understanding of cause and effect are totally destroyed. I heard of a child who broke one of the house rules and was locked in the closet until the next day. This punishment violated the child's sense of justice and later she developed claustrophobia as an adult. Sometimes children are abandoned, neglected, or brutally treated.

The cycle of abandonment and abuse and neglect can reach extreme proportions.

We have read and heard about horror stories. Children were tied up, beaten, burned with cigarettes, urinated on, raped, forced to perform perverted sexual acts on adults, forced to kill animals, and so on. At schools some children become victims of bullying. They grow up as victims and prisoners of their past. They believe that something must be profoundly wrong with them. Their shameful experiences of childhood may cause them feel inferior and worthless. Early emotional attitudes of their parents may have given them the feeling that they were not wanted. Childhood experiences such as illness or long hospitalization may have given them a feeling of separation and a lack of personal competence. Such episodes create a backlog of emotions about which a complex of inferiority feelings can grow and their sense of self-worth plunges.

REACTIONS TO VICTIMIZATION

Dr. E. Gene Rooney, in his book Amphorae, writes: "Although most of us intellectually know that hardships and heartaches are a natural part of human life, some of us come to believe that we will personally escape and be miraculously spared our share of normal strife. We become victims of what has been labeled the 'princess syndrome.' We begin to believe that if we are a good person, if we try hard, if we are sincere, if we have enough faith, etc., that somehow all the hurt and pain that comes to everyone else will mysteriously and mercifully pass over us. Then, when our universal share of disappointment and disillusionment happens, as it undoubtedly will, we receive this as a sign that we are not worthy, and that we have been singled out by a malevolent deity or by fickle fate for cruel and unusual punishment. Thus, since we have tied our self-concept to escaping discomfort and disappointment, every time problems happen in our lives, we react with self-doubt and self-loathing." (Rooney, *Amphora*, pp. 27-28)

Sometimes, some would turn their violence outward in the form of vandalism, assault, and criminal activity, while others would turn inward in the form of shame, self-rejection, and depression. According to Kay Arthur, "The first degree of depression is dejection (a lowness of spirit, a feeling of spiritual and emotional fatigue). If not reversed this dejection takes us down even further, plunging us into despair and finally into utter demoralization. At this stage of descent or disintegration, hope is entirely abandoned and is replaced by apathy and numbness. Fear becomes overwhelming and paralyzing and can degenerate further into disorder and reckless action that is heedless of consequences. Unresolved depression eventually can lead to untimely death." (Arthur, *As Silver Refined*, p. 13)

It is very important to note that there is a big difference between shame and guilt. Guilt is a sense of painful feeling comes from what *you* have done wrong, while shame is a sense of painful feeling comes from what *others* have done to you. But, these victims of the sexual abuse are confused that they are responsible for their pain and suffering. If we want to be free from a deep sense of shame, we must claim the God-given self-image.

I have addressed the composition of self-image in my previous book:

"One's self-image has three very important, very distinct, and very powerful components: self-evaluation (self-judgment), social–worth, and self-esteem...While self-evaluation deals with perceived personal competence and demonstrated performance and social-worth is derived from the evaluation of others, self-image is one's innate, God-given worth as human being who is created in the image of God...Being a person esteemed by God does little practical good until we act as a person esteemed by God. Living out the truth of our image, then, is every bit as important as coming to understand the concept that self-esteem is the foundation for self-image." (Cho-Kim, *God of Active Verbs*, pp. 233-234)

Cecil G. Osborne clarifies: "If you lack self-esteem, it is not because you do not have enough education or money, or because you are not physically attractive. It is solely because of your own evaluation of your self. And this has come about largely because of your early childhood. We get our basic sense of self-worth from parents and other authority figures. If you did not get enough affirmation and acceptance to make you feel worthwhile or okay, then you can begin to work to improve your self-image." (Osborne, *The Art of Becoming a Whole Person*, p.103)

Lack of self-esteem is not a rare phenomenon, observed only in emotionally damaged persons who suffer the pain of shame. The vast majority of human beings suffer from shame in some degree, chiefly because of impatient, or hostile, or unloving, un-accepting parents. Jesus deals with the tragic consequences of a weakened sense of self-esteem when he urges his listeners to deal ever so tenderly with small children:

> "If any of you put a stumbling block before one of these little ones who believe in me, it would be better for you if great mill stone were fastened around your neck and you were drowned in the depth of the sea. Woe to the world because of stumbling blocks! Occasions for stumbling are bound to come, but woe to the one by whom the stumbling block comes!" (Matthew 18:6-7)

PRINCIPLE WAYS TOWARD POSITIVE SELF-IMAGE

According to Dr. E. Gene Rooney, there are fourteen principles we may follow to assist us in the task of keeping our self-image strong and positive: (Rooney, *AMPHORE*, pp. 38-59).

1. *Developing an affirming spirit is fundamental.*

   A denying, punitive, judgmental spirit is never as corrective, as helpful or as useful as its possessor hopes it will be. The victims need to hear repeatedly:

   "It's not your fault!"

2. *Helping people identify with their successes rather than their defeats is an essential directional shift.*

   After each setback they merely pick themselves up, brush themselves off, learn from the painful experience and move on to the next challenge.

3. *Complementing people of their progress is very useful.*

   Realistically tell them what they're doing well helps them value themselves   regardless of successes or defeats.

4. *Learning to seek and tap into that inner space in everyone where s/he wants to feel good about her/himself is a major motivator.*

   Self-image is greatly enhanced when we tap into that wellspring.

5. *Knowing that people were created to respond to people is basic to understanding human nature.*

   Responding to others on a principled, caring, responsible level enhances self-worth in all parties.

6. *Accepting the fact that one's relationships with others and one's own self-image mutually interact and impact one another is fundamentally important.*

   It is vitally important to choose very wisely and carefully the company we keep.

   Our sense of self-value will have a hard time surviving regular, harsh attacks.

7. *Reframing all failures into feedback is essential for turning life's negative lessons into useful ones.*

   Whenever we fail, we ask the question, "What did I learn from this situation that I might not have learned had it been more successful?"

8. *Affirming the person while rejecting negative or harmful behavior is essential to both relationship and self-value.*

   All societies have learned the need for sensible boundaries, fair limits, and clear guidelines.

9. *Focusing on the positives in any given situation is basic mental health model of good self-image.*

It matters not how long you live, but how well you live. Life is like a cash register, in that every account, every thought, and every deed, like every sale, is registered and recorded. Those with good self-image have not always led better, easier, more sheltered lives with more joys, more rewards and more love. Those with low sense of self-worth are not always those that have been kicked around the most or the worst; the difference is not in external reality, but internal reality.

10. *Realizing your personal worth is the most important, most holy mission of your life. Know that you have the power to choose!*

Choose love, not hate; choose gentleness, not violence; choose holiness, not evil! Dare to believe that the Reign of Love and Peace is coming soon! Ready yourself for it!

11. *Giving yourself time is wise.*

The seed is a metaphor whose power has been almost totally lost on our culture. The seed is the way God works. With adequate time the seed grows, "first the blade, then the ear, then the full grain shall appear."

12. *Loving others provides the motivation for growth that we all innately need.*

We all need to accept the love of God; we all need to have self-love; we need to be loved by and to give love to our significant others. We need affection, approval, acceptance, achievement, acclamation, and attention.

13. *Releasing suppressed and repressed memories is a step towards healing a bruised self-image.*

Someone has said that repression means to have forgotten, and suppression means to have forgotten that you have forgotten. Unfortunately, out of sight is not out of mind. A picture out of focus, a voice out of tune, a feeling out of sync does not cease to exist. From the security of their hiding places, these memories carry on their horror work. Having forgotten we sent them to the dungeon, then hearing only the mournful moans in the dark, we come to believe that the "house" is haunted.

14. *Discovering the new whole person is the final step toward which all the other principles have been moving.*

Past traumas are brought up out of the darkness, defanged, faced, and accepted. The desires and the anxieties, the phobias and the fears, are transformed. Not renovated, not redecorated, not redefined, but transformed.

GOD-GIVEN SELF-WORTH

An authentic sense of self-worth is accompanied by accepting God's valuation of us in place of the self-evaluation, or the social-worth evaluations of our culture or of others. But, God's valuation of us as a person is based alone on our intrinsic human worth. Therefore, we no longer search to find out "Who am I?" Because we have the answer: "I am *a beloved* child of God who frees me from my sense of shame and guilt by uplifting my self-worth."

This God-given self-esteem can*not* be destroyed by storm or fire in life. It is an anchor that no hurricane of life can tear down. In this day of market place mentality, everything and everyone is valued by their capacity to produce, their balance sheet or their capital net profit. But, this concept of God-given self-esteem liberates us from being a thing with relative values to a person with an eternal value and infinite worth. It is based on our innate sacredness as human beings. We are God's image-bearers. Nothing in the world can ever make us question our self-esteem because nothing in the world can give it to us. It is created within us an innate gift and a permanent sacredness. This truth leads us to self-love with humility and humanity.

The key to mental and emotional stability and wellness is our fully accepting this God's gift of self-worth by radically trusting in his agape-love; by our steadfast hope of endurance, even when social worth perceptions and self-evaluation judgments go down. If we don't, our sense of self-worth fluctuates with the market. If we don't, our self-worth as a person is up for grabs. But, when we have an unshakable foundation upon which to rest our identity, nothing can shake us. Authentic self-esteem is never a question of accomplishment, or track record, or other's assessment of us, or even our own self-evaluation.

In the coming of the new world, God will not ask me, "Why were you not Oprah?" Rather, God will ask me, "Why were you not Hakyung?"

Let us pray to God: "Never let me be put to shame…so that all day long my tongue will talk of your righteous help, for those who tried to do me harm have been put to shame, and disgraced" (Psalm 71:1, 24).

HEALING FEARS BY TRUSTING GOD'S PROVIDENCE

In Appendix II, I have provided two worldviews (positive outlook vs. negative outlook on life) and how they affect our behaviors, our relationships, our characters, and our personalities. You want examine and study these thirty suggested poles and work on your weaknesses so that you may establish or increase your trust in God's providence.

ILLUSTRATION 8

Following is the story of Dr. J.P. Moreland, the Philosophy Professor at the Talbot Seminary, who suffered from a series of anxiety attacks that led to a debilitating depression for seven months. (Moreland and Issler, *In Search of Confident Faith*, pp. 145-147).

Almost immediately after sinking into an emotional and spiritual abyss, Dr. Moreland began to be plagued with doubts and self-criticism about his academic and scholarly work. He was filled with repeated self-accusations that he had wasted his life in his intellectual endeavors. This repeated thought plagued him for several weeks, plunging him into deeper depression. He felt his work had been meaningless and, as a result, that his whole life was basically meaningless. He was suffering from depression resulting from anxiety and the fear of failure.

In the midst of this plunge, he was invited to Columbia International University in Columbia, South Carolina, to deliver five-day lecture series. While he was there, he developed a severe migraine headache with so much pain that he ended up in a hospital emergency room at Irma, South Carolina, a long way from his home in Southern California. After about five minutes of triage work by the nurses, a doctor on call that evening walked in the room. He asked, "Are you Professor J.P. Moreland? Are you the one who teaches at Talbot Seminary?" He (JP) nodded. The emergency room doctor on call that evening was very excited and said: "Dr. Moreland, I can't thank you enough for what you have done in the intellectual world for the cause of Christ! I have read almost all your books, and, hey, you know that book *Body and Soul*, you wrote with Scott Rae? I teach ethics at a local community college, and I use that as a text. I can't believe I am getting to meet you!"

It turned out that Dr. Moreland had most likely eaten some bad shrimp at dinner the day before this happened, and he was told that it takes about twenty-four hours for food poisoning to hit someone. But as soon as this doctor shared with him the impact he had on him, it was like the Lord was speaking to him, saying, "I am well pleased with your academic work for my name's sake. You have done well. Keep trusting me." That's exactly what he needed. The experience helped him to trust in a God who consoles through a doctor to free him from his depression caused by the fear of failure.

After Dr. J.P. Moreland reflected on the event, he concluded: "It was one of *"incredible providential coincidences.* Sometimes God orchestrates a convergence of factors at just at the right moment to meet a need." (Ibid. p.147)

THE SOURCE OF FEAR OF INSECURITY

Persons in the Thinking Triad have issues with insecurity and vulnerability. They seek security and safety, and their underlying feeling is fear and anxiety. Their desire to be secure causes them to have a specific fear of being without support or guidance. They may have abandonment and deprivation issues in their childhood. Deprivation in early childhood is firmly imprinted in their heart and they are hungry for warm affection. They may accept substitutes (food, sex, drugs, information, money, power, adventure, etc.) to satisfy their hunger. And they search for more objects because the substitutes that have been working no longer satisfy them. They focus on what is missing rather than on what is available. When the missing substitutes are not found, panic sets in, then despair and chronic depression.

In the Psalm 55:4-6, the writer expresses his fear and horror... And he wishes to escape from his painful reality:

> "My heart is in anguish within me, the terrors of death
> have fallen upon me. Fear and trembling come upon me
> and horror overwhelms me. And I say, 'O that I had
> wings like dove! I would fly away and be at rest.'"

Like the Psalmist, people with the fear of insecurity and anxiety are suffering because they can find no sanctuary in life where they would be safe from "the wind and the storm." Life was too hard for them. They want to flee from their situations. This Psalm 55 is ancient writing, and yet those same realities—the threat of death, chaos in society, greed and fraud in the marketplace, overwhelming personal life, the possibility of betrayal by loved ones or friends as well as abandonment and deprivation issues in their childhood —can be heavy burden to any one, just as they were to the Psalmist.

There are other possible burdens that cause us to be insecure and anxious. Different people feel burdens differently. Some people are more sensitive to a stressor than others. Two different persons may react differently to a stressful situation. Those with the fear of insecurity and anxiety may overreact to a situation and to them the situation becomes their serious burden. When that happens, the Psalm invites them to "cast your burden upon the Lord, and he shall sustain you" (Psalm 55:22).

The text is very clear about the importance of our believing that God seeks to lessen our burdens and sustain us. Interestingly, the text does not say, "he shall remove it (the burden)." "God shall sustain you." means: with God's sustaining power, your soul will overcome the fear by healing your past memories and by renewing your mind.

<u>RELYING ON GOD'S PROVIDENCE</u>

Throughout different seasons of life, we have learned to rely upon God's consistent presence in all that happens. Ships leave or come into port on the tides that rise and fall at regular intervals. Farmers depend upon growing seasons with rain and sunshine. The sun rises each morning and sets each afternoon at clearly defined times.

This consistency of God makes us believe that nothing can befall us by chance, but by the direction of our most gracious God who watches over us with a paternal care, keeping all creatures so under his power that not a hair of our head (for they are all numbered), nor a sparrow, can fall to the ground, without the will of God, in whom we do entirely trust.

When we find ourselves having a panic attack, despair, or depression, we need to set apart a quiet time with God in a silent retreat. This is time to search our painful childhood memories—in the deep unconscious level-- and to ask God to reveal causes of our insecurity and anxiety and heal them. Once we identify past experiences of abandonment or deprivation, we can overcome the fear of insecurity by learning to trust God of Providence.

The root meaning of the term *providence* is *to foresee*, or *to provide*. The question of providence concerns how God thinks ahead to care for all creatures, fitting them for contingencies, for the challenges of history, and for potential self-actualization to the glory of God. God's providing looks ahead for needs as yet unrecognized by creatures. But more than simply foresight, providence has to do with the active, daily caring of God for the world in its hazards. Such caring requires not only formulating a plan but also acting patiently to carry out the plan over a long course of time.

Thomas C. Oden defends the traditional views of God's providence:

1. The faith in God's providence is not a pantheism, which confuses God and the world by absorbing God into world.

88

2. God of providence is quite different from the God of deism, which cuts God off from the world by making God the Creator of the world that God then abruptly leaves, as a watchmaker might leave a watch behind, implying complete separation between God and the world.

3. Providence is not a dualism which views the world as divided into two parts under a good power and a bad power that competes for control. Neither of which could be final, and therefore neither of which could be God.

4. Providence is distinguished from an in-determinism, which holds that the world is not under any intelligible control at all.

5. Providence is not a strict or unqualified determinism, which posits a control so absolute that it destroys human responsibility, freedom and accountability, viewing all events only in terms of their natural causal determination.

6. Providence is also sharply different from a view of God's Omni-causality that holds that God so does everything that all other agents do nothing.

7. Providence distinguishes itself from a doctrine of chance, which denies that the controlling power can be intelligible or personal or rational.

8. Finally, providence differs from a doctrine of fate, which denies that the ultimate power is benevolent.

Odon summarizes that "the theme of the providential caring of God for creation is widely dispersed throughout the Scriptures: God is preserving the creation in being; God is cooperating to enable creatures to act; God is guiding all creatures toward a purposeful end that exceeds the understanding of those being provided for." (Odon, *The Living God*, pp. 277-279)

GOD'S SPECIAL PROVIDENCE AND THE INTERCESSORY PRAYERS

As believers of the Bible, we pray because we believe in the God of both "general and special providence." Odon clarifies the difference:

> "Special providence means that God acts through particular events in special ways, as in the answering of intercessory prayers, and not just general providence alone. Rationalistic deism" resisted the notion of special or egocentric providence on the grounds that since God has created a good and intelligible system of natural order of the universe, God would not arbitrarily break that order on the whim of special supplications... Some argue on the strength of general providence in which God is powerless to intervene within the context of natural causality, and that it would be inconsistent with the divine majesty if God became enmeshed in special or petty occurrences of human history...Indeed, it must be admitted that special providence may be easily trivialized. Yet classical exegetes have generally argued both for general providence and for the special competence of God to become intimately involved at any particular point in human history while still respecting the intelligible natural order." (Odon, *The Living God*, p. 309)

Odon further states that "Without *general providence* the scope of divine care is <u>not universal</u>. Without *special providence* the <u>act of praying</u> is made absurd. For divine guidance occurs in whatever way is most fitting in caring for free, self-determining human agency, the wills of morally accountable persons, just as parental care looks for the most filling situational mode of guidance." (Prov. 4:11; Isa. 58:11; John 16:13)." (p. 309).

Abraham's faith that "The Lord will see and provide" (Genesis 22:8), manifested through testing, became the key paradigm of <u>faith in providence</u> for classical Jewish and Christian teaching (Hebrew 11:17). In the name *Jehovah-jireh (God provides)* the central insight of God's governing providence is contained. The Gospel of John would report the remarkable saying of Jesus, "Your father Abraham was overjoyed to see my day" (John 8:56). The implication is that Abraham trusted that God's promise would be fulfilled, even if it required a long and arduous history to accomplish. The end was clear, and he trusted that providence would find a means for the fulfillment of the promise. The Divine governance of the world is evident through nature, graces in history, and luminous disclosures in Scripture of the ways God uses evil for good and turns human wrath into praise (Psalm 70:10; Romans 8:28).

Oden's concluding remark of God's special providence gives us *courage*:

> "The teaching of providence is much closer to the daily life of the believer than at first might be supposed. It is interwoven with the power and courage to live the Christian life day by day, to persevere through trying difficulties, to celebrate divine guidance present in hostile environments. It is *faith in the special providence* that enables Christians to pray that God will carry them

through hazards, care for them, and be present to them amid ordinary and extraordinary human struggles. Without God's providing, the act of [intercessory] praying would be absurd." (Oden, *the Living God*, pp. 217-218)

The prayer in Psalm 71 expresses tremendous assurance in God's faithfulness, which results in praises. Even if we live in a world filled with adversity, suffering, and challenges, we can remain faithful and trust God who is <u>in control</u> of our lives. When we have that trust in the God of providence (both general and special), our <u>praise</u> becomes our lifestyle rather than an occasional ritual act.

I have a <u>fear of drowning</u> because my legs cramp easily in cold water. Learning to trust in God's providence is like learning <u>how to swim</u>. In spite of my fear I learned the right movements of arms and legs, and then I practiced turning my head at just a right angle for breathing with the minimum interruption of my speed. These skills allowed me to float in the water with great efficiency. But before I swim across a pool, I had to learn to trust the water's buoyancy. Just as it lifts my body up from the water, God's love has lifted me up when nothing else could help me from my sinking deep in sin... "But the Master of the sea heard my despairing cry, from the waters he lifted me now safe am I. Love lifted me! Love lifted me!" (Words by James Row)

Unless I learn to trust the water, swimming becomes useless kicking and stroking—it depletes my energy and it doesn't take too long I get panic and quit swimming because of my leg cramps. When we trust God who provides, He will lift you by his love out of the angry waves. When we willingly surrender to the buoyant power of the loving God, we will surely transcend the fear of adversity as well as insecurity. A strong and well-grounded confident trust (faith) in God's provision and protection stands as the best remedy for healing insecurity and anxiety.

And when someone asks us, "How is your soul?" With confident faith in God, we are able to respond: "It is well with my soul."

My favorite Hymn is, "It Is Well with My Soul." It is written by Horatio Stafford. In my previous book I have written about the background story. (Cho-Kim, *God of Active Verbs*, pp. 268-270)

The words are a prayer that God would help him to regain his faith and hope when he and his wife lost their four daughters during a Mid-Atlantic voyage as they headed toward Jerusalem as missionaries. As he was in deep sorrow, he was able to write these words:

"When peace, like a river, attended my way,
When sorrow like sea billows roll;
Whatever my lot, thou hast taught me to say,
It is well, it is well with my soul.

And, Lord, haste the day when my faith shall be sight,
The clouds be rolled back as a scroll;
The trump shall resound, and the Lord shall descend;
Even so, it is well with my soul." (The UMH, #377).

CHAPTER 3

HEALING AND WELLNESS IN THE SIRITUAL DIMENSION

NOTICING GOD IN OUR DAILY LIVING

The God of the Bible is indeed alive and is actively involved in our personal lives in the contemporary world. This God whose inner nature is compassion for the hurting world is busy doing something so that good can come out of the human brokenness, disharmony, and incompleteness. With St. Paul we proclaim: "We know that all things work together for good for those who *love* God, who *are called* to according to his *purpose*" (Romans 8:28).

I confidently proclaim that "the uniqueness of Christianity is to believe in the triune God who reveals Godself in three different ways. This faith leads each of us toward an intimate relationship with the triune God and toward a more mature Christian; a relevant, compassionate witness in the world. It also guides each of us to establish balanced experiences with God who is working in the world in creating, redeeming, and sustaining ways:

a. The Transcendent, Creator God who exists and works beyond the world (the planet earth) as God *above* us;

b. The human face of redeeming God who is revealed in the person of Jesus Christ as God *among* us;

c. The immanent, sustaining God who is present and active throughout the world as the Spirit of God *within* us.

Our personal encounters with the triune God in our daily lives would make us believe in the gospel of peace (*shalom*) and make us respond to his love according to the Appendix I of my previous book, the *God of Active Verbs, A to Z*: It demonstrates that our experience of God's loving compassion can establish our willingness to respond to others in need with compassion. Therefore, we need to learn to "notice" or "discern" God's Presence in our ordinary daily lives by opening our whole beings to his work of compassion to the hurting world. (see Appendix I)

Our discipline (practice) in meditation and prayer fosters an attitude, which facilitates religious experience. The discipline then, functions to sharpen religious awareness and understanding, so that one can be more open to God's presence, and be more sensitive and reflective on our life events. We may come to realize that it was God who acted in them, even though we may have not recognized the divine Presence right at those moments.

Our realization of God's presence and God's loving actions in our lives comes after our discerning meditation and prayerful reflections. Jacques Ellul enlightens us: "Everything always has to be viewed in a retroactive light and what happens afterward makes you understand what went before. We shall never know it as a *God moment* when that encounter is taking place. It is always afterward that we can say, with astonishment, that strange situation, that impression, that unexplainable event was God." (Ellul, *Living Faith: Belief and Doubt in a Perilous World*, p. 267)

WANDERING IN THE WILDERNESS

A spiritual journey toward wholeness (holiness) may be compared to the Israel people's wilderness journey toward the Promised Land (Canaan) of "milk and honey." The journey began after the miracle of the Exodus event for their freedom from the bondage of Egyptian slavery. God led his people: "The Lord went in front of them in *a pillar of cloud* by day, to lead them along the way, in *a pillar of fire* by night, to give them light, so that they might travel by day and by night" (Exodus 13:21).

The history of the people of Israel is expressed in Psalm 78 that includes a long list of God's goodness and Israel's ingratitude:
*The rebellion of Israel peoples against the most High in a poetic way (vv. 9-31);
*The stubbornness of the Wilderness first generation—providing a monotonous succession of sin, punishment, repentance, and pardon (vv. 32-39);
*The deliverance (Exodus) from Egypt (vv. 40-53);
*The Conquest of Canaan (vv. 54-55);
* Israel's infidelity, willful stubbornness, and rebellion against God (vv. 56-66);
*God's rejection of Ephraim and the election of Zion—David as the shepherd of Jacob about 1000 BC (vv. 62-72).

By telling the story, the Psalmist hopes that the following generations will not be like their ancestors. The writer tells future generations about God's provision through blatant improbabilities of nature: God divided the sea; God made a cloud by day and a fire by night to lead Israel people; God provided them food from the air and water from the rock.

We often wonder why they did not soften their hearts after experiencing such miracles of above-mentioned improbabilities and they rebelled against God's leading of their wilderness journey. Sadly, the people of Israel neither showed gratitude nor fidelity toward Yahweh who delivered them out of slavery in Egypt because of their "spiritual amnesia." As the consequence, the first generation of Israelites died in the wilderness, except Joshua and Caleb, and the second generation of Israelites eventually arrived in the Promised Land after 40 years of wandering in the wilderness. This warns us that we too easily stumble by becoming ungrateful, thus committing the sin of spiritual amnesia (2 Peter 1:9-10), reminding us that we cannot achieve holiness (wholeness) by our human strength and efforts; only with the *sanctifying grace* of God.

GOD'S AMAZING GRACE AND OUR LIFE JOURNEYS

The Jesus' public ministry began with his baptism, followed by the descending of the Holy Spirit on him like a dove. John, the Baptist, testified: I heard a voice from heaven saying, "This is my Son, the Beloved; with whom I am well pleased" (Matthew 3:16-17). Jesus began his ministry of God's redemptive work after he was filled with the Spirit and was tempted by Satan in the wilderness for 40 days. We also begin our spiritual journey toward wholeness by accepting God's offering of salvation from the human bondage of sin and death by baptism (cleansing) of water and of the Holy Spirit.

This is a turning point of each person's life when he or she hears the God's awakening *call*: "Wake up, O sleeper, rise from the dead, and Christ will shine on you" (Ephesians 5:14). God calls all sleepers to salvation through his *prevenient grace*—the grace that precedes human response and prepares the hurting and lost souls for receiving God's salvation--caring and curing.

The *prevenient grace* is available in principle to *all* persons, but not everyone answers his wake-up call. Do you hear the Christ's calling now? He says, "Listen! I stand at the door and knock. If you hear my voice and open the door, I will come in to you and eat with you, and you with me (Revelation 3:20)." Those who accept this fantastic offer of salvation, saved from the power of sin and death, become free human beings who are living in Christ.

We see the evidence of God's *double grace* (justification and sanctification) in the life of the Apostle Paul. His conversion experience on the road to Damascus was recorded three times in the Book of Acts (Chapters, 9, 22, and 26). The powerful conversion story of Saul (Paul's name before his conversion) is inspirational because it shows how an angry Jewish persecutor against believers of the Way of Jesus was transformed to the Apostle Paul with the mission and vision to spread the gospel message of the *salvation* to the Gentiles of the day.

Many preachers love to proclaim this story and usually end it by saying: "He turned the world upside down for Jesus Christ *immediately*." But, they forgot to mention that it took some eighteen years of discipleship and learning about Jesus Christ. He interviewed Mary, the mother of Jesus, and Mark, who wrote the Gospel according to Mark. He spent three years in Damascus and the Arabian Desert, fourteen years in Tarsus, and a year in Antioch. He visited Jerusalem several occasions to validate his experiences with the Apostles Peter and James. He was on the life-long journey of sanctification in the Spirit of God.

INNER CONFLICTS WITHIN THE HUMAN SOULS

After Paul preached the gospel to the Gentiles far and wide, he wrote to the Christian congregation in Rome about his inner conflict and struggles:

> "...I do not understand my own actions. For I do not do what I want, but I do the very thing I hate...For I delight in the law of God in my inmost self, but I see in my members another law at war with the law of my mind, making me captive to the law of sin that dwells in my members. Wretched man that I am! Who will rescue me from this body of death?" (Romans 7:14-24)

It is alarming to hear the Apostle Paul's crying out, "Wretched man that I am! Who will rescue me from this body of death?" The anguish is coming from his awareness that there was a major inner conflict within his inmost self. He realized that the inner conflict is between the profound riches of the Essence -- the True Self -- and the more superficial, automatic, ego-inflated personality – the religious False Self.

Riso and Hudson enlighten us on this matter:

> "When the mechanisms of the personality are running the show, the most dire things can happen. All of us can think of dozens of times when we came very close to causing a disaster, something intervened to avert it. For instance, if wrong words had been spoken or if we had allowed rage, sarcasm, or pride to take over, the rest of our lives would have taken a different turn.

> That something was awareness. Suddenly we were able to wake up to the danger, the foolishness, and the

self-destructiveness of what we had been doing, and to stop it before things got worse. In retrospect, we may get cold shivers when we think about how close we came to losing a job, our best friend, and our marriage, or to alienating our children.

If something in us had not been awakened to see what we were *unconsciously* doing, the rest of our lives would be very different. The fact that we were present (aware) in those crucial moments changed the course of our own history and made all the difference...Awareness is part of our Essential nature [the Essence]: it is the aspect of our Being that registers our experience. Awareness is such a fundamental capacity, that it is almost impossible to imagine what our life would be like to be without it. We can also recognize awareness as our capacity to pay attention. Unfortunately, our attention is usually drawn into deep identifications with the preoccupations of our personality -- into fantasies, anxieties, reactions and subjective memories.

When our awareness becomes identified with these aspects of our personality, we lose contact with the immediacy of our lived experience. Our attention shrinks away from a broader perspective and from what is actually occurring around us. It contracts into narrow concerns or reactions and we "fall asleep." (Riso and Hudson, Understanding the Enneagram, pp. 13-14)

The Apostle Paul cried out, because he had a new awareness of his inner conflict and consequent "wake-up call." The Apostle Paul, after his conversion experience of the risen Lord on the road to Damascus, became a Spirit-filled missionary to the Gentiles, and yet he was tormented because he was losing *the war within*. He said: "I do not understand my own actions. For I do not do what I want, but I do the very thing I hate." When we receive our own "wake-up calls" it is the time for each one of us to begin the journey toward personality transformation which moves us forward on a deeper journey toward wholeness: the spiritual maturity.

LIVING IN THE CONTEMPORARY WORLD

In 1977 (37 years ago), Dr. Paul Tournier boldly diagnosed the inner conflict of modern man as repression of the Spirit, the very principle of the inner harmony:

> "Thus modern man [humanity], like an adolescent in profound crisis, appears to us to present a strange and contradictory mixture of naïve superstition, disillusioned skepticism, and partisan spirit. For in repressing values [conscience] without having freed himself from them, without ever being able to free himself from them—he has repressed the very principle of his inner harmony: the Spirit.

> Ever since human beings suppressed God, they have lost the concept of personhood. Because they have closed their eyes to the world of the Spirit, they have lost the sense of personhood. They cannot comprehend that they may become spiritual persons...

> For more than a hundred years now, medical science has pursued the direction of "materialism." And from that point of view a human being is compared with an

automobile with various parts—cylinders, ignition system, carburetor, headlights, and etc....The ideal of science is to separate these machine parts from the assemblage and to study them individually in order understand how each of them function. Then, each can be reduced to physico-chemical processes that are not alive. At least, they have to admit that different models of cars have <u>designers</u>. But in the case of human beings, they insist that different organs and their various chemico-physical functions merely happened <u>by accident</u> to come together to form an organism. Science rejects any argument from God being the Designer and the Creator...As an <u>individual</u> [part] human being belongs to the human species, to society, consequently to the state...But as a <u>person</u> he [she] belongs to God." (Tournier, *The Whole Person in a Broken World,* p. 34)

Dr. Paul Tournier was a prophet who warned us four decades ago:

"Today the person is regarded as a mere machine; the importance of the spiritual dimension of human beings is not recognized; the sense of humanity and justice is wounded; aggressive reactions against Christianity are unleashed. Then all the conflicts that result provoke fresh acts of violence and multiply the injustices. At the same time, we see how the problem of the person and the problem of the world are interrelated. If we ignore the human spirit in our concept of man (humanity), then society, the state, industry, and science, likewise, ignore the spiritual needs of human beings. They wound others and thus bring about that flood of aggressive reactions and conflicts which go on increasing in a vicious circle." (Ibid. p. 71)

Lyman Coleman agrees with Dr. Tournier's warning by writing,

"We live in a time considered to be a scientific and technological age. However, we have discovered that science and technology can't give us all we are searching for in life. These scientific disciplines can give us certain tools for living, but no direction for living...We are searching for more than they can give us. Because we are searching in a society, which has for so long, denied the reality of anything beyond the physical, our hunger [and thirst for righteousness for the spiritual dimension] is especially intense. The only problem is that we are uncertain where to find it! Our increased hunger has driven us to seek answers in astrology, connection with the earth, and on understanding of life beyond the physical through new age mysticism. While these avenues satisfy some, they leave many others confused and spiritually frustrated. Many are beginning to believe that it is time to rediscover biblical Christianity and the importance of the spiritual dimension of our life." (Coleman, *Whol-I-ness: Holy, Wholly, Holley*, p. 13)

NATURAL PERSON VS. SPIRITUAL PERSON

St. Paul explains the difference between a natural (unspiritual) person and a spiritual person: "Those who are unspiritual (natural) do not receive the gifts of God's Spirit, for they are foolishness to them, and they are unable to understand them because they are spiritually discerned. Those who are spiritual persons discern all things, and they are themselves subject to no one else's scrutiny" (1 Corinthians 2:14-15).

John Wesley, the father of the Methodist Movement, taught his followers his description of a natural man:

> "His soul is in deep sleep; his spiritual sense is not awake, s/he discerns neither spiritual good nor evil. This person is utterly ignorant of God, knowing nothing concerning him or her as he or she ought to know. He has no conception that evangelical holiness, without which no man shall see the Lord; nor of the happiness which only they find whose 'life is hid with Christ in God' (Colossians 3:3). And, for this very reason, s/he is fast asleep... and is blind."

Now is the time that we must reject the materialistic worldview and re-claim the biblical truth-- "that human beings are created in the image of God." Now is the time that we reclaim that God is the Spirit and we are spiritual beings with indwelling Spirit. Therefore, we must affirm and share our conviction that we are sacred human beings with the body, soul (mind), and spirit.

CONVERSION OF *JACOB* TO *ISRAEL,* FATHER OF THE NATION, ISRAEL

In Genesis 28, we meet Jacob. Here we see a natural man if there ever was one. He looks only to his own interests to interpret life. When we pick up Jacob's story, he has already made a big mess of things. He is more crooked than the Pennsylvania Turnpike. He has cheated his twin brother, Esau, out of his birthright and deceived his blind old father, Isaac, on his deathbed into giving him the blessing meant for Esau.

Esau was so mad that he plotted to kill Jacob. Jacob, following the advice of his mother Rebekah, fled to his uncle, Laban, his mother's brother. Jacob left his home, Beersheba, on foot on his journey of more than 400 miles to Haran with no map and no companion. You may recall that Haran was the home of Abraham (Jacob's grandfather) before he immigrated to Canaan. Abraham represents God's promise and covenant with Hebrew people. God's promise continues through the family of Abraham and Sarah, coming to rest with the twin sons, Esau and Jacob. Jacob's wresting of the birthright from his brother sends him off to live with his uncle.

Jacob spent his first night near Bethel, 10 miles north of Jerusalem and 64 miles north of his home Beersheba. Perhaps it was the first night in his life away from home alone and he lies down with nothing but a cold stone as his pillow. But it was also the first time in his life that he had a marvelous experience of a host of angels and the voice of God saying:

> "I am the God of Abraham and Isaac; the land on which you lie I will give to you...and all the families of the earth shall be blessed by you...know that I am with you and I will keep you wherever you go, and I will bring you back to this land for I will not leave you until I have done what I have promised you" (Genesis 28:13-15).

When Jacob awakes, he is perceptive enough to realize that something awesome has happened, and that although Jacob has not expected it, the Lord really was in that place. Jacob anoints the stone he has used as a pillow and confesses: "Surely the Lord is in this place...This place is none other than the house of God, and this is the gate of heaven." But, Jacob was still very much a 'natural man' because his prayer was a *conditional prayer.* His prayer goes like this: "[If God] will be with me, and [if God] will keep me in this way that I go, and [if God] will give me bread to eat and clothing to wear, so that I come again to my father's house in peace, *then the Lord shall be my God.*"

What came out of his mouth shows us that the spiritual encounter with God has not changed Jacob's inner person; he was still a schemer and a natural man. His prayer does not show any remorse of his heart, but expresses what Jacob wants to get out of this prayer. Still, that's not to say that he should not have prayed at all. It is better to have prayed what was really in his heart than to speak some pious platitudes he had no intention of keeping.

However, God has kept his promise and blessed Jacob with twelve sons and one daughter from his two wives (Rachel and Leah) and two concubines. He is now wealthy man with servants and flocks. During the twenty years living in Haran (from Genesis 31-41), the two brothers (Jacob and Esau) exchanged no words. We can understand some of Jacob's distress at the thought of returning home.

Jacob's servants who went before him, returned to report to him that his brother Esau with 400 men are approaching. Jacob realizes that this is not a warm homecoming welcome. He quickly divides his group into two camps, reasoning that if Esau should come upon one camp and destroy it; the remaining camp would have time to escape in the opposite direction.

Jacob's life will change substantially at the Jabbok River (from Genesis 32:24-32). After sending his family across the Jabbok, Jacob remains alone to face the future and to think abut his destiny. Jacob wrestles with a man all night long until the breaking of day. This wrestling match changes Jacob from what he is to what he can become, and he receives the new name of *Israel* ((meaning *the one God rules*). Hence the birthright is fulfilled; Jacob (meaning *supplanter or usurper*) is now Israel, the continued life of Abraham and carrier of the Abrahamic Covenant. Wrestling with God is serious business, and it may leave us bent out of shape for our own desires but put us in shape for God's desires. Wrestling with God heightens our awareness of our relationship with God and of God's expectations of us. We may take an inventory of our behavior as Christians; intentionally assessing whether we have experienced life-changing moments in Christ or whether we are just drifting away. To struggle with God's demands is challenging, and frequently takes us where we would not choose to go. The joy comes in knowing that we never go alone, God has gone before us and goes with us.

This is a wonderful illustration of how a natural man can be <u>transformed</u> to a spiritual man through the power of the Spirit of God, and Israel (Jacob's new name) called this place Penuel. With a new name, Israel, he became the <u>father of the nation, Israel</u> consisting of the twelve Tribes from the descendants of his twelve sons. Finally, the Abrahamic Covenant was fulfilled in Jacob, not in Esau!

NATURAL MAN'S PRAYERS

In the middle of the last century, British author David Head wrote a wonderful little book entitled, *He sent Leanness: A book of Prayers for the Natural Man.* He wrote about prayers of the natural or unspiritual persons and here are samples I received in an e-mail:

"We have done wrong, but we hope nobody will find out."

"Don't let our witness for Christ make things awkward for us."

"O God, I hope the sermon doesn't last more than 15 minutes."

"O Lord, if I can get away with it this time, I promise I'll never steal again."

Listen to the prayer of a natural man about to be married:

"May she be always useful and always beautiful, full of interesting conversation, witty in private and sparkling in public, blind to my fault, tolerant with my follies, never weary, never demanding, not getting too involved with female friends, performing miracles with her housekeeping and cooking, and always grateful that I married her."

Listen to the prayer of people who live in the more wealthy parts of the world and think about people living in Third world countries:

"We who seek to maintain a shaky civilization do pray most earnestly that the countries which suffer exploitation may not be angry with the exploiters, that the hungry may not harbor resentment against those who have food, that the downtrodden may take it patiently, that nations with empty lenders may prefer starvation to communism that the 'have-not' people may rejoice in the prosperity of those that have, and that all people who have been deeply insulted and despised may have short memories. You can do all things, Oh God." Here is the wish of a rich farmer from the Jesus' parable of the rich fool who prayed: "Soul, you have ample foods laid up for many years; relax, eat, drink, and be merry" (Luke 12:19).

When we pray out of our natural or unspiritual state, we miss out on the greater riches of God, because the prayers of the natural person are motivated only by what we want, instead of seeking what God's will is for us by prayerful listening and reading the Word of God. If you have been praying the natural man's prayers of self-centered, conditional prayers, you must repent and earnestly ask God for the filling of the Holy Spirit. Then, you may be changed and transformed to become a spirit-filled person who prays:
"Spirit of the living God, fall afresh on me,
Spirit of the living God, fall afresh on me.
Melt me, mold me, fill me, [and] use me.
Spirit of the living God, fall afresh on me." (The UMH, #393)

HUMAN TEMPTATIONS ACCORDING TO THE TRIADS

In Chapter 3 we considered that the **Triads** (the Instinctive, the Feeling, and the Thinking Intelligence Centers) are important for transformational work because they specify where our life's energy imbalance lies.

The Triads represent the three main clusters of issues and defenses of the ego self. They reveal the principal ways in which we *contract* our awareness and limit our selves. Different characteristics of the Triads also give us a clue to what particular temptations we are to watch out for and overcome.

The Instinctive Triad (the doing persons) are concerned with the intelligence of the body, with resistance and control of the environment. The instinctive persons have issues with aggression and repression. They seek *autonomy.* Underneath their ego defenses they carry a great deal of *rage (anger).* Their *spiritual fear* is of giving up, allowing the self to be taken over by anyone or anything. They say 'no' because 'yes' would imply a caving-in of autonomy, after which there would be nothing left to be angry about. If they engage in intentional spiritual searching at all, they may be drawn to a simplistic religion that can be interpreted according to their own needs. Similarly, they may be attracted to forms of magic or sorcery that promise great personal power. In short, the primary temptation of the instinctive type is *power*-**seeking via control.**

The Feeling Triad (the feeling persons) are concerned with love of false self and self-image. The feeling persons have issues with identity and hostility resulting from their "narcissistic wounding." They seek *attention.* Underneath their ego defenses they carry a great deal of shame and guilt. Their *spiritual fear* is of being abandoned after having given up oneself. Surrender may come more easily, but it is often brief and superficial. They are likely to commit themselves enthusiastically to a variety of spiritual enterprises, only to drop them at the first sign of possible rejection. There is a tendency to gravitate toward affective (emotional) spirituality, often without adequate intellectual testing or critique. This is often combined with the use of human relationships as substitutes for universal belonging. This leads to a special susceptibility to being taken in by anything that comes along. In short, the primary temptation the feeling type is *popularity*-**seeking via sensationalism.**

While the Instinctive Triad is about maintaining a felt sense of self and the Feeling Triad is about maintaining a personal identity, *the Thinking Triad* (the thinking persons) are concerned with finding a sense of inner guidance and support. The thinking persons have issues with insecurity and anxiety. They seek *security*. Underneath their ego defenses their underlying feeling is fear and anxiety. Convinced that a proper relationship with God must be earned, they have difficulty in trusting either himself or herself or God to respond naturally and with love. This is manifested in a fear of anything that looks like *losing safety and control.* Therefore, they are drawn more to the metaphysical, interpretive, intellectual dimension of spirituality. Although they long for a spiritual experience, they often wind up talking, thinking, or reading about spirituality instead of relinquishing control and devoting themselves to it. In short, the primary temptation of the thinking type is *possession*-**seeking via hoarding**.

LIVING IN BALANCE AND HARMONY IN THE THREE DIMENSIONS

Joel Levey and Michele Levey write about our living in balance and harmony in the three dimensions of mind-body-spirit. Loss of balance in our outer lives reflects a cascade of inner imbalances. They explain further how they are interrelated:

> "Imbalance in our behavior is often reflective of our emotional imbalance, and emotional imbalance reflects imbalance in our biochemical and physiological systems... Our mental imbalance is rooted in the conscious or unconscious conflicts that arise when we relate to the world from the point of view of separation and alienation

instead of connectedness, communication, and whole-ness." (Levey and Levey, *Living in Balance,* p.71)

More and more medical centers are offering mind/body interventions to their patients and encouraging research on *psychosomatic* medicine. It is well documented that stress causes adverse effects on the immune system, personality, and spiritual vitality. A wise person said: "we cannot understand disease unless we understand the person who has the disease."

Being well in the physical dimension is a healthy body without ill symptoms; being well in the psychological dimension is inner peace without inner conflict; being well in the spiritual dimension is blessed-ness (happiness) of growing as a child of God without spiritual poverty. Medical researchers deal with physiology, psychology, and neuropathol-ogy, but not the spiritual dimension of human beings. As spiritual persons our goal is to grow and mature in the Spirit who empowers us to become whole persons by integrating the physical, psychological, and spiritual dimensions. Also we want to share with others the abundant life in all its fullness -- spiritual, physical, psychological (mental and emotional), relational, vocational, aesthetic, volitional, ethical, and moral dimensions.

"THORN IN THE FLESH."

In his workshop Dr. E. Gene Rooney tells a story, called "Thorn in the Flesh."

"It was 2 AM at night when the urgent call came for old Doc. Johnston, a veterinarian from a local farmer.

"Hey, Doc, I'm awfully sorry to call at this hour. You know I wouldn't if it weren't an emergency."

"What's wrong?" inquired Doc.

"It's that new cattle dog we got a few months back. He's awful sick."

"What seems to be the trouble?" asked Doc.

"Well, last night when we brought the herd into the barn I noticed he was limping.

I thought maybe he'd sprained is leg. But he's running a high temperature now and he seems to be in a lot of pain. His whimpering and howling woke us up."

It didn't take Doc long to make the trip to the farmer's home.

After examining the dog, Doc said, "It's not a sprain. There's a thorn deep inside his paw. It's broken off and his pad has closed up so you can't see the wound. It's got to come out, but it will only take a minute."

The wise old "vet" removed the poisonous thorn tip so deftly, the pup hardly noticed. He cleaned the wound, gave him a good dose of antibiotics, bandaged the foot, patted the dog, shook the grateful farmer's hand and sleepily drove back to town and his waiting bed.

In his hand he held the tiny broken thorn tip had taken from the dog's foot. The young pup probably weighed over thirty pounds already, and would one day be a great, stocky dog. The torn tip weighed less than $1,000^{th}$ of an ounce. Doc reflected on how small an external agent could be and still wreak havoc in an animal millions of times its size. Some things simply don't belong inside a dog's foot, and as long as the invading agents are in there, they will cause more and more trouble.

Doc found himself reflecting about how much the dog's problem was like some of people's problems, as well. A person may pretend that all is well when, in fact, there's an infection forming deep inside. A soul can become festered by the presence of deeply embedded hatred and prejudice. A mind can be poisoned by a warped belief, such as a "holy war." Fear or hatred can infect a person's insides in a dozen different ways, causing him or her to limp through life worse than the unfortunate pup. Grief can alter the chemistry of a life until the heart is sick deep within. "No sir," thought Doc, "there are some things the good Lord didn't intend us to have broken off inside, poisoning and rotting us from within. Some things just have to come out and be done away with. And with that, Doc threw the thorn out his car window, drove home and went to bed."

The story brings few questions for us to consider:

• Why does it seem so very natural for us to seek help for physical infections, and yet, we avoid help for psychological or spiritual "infections"?

- With all the current research showing so powerfully the direct and/or indirect connection **between** inner conflicts such as resentment, anger, hatred, stress, fear, unresolved grief, unremitting guilt, or doubt **and** psycho-somatic (mind-body) syndromes, why do you suppose there is still **not** much attention being given to the body-mind-spirit connection.

PART TWO

Integration of the Enneagram and Spirituality
toward Personality Transformation

PART TWO

CHAPTER 4

SELF-KNOWLEDGE

INTRODUCTION TO THE ENNEAGRAM

The Enneagram was brought to the West by the Russian spiritual teacher, George Ivanovitch Gurdjieff, around the turn of the century and further developed by the Bolivian mystic, Oscar Ichazo, beginning in the 1960s. Ichazo brought the Enneagram to the United States in 1970, and within a few years, awareness of this powerful typology quickly spread around North America.

Gurdjieff reintroduced the phenomenon of "the Law of Three," taught by almost all of the major religions to the Western logic of duality. The most ancient religious traditions taught that the universe is a manifestation of trinity, not a duality. But, the Western way of looking at reality has been pairs of opposites, such as good and bad, black and white, male and female, introvert and extrovert, and so forth. The ancient traditions look at life in trinity: man, woman, and child; black, white, and gray, and heaven, earth, and humans... "The Law of Three" sees that everything that exists is the result of the interaction of three forces (whatever they may be in a given situation or dimension).

The *circle* in the Enneagram's symbol refers to unity, wholeness, and integration, and it symbolizes the idea that *God is One,* the distinguishing feature of the major Western religions, Judaism, Christianity, and Islam. Gurdjieff explained that the Enneagram's symbol has three parts: the *circle*, the *triangle*, and the *hexad*. This triple symbol represents the interdependent and mutually sustaining parts of the whole within the circle. In the circle we find the next symbol of the *triangle*. It refers the Trinity, the Three Intelligence Centers (the figure tracing the numbers 6-9-3), and the three Essential attributes (faith, hope, and love). The third symbol is the hexad (the figure tracing the numbers 5-8-2-4-1-7-5, the Law of Seven). When we put these three elements together, we get the Enneagram. It is a symbol that shows the wholeness of a thing (the circle), how its identity is the result of the interaction of three forces (triangle), and how it evolves or changes over time (the hexad). (Riso and Hudson, the Wisdom of Enneagram, pp. 20-22)

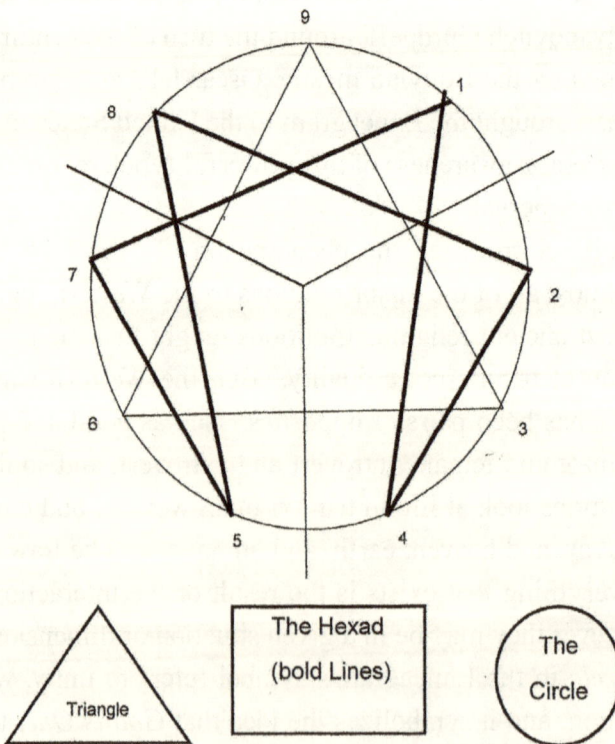

Figure 2. The Traditional Enneagram Symbol with the Triads

In 1975 Don Riso, a Jesuit seminarian, began developing the Enneagram in light of modern psychology, adding his own insights and discoveries to the original body of knowledge. While Gurdjieff and Ichazo were the first who attempted to communicate the Enneagram to a modern audience, Riso developed the descriptions of the personality types and the underlying theory. In 1977, there was a major breakthrough when he discovered the Levels of Development within each personality type. The Levels (Unhealthy, Average, Healthy) for each personality type revealed the *vertical* graduations of growth and deterioration that people actually move through in their lives. For forty years he committed and devoted himself to the further development and education of the wisdom of Enneagram until his death in 2012. Now we are looking to leadership of Russ Hudson in continuing the legacy of Don Richard Riso.

The word Enneagram comes from the Greek for 'nine' (pronounce 'ANY') and 'figure' (*gram*); thus, it is a 'nine-pointed figure.' The Enneagram is a geometric figure that maps out the nine fundamental personality types of human nature and their complex inter-relationships.

Riso and Hudson point out the importance of human diversity:

> "Any effective approach to growth must therefore take into account the fact that there are different kinds of people—different personality types. Historically many psychological and spiritual systems have attempted to address this key insight: astrology, numerology, the four classic tempera-ments (phlegmatic, choleric, melancholic, and sanguine), the Jung's system of psychological types (four pairs of ex-trovert/introvert orientations, sensing/intuition, feeling/ thinking, judging/perceiving functions), and many others. Furthermore, recent studies in infant development and in brain science have indicted that fundamental differences in temperament between different types of people have a

biological basis. This diversity explains why what is good advice for one person can be disastrous for another. Telling some types that they need to focus more on their feelings is like throwing water on a drowning man. Telling other types that they need to assert themselves more is as foolish as putting an anorexic person on a diet. In understanding ourselves, our relationships, our spiritual growth, and many other important issues, we will see that type, not gender, not culture, not generational differences—is the crucial factor." (Riso and Hudson, *The Wisdom of the Enneagram,* pp. 2-3) The profiles of nine personality types according to the Riso-Hudson's Enneagram are presented in pages 90-98.

The Riso-Hudson's Enneagram

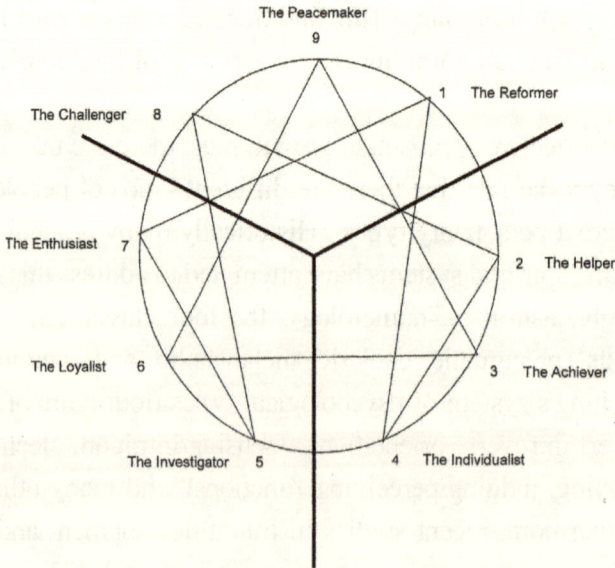

Figure 3. The Riso-Hudson Enneagram

Riso and Hudson point out the importance of human diversity by stressing that

> "Any effective approach to growth must therefore take into account the fact that there are different kinds of people—different personality types." Historically many psychological and spiritual systems have attempted to address this key insight: astrology, numerology, the four classic temperaments (phlegmatic, choleric, melancholic, and sanguine), the Jung's system of psychological types (four pairs of extrovert/introvert orientations, sensing/intuition, feeling/thinking, judging/perceiving functions), and many others.

They report recent studies in infant development and in brain science have indicted that fundamental differences in temperament between different types of people have a biological basis:

> This diversity explains why what is good advice for one person can be disastrous for another. Telling some types that they need to focus more on their feelings is like throwing water on a drowning man. Telling other types that they need to assert themselves more is as foolish as putting an anorexic person on a diet. In understanding ourselves, our relationships, our spiritual growth, and many other important issues, we will see that type, not gender, not culture, not generational differences—is the crucial factor." (Riso and Hudson, *The Wisdom of the Enneagram*, pp. 2-3)

THE RISO-HUDSON'S ENNEAGRAM

Riso and Hudson have taught their many students for the past two decades that the Enneagram is a psychological system that *offers* following benefits:

1. Enneagram is a system that could enable us to have more insight into others and ourselves.

2. This system could help us discern our filters more clearly and take them into proper account. We can use our personality type as the main filter to understand the world around us so that we can express and defend ourselves; we deal with our past and anticipate our future; we learn, rejoice, and fall in love.

3. This system can show us our psychological issues as well as our inter-personal strengths and weaknesses.

4. This system does not depend on the pronouncements of experts or gurus, or on our birth date, or our birth order, but on our personality patterns and our willingness to honestly explore ourselves.

5. This system could show us not only what are our inner conflicts, but also point out effective ways to deal with them.

6. It helps us identify hurtful memories of the past by bringing to light what was formerly hidden from our consciousness.

7. It helps us to isolate the causes of anger, shame (guilt), and fear expressed by the personality type of each individual and heals them.

8. By understanding the mechanical aspects of our personality (that is, our automatic, reactive, defensive patterns), we learn how to avoid them in the future.

9. We identify shackles of our ego-inflated personality and we relinquish them. Then, we can begin to recognize our truest self (the Divine Essence).

10. It also provides a way out of our conflicts and confusions and helps us to be hopeful in moments of darkness and despair.

11. It helps us to be free from inner conflicts and neurosis by reversing the vicious circle caused by our typical [ego] fixations.

12. By turning our lives around (from the false self to the true self), we find that life becomes easier because our time and energy can be used now for living creatively rather than be wasted in turmoil and inner conflicts.

13. Once we discover our true self, we naturally move toward self-transcendence. The Enneagram points out each type's path of self-transcendence through the directions of integration.

14. This system could direct us toward the depth (Essence) of our soul and help us discover true self.

15. The Enneagram is indeed a tool that integrates psychology and spirituality (theology) for the transformation of the core of human beings.

In conclusion, the Enneagram is a wise guide in our paths toward personality transformation: self-knowledge, self-realization, and self-transcendence. It is not only profound psychological tool, but also provides a spiritual path since true self-knowledge is the first step toward spiritual formation.

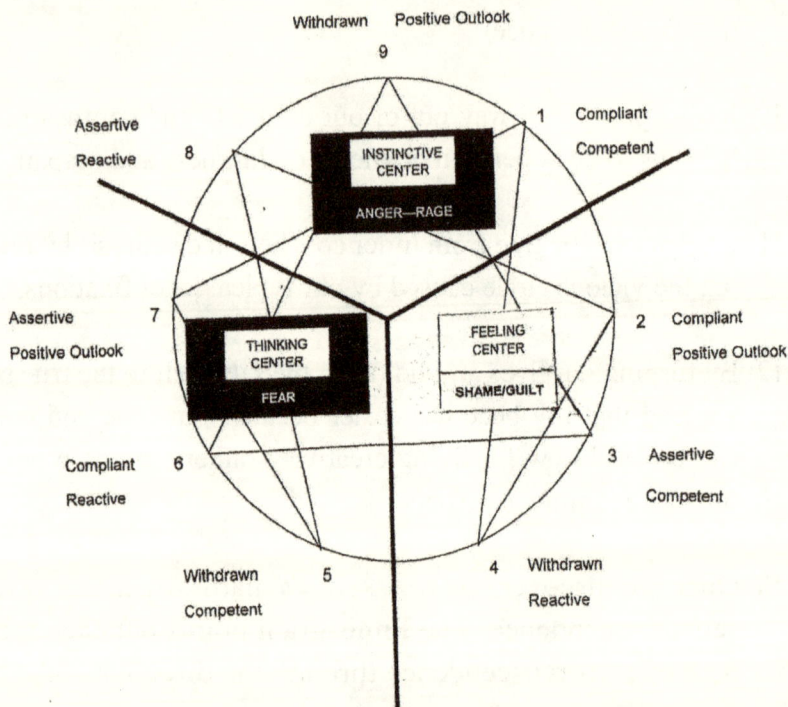

Figure 4. Summary of the Triadic Self

HOW TO DISCOVER YOUR PERSONALITY TYPE

The first questionnaire is the Riso-Hudson QUEST, the *Quick Enneagram Sorting Test* (*the Wisdom of Enneagram*, pp.14-15). This test will help you narrow down the possibilities for your type in less than five minutes with about 70 percent accuracy.

The second set of questionnaires is the Riso-Hudson TAS, or Type Attitude Sorter. At the beginning of each of the Nine Type Chapters (pp. 97-340) is a set of 15 statements that are highly characteristic of the type under consideration. If you are interested in taking a self-sorting computerized Enneagram Test, you can do so by taking RHETI questionnaire on-line at www.EnneagramInstitute.com

INTERPRETATION OF THE TRIADIC SELF

(Extracted from Riso-Hudson's *The Wisdom of the Enneagram*, pp. 49-68)

A. THE FEELING TRIAD (TYPES TWO, THREE, AND FOUR)

From the Appendix IV: "The Three Intelligence Centers," we can easily decide to which Triad we belong.

1. When we decide that we are feeling people, and then we must learn:

The people in the Feeling Triad are most concerned with our "narcissistic wounding, that is, not being valued for who we really were as children. Because no one graduates from childhood without some degree of narcissistic damage, as adults, we have a lot of difficulty being authentic with one another. There is always the fear that, when all is said and done, we are really empty and worthless. The tragic result is that we almost never actually see each other or allow ourselves to be seen, no matter what type we are. We are resolved to correct this dilemma in three different approaches:

a. By going out to please others so that people will like us (Type Two). Our social style group is the *compliants* (Horney's "moving toward people"). We are super-ego driven. Our coping style when faced with loss and disappointment is the Horney's *positive outlook* group. We usually maintain a positive outlook and feel that things will work out for the best. We can usually find something to be enthusiastic about and different ways to occupy ourselves. But, staying positive has sometimes meant that we have put off dealing with our own problems for too long.

b. By achieving things and becoming outstanding in some way so that people will admire and affirm us (Type Three). Our social style group is the *assertives* (The Horney's "moving against people"). We are ego-driven. Our coping style when faced with loss and disappointment is the Horney's *competency* group. We tend to be self-controlled and logical and efficient. When there are problems or personal conflicts, we focus on the issue and avoid emotional reactions that distract them from hat's really important to them.

c. By having an elaborate story about us and attaching tremendous significance to all of our personal characteristics (Type Four). Our social style group is the *withdrawns* (the Horney's "moving away people").

2. Our coping style when faced with loss and disappointment is the Horney's *reactive* group. Two major issues of the Feeling Triad types are identity and hostility. We have strong feelings about things – most people can tell when we are unhappy. When we

126

are upset about something, we want others to respond and to get as worked as we are.

c. When Twos do not obtain favorable reactions by giving people our energy and attention, we feel unappreciated, although, as much as possible, we must conceal the hostile feelings that this generates;

d. Type Three, the central type of this Triad (the type positioned on the equilateral triangle), directs attention and energy both inward and outward. Like Twos, Threes need the positive feedback and affirmation of others. Threes primarily seek self-identity through accomplishment. We are always in danger of 'believing our own press releases' more than the truth.

e. In Type Four our energy and attention go inward to maintain a self-image based on feeling, fantasies, and stories from the past. Our identity centers on being 'different,' and 'being unique,' and as a result, we often feel estranged from people. Our emphasis of the all the tragedies and abuses that have befallen us, is our way of eliciting attention and pity from others and, hence some degree of validation.

3. All the individuals in the Feeling Triad (Twos, Threes, and Fours) must learn that: "At the deepest level, *our hearts qualities are the source of our identity.* When our heart opens, we know who we are and 'who we are' has nothing to do with our past history. We have a particular quality, a flavor, something that is unique and intimately *ours.* It is through the heart that we recognize and appreciate our true nature. When we are in contact with the heart, we feel loved and valued. Moreover, as the great spiritual traditions teach, the heart reveals that we are *loved* and *valued.*"

Our share in the Divine nature means not only that we are
loved by God, but that the presence of love resides in us
and we are the conduit through which love comes into the
world. When our hearts are closed off and blocked, however, not only do we lose contact with our true identity, but
we do not feel valued or loved. This loss is intolerable, so
the personality steps in to create a substitute identity and
to find other things to give us a sense of value, usually by
seeking attention and external affirmation from others."
(Ibid. p. 55)

B. THE THINKING TRIAD (TYPES FIVE, SIX, AND SEVEN)

From the Appendix IV: "The Three Intelligence Centers," we can easily
decide which Triad we belong to. We who belong to this Triad suffer
from "chattering childhood memories" and "inner dialogues." We must
screen our thoughts by the filters of the truth, the goodness and the beauty.
When we are certain that we are thinking persons, then we must learn:

1. How we master our fear so that we may feel safe enough to come
   out of hiding?

   a. As the Fives we flee <u>inward</u> due to fear of aspects of the out-
      side of the world. Our social style group is the *withdrawns* (the
      Horney's "moving away people"). Our coping style when faced
      with loss and disappointment is <u>the Horney's *competency* group.</u>
      (Read the Feeling Triad)

128

b. Type Six, the central type in the Triad (the type positioned on the equilateral triangle), tries to hold our ego boundaries in both areas, internal and external. As the Sixes we flee inward to avoid external threats and outward to avoid internal fears. Our social style group is the *compliants* (the Horney's "moving toward people"). Our coping style when faced with loss and disappointment is the Horney's *reactive* group. (Read the Feeling Triad)

c. As the Sevens we flee outward due to fear of aspects of our inner world. Our social style group is the *assertives* (the Horney's "moving against people"). Our coping style when faced with loss and disappointment is the Horney's *positive outlook* group. (Read the Feeling Triad)

2. How do we meet our primary need of security? According to the Hornevian Social Groups we employ these strategies to get our need met:

a. As the *assertive* type (the Seven) we *insist or demand* that we get what we want from others. Our approach is active and direct as we go after what we believe what we need.

b. As the *compliant* type (the Six) we attempt to *earn* something by placating our superego to get what we want. We do our best to be "good boys and girls" to get what we need.

c. As the *withdrawn* type (the Five) we *withdraw* to get what we want. We disengage from others to deal with our needs.

C. THE INSTINCTIVE TRIAD (TYPES EIGHT, NINE, AND ONE)

From the Appendix IV: "The Three Intelligence Centers," we can easily decide which Triad we belong to. Those who belong to this Triad are mostly influenced by instinctive childhood temperaments. When we decide that we are instinctive persons, then we must learn about our strong ego boundaries created by our false sense of autonomy. While all of the personality types employ ego boundaries, as the Eight, Nine, and One we do so for a particular reason—"We are attempting to use our will to affect the world without being affected by it."

1. How do the Instinctive Types master our fear?

a. In Type Eight individuals the ego boundary is primarily focused outward, against the environment. The focus of attention is also outward. As the Eights we are constantly putting out energy so that nothing can get too close and hurt us. The more wounded the individual is from childhood, the thicker our ego boundary, and the tougher we are going to make it for others to get through to us. As the Eights we flee outward due to the fear of aspects of our inner world. Our social style group is the *assertives* (the Horney's "moving against people"). Our coping style when faced with loss and disappointment is the Horney's *reactive* group. (Read the Feeling Triad)

b. In Type Nine, the central type in the Triad (the type positioned on the equilateral triangle), individuals we try to hold our ego boundaries in both areas, internal and external. We do not want certain feelings and states to disturb our equilibrium. We often engage in passive-aggressive behaviors and turn a blind eye to whatever threatens our peace.

As the Nines we flee <u>inward</u> due to the fear of aspects of our outer world. Our social style group is the *withdrawns* (the Horney's "moving from people"). Our coping style when faced with loss and disappointment is the <u>Horney's</u> *positive outlook* <u>group.</u> (Read the Feeling Triad)

c. Type One individuals also hold a boundary against the outside world, but we are far more invested in maintaining our internal boundary. We expend enormous energy trying to hold back certain unconscious impulses, trying to keep them from getting into our consciousness. We create a great deal of physical tension to maintain our inner boundaries and hold aspects of our own inner nature at bay.

As the Ones we flee <u>outward</u> due to the fear of aspects of our inner world. Our social style group is the *assertives* (the Horney's "moving toward people"). Our coping style when faced with loss and disappointment is the <u>Horney's</u> *competency* <u>group.</u> (Read the Feeling Triad)

2. How do we get our need of autonomy?

According to the <u>Hornevian Social Groups</u> we employ the strategies or tactics to get our need met.

a. As the *assertive* type (the Eight) we *insist or demand* that we get what we want (autonomy) from others. Our approach is active and direct as we go after what we believe what we need.

b. As the *withdrawn* type (the Nine) we *withdraw* to get what we want. We disengage from others to deal with our needs (to have our own space).

c. As the *compliant* type (the One) we attempt to *earn* autonomy (feeling that if we are perfect, others will not interfere with us).

PROFILES OF THE RISO-HUDSON'S NINE PERSONALITY TYPES

(Following profiles are extracted from *The Wisdom of Enneagram*, pp. 95-314)

PERSONALITY TYPE TWO: THE HELPER. THE CARING, INTERPERSONAL TYPE.

PROFILE DESCRIPTION:

> "Twos are empathetic, sincere, and warm-hearted. We are friendly, generous, and self-sacrificing, but we can also be sentimental, flattering, and we are driven to be close to others, and we often do things for others in order to be needed. We typically have problems taking care of ourselves and acknowledging our own needs. *At best*, healthy Twos are unselfish and altruistic and have unconditional love for themselves and others."
> (Ibid. p. 11)

-One of the <u>Feeling Triad.</u>
-Wing Subtype Names: 2 w1 (The Servant); 2w3 (The Host/ The Hostess). (Ibid. p. 70)

-Basic Fear: Being unworthy of being loved.

-Passion (Deadly Sin): Pride.

-Basic Desire and Its Distortion: The desire to be loved. It deteriorates into the need to be loved.

-Nurturing/Protective Figure(s): Rejection.

-Superego Message: "You are good or okay if you are loving and close to others."

-Ego-Fixation: Flattery.

-Unconscious Childhood Message: "It's not okay to have your own needs."

-Lost Childhood Message: "You are wanted."

-Sense of Self (Mask): "I am loving."

-Defense Mechanisms: Identification, reaction formation, denial.

-Characteristic Temptation: People-pleasing

-Religiosity: *Possessive* of "my God."

-Lost Holy Ideas: Holy Will; Holy Freedom; Virtue of Humility.

-Motivational Invitation: *To nurture yourself and others.* Remember that it is your true nature to be good to your self and to have goodwill and compassion for others.

PERSONALITY TYPE THREE: THE ACHIEVER. THE ADAPTABLE, SUCCESS-ORIENTED TYPE.

PROFILE DESCRIPTION:

"Threes are self-assured, attractive, and charming. Ambitious, competent, and energetic, we can also be status-conscious and highly driven for personal advancement. Threes are often concerned about our image and what others think of us. We typically have problems with workaholism and competitiveness. *At best,* healthy Threes are self-accepting, authentic, and everything we seem to be—role models who inspire others."

-One of the <u>Feeling Triad.</u>

-Wing Subtype Names: 3w2 (The Charmer); 3w4 (The Professional).

-Basic Fear: Fear of being worthless or without inherent value.

- Passion (Deadly Sin): Deceit.

-Basic Desire and Its Distortion: The desire to be valuable. It deteriorates into chasing after success.

-Nurturing/Protective Figure(s): Connection.

-Superego Message: "You are good or okay, if you are successful and others think well of you."

-Ego-Fixation: Vanity.

-Unconscious Childhood Message: "It's not okay to have your own feelings and identity."

-Lost Childhood Message: "You are loved for yourself."

-Sense of Self (Mask): "I am outstanding."

-Defense Mechanism: Repression, projection, displacement.

-Characteristic Temptation: Highly driven to excel.

-Religiosity: Façade (outward form of godliness but deny its power).

-Lost Holy Ideas: Holy Law; Holy Hope; Virtue of Truthfulness.

-Motivational Invitation: *To develop yourself and set an example for others.* Remember that it is your true nature to take pleasure in your existence and to esteem and value others.

PERSONALITY TYPE FOUR: THE INDIVIDUALIST.
THE ROMANTIC, INTROSPECTIVE TYPE.

PROFILE DESCRIPTION:

"Fours are self-aware, sensitive, reserved, and quite. We are self-revealing, emotionally honest, and personal, but we can also be moody and self-conscious. Withholding ourselves from others due to feeling vulnerable and de- fective, we can also feel disdainful and exempt from or- dinary ways of living. We typically have problems with self-indulgence and self-pity. At our best, healthy Fours are inspired and highly creative, able to renew ourselves and transform our experiences." (Ibid. p.11)

-One of the <u>Feeling Triad.</u>
-Wing Subtype Names: 4w3 (The Aristocrat); 4w5 (The Bohemian).
-Basic Fear: Fear of being without identity or personal significance.
-Deadly Passion: Envy.
-Basic Desire and Its Distortion: The desire to be oneself. It deteriorates into self- indulgence.
-Nurturing/Protective Figure(s): Frustration.
-Superego Message: "You are good or okay, if you feel something unique and true to yourself."
-Ego-Fixation: Melancholy.
-Unconscious Childhood Message: "It's not okay to be too functional or too happy."
-Lost Childhood Message: "You are seen for who you are."

-Sense of Self (Mask): "I am unique."

-Defense Mechanisms: Introjection, displacement, splitting, turning against the self.

-Characteristic Temptation: Given to fantasy and mood.

-Religiosity: Destructive criticism and poisonous divisiveness.

-Lost Holy Idea: Holy Origin: Virtue of Equanimity (emotional stability).

-Motivational Invitation: *To let go of the past and be renewed by your experiences.* Remember that it is your true nature to be forgiving and to use everything in life for your growth and renewal.

PERSONALITY TYPE FIVE: THE INVESTIGATOR.
THE INTENSE, CEREBRAL TYPE.

PROFILE DESCRIPTION:

"Fives are alert, insightful, and curious. We are able to concentrate and focus on developing complex ideas and skills. Independent and innovative, we can become pre-occupied with our thoughts and imaginary constructs. We become detached, yet high-strung and intense. We typically have problems with isolation, eccentricity, and nihilism. *At our best*, healthy Fives invest are vision-ary pioneers, often ahead of our time and able to see the world in an entirely new way."

-One of the Thinking Triad.

-Wing Subtype Names: 5w4 (The Iconoclast); 5w6 (The Problem-Solver).

-Basic Fear: Fear of being useless, incapable, or incompetent.

-Deadly Passion: Avarice (stinginess).

-Basic Desire and Its Distortion: The desire to be competent. It deteriorates into useless specialization.

-Nurturing/Protective Figure(s): Rejection.

-Superego Message: "You are good or okay, if you know and mastered something."

-Ego-Fixation: Stinginess.

-Unconscious Childhood Message: "It's not okay to be comfortable in this world."

-Lost Childhood Message: "Your needs are not a problem."

-Sense of Self (Mask): "I am perceptive."

-Defense Mechanisms: Displacement, projection, isolation.

-Characteristic Temptations: Conceptual and removed from immediacy.

-Religiosity: Extreme intolerance to protect "their God" and their dogmas.

-Lost Holy Ideas: Holy Omniscience; Holy Transparency; Virtue of Nonattachment.

-Motivational Invitation: *To observe yourself and others without judgment or expectations.* Remember that it is your true nature to be   engaged with reality, contemplating the infinite riches of the world.

PERSONALITY TYPE SIX: THE LOYALIST. THE COMMITTED, SECURITY-ORIENTED TYPE.

PROFILE DESCRIPTION:

"Sixes are reliable, hardworking, and responsible, but we can also be defensive, evasive, and highly anxious—running on stress while complaining about it. We are often cautious and indecisive but can also be reactive, defiant, and rebellious. We typically have problems with self-doubt and suspicion. At our best, healthy Sixes are internally stable, self-confident, and self-reliant, courageously supporting the weak and powerless."

-One of the <u>Thinking Triad.</u>
-Wing Subtype Names: 6w5 (The Defender); 6w7 (The Buddy).
-Basic Fear: Fear of being without support or guidance.
-Deadly Passion: Fear.
-Basic Desire and Its Distortion: The desire to be secure. It deteriorates into an attachment to beliefs.
-Nurturing/Protective Figure(s): Connection.
-Superego Message: "You are good or okay, if you are responsible and do what is expected of you."
-Ego-Fixation: Cowardice.
-Unconscious Childhood Message: "It's not okay to trust yourself."
-Lost Childhood Message: "You are safe."
-Sense of Self (Mask): "I am reliable."
-Defense Mechanisms: Identification, displacement, projection.
-Characteristic Temptation: Invested in external sources of security.
-Religiosity: Manipulative faith to gain our own agendas, not God's purposes.
-Lost Holy Idea: Holy Faith; Virtue of Courage.
-Motivational Invitation: *To have faith in yourself and trust in the goodness of life.* Remember that it is your true nature to be courageous and capable of dealing with life under all conditions.

PERSONALITY TYPE SEVEN: THE ENTHUSIAST.
THE BUSY, PRODUCTIVE TYPE.

PROFILE DESCRIPTION:

"Sevens are versatile, optimistic, and spontaneous. Playful, high-spirited, and practical, we can also be over-extended, scattered, and undisciplined. We constantly seek new and exciting experiences, but we can become distracted and exhausted by staying on the go. We typically have problems with superficiality and impulsiveness. *At our best*, healthy Sevens focus our talents on worthwhile goals, becoming joyous, highly accomplished, and full of gratitude."

-One of the Thinking Triad.
-Wing Subtype Names: 7w6 (The Entertainer); 7w8 (The Realist).
-Basic Fear: Fear of being deprived or trapped in pain.
-Deadly Passion: Gluttony.
-Basic Desire and Its Distortion: The desire to be happy. It deteriorates into frenetic escapism.
-Nurturing/Protective Figure(s): Frustration.
-Superego Message: "You are good or okay, if you are happy and getting what you need."
-Ego-Fixation: Planning.
-Unconscious Childhood Message: "It's not okay to depend on anyone for anything."
-Lost Childhood Message: "You will be taken care of."
-Sense of Self (Mask): "I am enthusiastic."

-Defense Mechanisms: Repression, externalization, acting out.

-Characteristic Temptations: Mentally restless and acquisitive.

-Religiosity: Indulgence in certain styles of religious practices or an incessant quest forever new and more fulfilling forms of liturgy and discipline practice.

-Lost Holy Ideas: Holy Wisdom; Holy Plan; Virtue of Sobriety.

-Motivational Invitation: *To joyously celebrate existence and share your happiness.* Remember that it is your true nature to be happy and to add to the richness of experience for every.

PERSONALITY TYPE EIGHT: THE CHALLENGER.
THE POWERFUL, DOMINATING TYPE.

PROFILE DESCRIPTION:

"Eights are self-confident, strong, and assertive. Protective, resourceful, and decisive, we can also be proud and domineering. Eights feel that we must control our environment, often becoming confrontational and intimidating. We typically have problems with allowing ourselves to be close to others. *At our best,* healthy Eights are self-mastering—we use our strength to improve others' lives, becoming heroic, magnanimous, and sometimes historically great."

-One of the Instinctive Triad.

-Wing Subtype Names: 8w7 (The Independent); 8w9 (The Bear).

-Basic Fear: Fear of being harmed or controlled by others.

-Deadly Passion: Lust.

-Basic Desire and Its Distortion: The desire to protect oneself. It deteriorates into constant fighting.

-Nurturing/Protective Figure(s): Rejection.

-Superego Message: "You are good or okay, if you are strong and in control of the situation."

-Ego-Fixation: Vengeance.

-Unconscious Childhood Message: "It's not okay to be vulnerable or to trust anyone."

-Lost Childhood Message: "You will not be betrayed."

-Sense of self (Mask): "I am strong."

-Defense Mechanisms: Repression, displacement, denial.

-Characteristic Temptations: Highly pragmatic and self-sufficient.

-Religiosity: Distinction-making between those of various theological persuasions.

-Lost Holy Idea: Holy Truth; Virtue of Innocence.

-Motivational Invitation: *To stand up for yourself and to speak out for what you believe.* Remember that it is your true nature to be strong and capable of affecting the world in many different positive ways.

PERSONALITY TYPE NINE: THE PEACEMAKER.
THE EASY-GOING, SELF-EFFACING TYPE.

PROFILE DESCRIPTION:

"Nines are accepting, trusting, and stable. We are good-natured, kind-hearted, easygoing, and supportive but can also be too willing to go along with others to keep the peace. We want everything to be without conflict but can tend to be complacent and minimize anything upsetting. We typically have problems with passivity and stubbornness. At our best, healthy Nines are indomitable and all-embracing; we are able to bring people together and heal conflicts."

-One of the <u>Instinctive Triad.</u>
-Wing Subtype Names: 9w8 (The Referee); 9w1 (The Dreamer).
-Basic Fear: Fear of loss of connection, of fragmentation.
-Deadly Passion: Sloth.
-Basic Desire and Its Distortion: The desire to be at peace. It deteriorates into stubborn neglectfulness.
-Nurturing/Protective Figure(s): Connection.
-Superego Message: "You are good or okay, if you are at peace and those around you are okay."
-Ego-Fixation: Indolence (avoid exertion).
-Unconscious Childhood Message: "It's not okay to assert yourself."
-Lost Childhood Message: "Your presence matters."
-Sense of Self (Mask): "I am peaceful."
-Defense Mechanisms: Repression, dissociation, denial.
-Characteristic Temptation: Highly accommodating.
-Religiosity: Playing 'god' in life being self-centered and with false-serenity.
-Lost Holy Idea: Holy Love; Virtue of Action.
-Motivational Invitation: *To bring peace and healing into your world.* Remember that it is your true nature to be an inexhaustible front of serenity, acceptance, and kindness.

PERSONALITY TYPE ONE: THE REFORMER. THE PRINCIPLED, IDEALISTIC TYPE.

PROFILE DESCRIPTION:

"Ones are ethical and conscientious, with a strong sense of right and wrong. We are teachers and crusaders, always striving to improve things but afraid of making a mistake. Well-organized, orderly, and fastidious, we try to maintain high standards but can slip into being critical and perfectionistic. We typically have problems with repressed anger and impatience. *At our best*, healthy Ones are wise, discerning, realistic, and noble, as well as morally heroic."

-One of the <u>Instinctive Triad.</u>
-Wing Subtype Names: 1w9 (The Idealist); 1w2 (The Advocate).
-Basic Fear: Fear of being bad, corrupt, evil, or defective.
-Deadly Passion: Anger.
-Basic Desire and Its Distortion: The desire to have integrity. It deteriorates into critical perfectionism.
-Nurturing/Protective Figure(s): Frustration.
-Superego Message: "You are good or okay, if you are good and do what is right."
-Ego-Fixation: Resentful and judgmental.
-Unconscious Childhood Message: "It's not okay to make mistakes."
-Lost Childhood Message: "You are good."
-Sense of Self (Mask): "I am reasonable."
-Defense Mechanisms: Repression, reaction formation, displacement.

-Characteristic Temptation: Personally obligated.
-Religiosity: Self-righteousness; fearful and angry; frenetic performance
         to authenticate their identity and their "idol in its box."
-Lost Holy Idea: Holy Perfection; Serenity with Realism.
-Motivational Invitation: *To live for a Higher Purpose.* Remember that
         it is your true nature to be wise and discerning.

TEMPERAMENT AND PERSONALITY

Temperament is that genetic inborn part of a human being that determines how one reacts to people, places, and things. In short, how humans interact with the environment around him or her. However, Sigmund Freud insisted that humans are born "blank." He believed the environment and developmental stages that each human goes through determine one's behavior. But, we know inborn babies are different. If they were born "blank," the babies in the nursery would all behave same way. Yet, as we all know, their behaviors differ from crib to crib. We are reminded of the Bible story of Esau and Jacob who were twins (Genesis 25:21-28).

The first building block of human behavior is God-given and called temperament – the genetic inborn characteristic of a human.

The second building block of human behavior is called character (environment-made); it is resulted from the temperament interacting with the environment.

The third building block of human behavior is self-made and called personality. This is the way the individual perceives that they must behave to survive in the world in which one lives, either moving toward, against, or away from others.

Personality is a mask we wear for the world, and as with any other mask, it cannot be worn long, so one reverts back to temperament character. We know that our behaviors at home are different from those at work. Temperament determines how much inclusion, affection, and control we would receive or give.

Riso and Hudson points out our dilemma of the parent-child relationships: "Since parents usually play an extremely significant role in the crystallization of their child's overall personality pattern, it is imperative to consider: "How good is the temperamental match between the parent and the child? How are the needs of the child matched with the needs of the parents? How realistic are the expectations of the parents for their child, given the innate temperament of the child they are actually presented with? How can the child be validated and mirrored when given a 'poor' match?" (Riso and Hudson, *Understanding the Enneagram*, p. 314)

Riso and Hudson quote words of Oscar Ichazo, who addressed how the nine personality types have developed:

> "We have to distinguish between a (hu)man *as* one is in [divine] Essence and *as* one is in inflated ego or false self. In [divine] Essence every person is perfect, fearless, and in loving unity with the entire cosmos; there is no conflict within the person between head, heart, and stomach [gut] or between the person and others. Then something happened...Humans lost the unity in our "Triadic Center" and became distorted and divided in our thinking, feeling, and doing; thus there are nine ways that we forgot our connection with the Divine [Essence], thus resulting in nine personality types... Actual soul qualities of the Essence became distorted, or contracted, into states of [inflated] ego or personalities [false selves]." (Ibid. pp. 33-34)

CHAPTER 5

SELF-REALIZATION

DO YOU LIKE BEING YOU?

Not only does the Enneagram provide us with our basic nine personality types, but it also describes nine distinct ways that human nature expresses itself, nine different perspectives on life, and nine modes of being in the world.

Don Riso enlightens us: "Through the self-knowledge our attention is constantly possessed by ever-changing fears and desires, fantasies, and associations, which lead us nowhere, while keeping us out of touch with our deeper true self. Ironically, we build our identity out of these chaotic and unconscious impulses—embracing them as our [real] self, and defending them with our life." (Riso, *Enneagram Transformations*, p. 4)

The Enneagram shows us where our personality most 'trips us up.' It highlights both what is possible for us and how self-defeating and unnecessary many of our old reactions and behaviors are. This is why, when we identify with the personality, we are settling for being much less than who we really are. It is as though we were given a mansion to live in, with rich furnishings and beautifully kept grounds, but have confined ourselves to a small dark closet in the basement. Most of us have forgotten that the rest of the mansion exists, or that we are really its owner.

PART 2

WAKE-UP CALLS

Riso and Hudson have taught that teachers through out the ages have pointed out that *we have fallen asleep to ourselves and to our own lives.* The Wake-up Call is an invitation to wake-up *before* we move deeper into the Average Levels and further into fixation and increasing "sleep." Most of the day we walk around preoccupied with ideas, anxieties, worries, and mental pictures. Seldom are we present to ourselves and to our immediate experience. As we begin to work on ourselves, however, we begin to see that our attention has been taken or 'magnetized' by the preoccupations and features of our personality, and that we are actually sleepwalking through much of life. This view of things is contrary to common sense and often feels insulting to the way we see ourselves—as self-determining, conscious, and in control.

They also emphasize:

> "At the same time, our personality is not bad. Our personality is an important part of our development and is necessary for the refinement of our Essential nature. The problem is that we become stuck in personality and do not know how to move on to the next phase. This is not the result of any inherent flaw in us; rather it is an arrested development that occurs because almost no one in our formative years was aware that any more was possible. Our parents and teachers may have had some glimmers of their true nature, but like us, they generally did not recognize them, much less live as expressions of them." (Riso and Hudson, *The Wisdom of the Enneagram*, p.80)

When we receive our wake-up calls, we begin the process of personality transformation. That's because the pain of inner conflict of staying

147

the same is much greater than the pain of changing. Consequences give us the pain that motivates us to change. Instead of denying inner conflict, we are to embrace it and understand it and transform it.

Thomas F. Crum insists that conflict becomes one of the greatest gifts we have for positive growth and change -- an empowering and energizing opportunity:

> "There is truly magical quality about conflict which can call out the best in us, that which is not summoned under ordinary circumstances…. As we begin to embrace conflict as a prime motivator for change in our lives, we begin to see it as an opportunity. We are able to use it effectively for nurturing growth in ourselves and in our relationships." (Crum, *The Magic of Conflict*, p. 35)

Gurdijieff taught that the nine types of Enneagram are detailed reminders of "waking up from our sleep" of "who we are not," rather than identities that cause further attachment to our ego and the perpetuation of our illusions and suffering. The Wake-Up Call serves as an indicator that we must **stop** our self-destructive patterns of idolizing ourselves. We wake up to see ourselves more objectively and compassionately. Our waking up is the beginning of the process of transformation (Riso and Hudson, *The Wisdom of the Enneagram*, p. 80)

"WAKE-UP CALLS" ACCORDING TO TYPES

They consist of <u>awareness</u> of our habits of:
Feeling a sense of personal obligation to fix everything themselves – Type 1;
Believing that they must go out to others to win them over – Type 2;
Beginning to drive themselves for status and attention -- Type 3;

Holding on to and intensifying feeling through the imagination -- Type 4;
Withdrawing from reality into concepts and mental world -- Type 5;
Becoming dependent on something outside the self for guidance -- Type 6;
Feeling that something better is available somewhere else -- Type 7;
Feeling that they must push and struggle to make things happen -- Type 8;
Outwardly, accommodating themselves to others -- Type 9.

In conclusion, the Enneagram helps us take concrete steps toward recovering our true self, our spiritual new self. But even the most dedicated spiritual seekers generally do not reach spiritual realization without a lot of significant *inner work* over a long period of time depending on a person's degree of integration (Please refer to the Appendix III). As a Christian, I believe that this inner work can be accelerated by God's grace through the sanctification process. (Refer to PART THREE)

WOUNDS FROM THE EARLY CHILDHOOD

The painful events of early childhood create a particular way of interpreting our experiences so that later life events reinforce our beliefs about our self and the world.

A study of historical sources reveals that loving, tender compassionate care of children is a fairly recent experience. Until the last century the beating of children was considered quite appropriate. Throughout history it was commonplace for children to be killed, abandoned, sexually abused, and terrorized by adults.

According to Cecil G, Osborne, "A child, made to feel inadequate and inferior, experiences a need to compensate in some way for the degradation suffered at the hands of others, particularly parents. One consequence is the need to alleviate or balance self-contempt with attention, regard, appreciation, admiration, or love from others. The pursuit of such attention is compulsive, because of the compelling need not to be at the mercy of self-contempt...and may amount to an all-consuming life goal. The result is total dependence on others for self-evaluation. It rises or falls with the attitude of others toward him or her." (Osborne, *The Art of Becoming a Whole Person*, pp. 30-31)

He continues: "The neurotics [same as personalities] come to despise themselves, as they felt themselves to be rejected by others in early childhood. As a consequence, they may dislike their faces, their names, their bodies, their limitations, their mental faculties, and/or their performance as human beings. For instance, the aggressive, vindictive type personality will despise in oneself most deeply anything he or she conceives as 'weakness." (Ibid. p. 31)

For instance, Ann was forty years old and was very active in her church. But a nameless fear made it impossible for her to speak in public. After a number of therapy sessions, she became aware of an almost totally buried hostility toward her father, a rage so deep that she dare not allow it into consciousness. Its power crippled and immobilized her. It took her two years of group therapy before full relief came. She realized that the discharge of her self-hatred came from hatred of the way she had been treated by her father.

The following demonstrates how personality types are affected by imperfect parents' treatment of their children:

As children they were physically punished for being wrong – Type 1;

As children they were put down and not loved – Type 2 Personality;

As children they were compared to high standards -- Type 3 Personality;

As children they were sexually abused – Type 4 Personality;

As children they experienced poverty and insecurity – Type 5 Personality;

As children they were forced into constant obedience – Type 6 Personality;

As children they were growing up in dysfunctional families – Type 7 Personality;
As children they were deprived and harmed – Type 8 Personality;
As children they were frustrated without parental guidance – Type 9.

Riso and Hudson stresses: "A child born into a dysfunctional family will most likely have to learn to defend oneself and build an identity in whatever degree of dysfunction exists. Destructive, abusive, or neglectful parents will, of course, make a major difference in the kinds of adaptations the child will have make... Two children of the same basic temperament will crystallize at different Levels of Development, depending on the differences of health or unhealthiness in their family of origin." (Riso and Hudson, *Understanding the Enneagram*, p. 314)

INNER HEALING OF WOUNDS OF CHILDHOOD

People attending church on a given Sunday morning consist of a great variety of personalities with different backgrounds and circumstances. Many of them are struggling with many different problems and issues in life -- some in financial crisis, some in addiction, some in domestic violence, and some in dysfunctional family...

But the most critical issue is our living in pretension by wearing the masks of personality. That's because we still carry our past wounds from past environmental conditions, life circumstances, bad memories, and wrong scripts from our childhood. That's why we have different personality types. We need to be free from our irrational fears, resentments, and inner conflicts. We need to be freed from our unresolved childhood issues; from our wayward passions and compulsions; from our distorted ego-driven desires.

The Enneagram can help us in the inner healing of our wounds of childhood so that we can move toward transformational processes. By understanding the structures of our own personality type, we realize how and why we have closed down and become blocked in our real growth and transformation. It also shows us with great *specificity* how our personality has limited us, what our path of growth is, and where real fulfillment can be found.

From *The Wisdom of the Enneagram* we can learn that our basic personality type reveals the psychological mechanisms by which we *forget* or *disconnect* from our true nature -- the Essence. This is how we abandon our true self. Our personalities draw upon the capacities of our inborn temperaments (introverts, extroverts, sensors, intuitive) to develop defenses and compensations for where we have been hurt in childhood. In order to survive whatever difficulties we encountered at that time, we unwittingly mastered a limited repertoire of strategies, self-images, and behaviors that allowed us to *cope* with and *survive* in our early environment. Each of us therefore has become an 'expert' at a particular form of coping which, if used excessively, also becomes the core of the dysfunctional area of our personality.

It is well established that children are equipped with an innate ability called ego defenses to defend their conscious awareness against threats and intolerable situations. The defenses are archaic and they function automatically and unconsciously once they are formed. The unconscious quality of these defenses is very damaging to all psychological systems, ranging from those of psychotics to fully functioning individuals.

As the defenses and strategies of our personality become more structured, our personalities cause us to lose contact with our direct experience of the True Self or the Essence. The personality, rather than contact with our inmost being, becomes the source our identity. Our sense of ourselves is based increasingly on internal images, memories,

152

and learned behaviors rather than on the spontaneous expression of our true nature. This loss of contact with our Essence (True Self) causes deep anxiety, taking the form of one of the nine [ego-driven] Passions. Once in place, these Passions, which are usually <u>uncon-scious</u> and <u>invisible</u> to us, begin to drive our personality.

Understanding our personality type and its dynamics, therefore, offers an especially potent approach to the unconscious, to our wounds and compensations, and ultimately, to our healing and transformation." (Riso, *Enneagram Transformation,* p. 125)

Michael Scanlan, the Roman Catholic Priest, in his book called, *Inner Healing,* makes important distinction between surface memories (the iceberg above the water) and root memories (the iceberg below the water). At times, there is a single surface memory of an embarrassing act, an incident filled with guilt feelings or a single moment of fright; and this memory can be recalled into the consciousness of the person easily. Following a prayer it is common for the person to experience new peace in the memory. (Scanlan, *Inner Healing,* pp. 47-51)

When a root memory is involved, there are many disturbing memories built upon one root memory like layers of an onion. Praying for individual surface memories would yield some success. These root memories are the parts of the iceberg below the water. The root (the deeply repressed) memories are not easily healed because they are not easily recalled to the conscious level. But, when the root memory is recalled to conscious level through the grace of God, we can experience new peace in the memory through healing prayers. Then, a new freedom of transparency is experienced with a whole series of other memories being healed.

A childhood memory of being alone at night in the dark, being lost amidst a crowd or being unwanted by parents can be the foundation for later fears of darkness, of strangers or of intimacy. Memory of a tyrannical father can be the root memory of many subsequent bad authority experiences. At times, the root is so deep and the healing is so radical that the release of new peace and love is an experience comparable or exceeding the original release of the Baptism of the Holy Spirit.

These deeply rooted memories are frequently healed with the aid of a visualization process. If the person was frightened at an early age, the minister prays aloud that the person will see Jesus now doing the very thing that would have most helped the person at the time of the original incident.

Father Scanlon shares his experience of helping persons to visualize Jesus protecting them from some feared danger, Jesus taking them to the God, the Parent, and introducing them to the first fatherly or motherly love they have known. Whatever the true need is, the loving heart of the Lord desires for that need to be filled with his saving love; the visualization is just a form of accepting the love that the Lord offers.

The scars of an unloving parent are so much at the root of other problems with authority figures. If only the current problems are dealt with, then the basic situation will remain unhealed and the series of current problems and sins will continue.

Dr. Paul Tournier presents an example of a doctor's dilemma of caring for a neurotic young adult who is suffering from an inner conflict between a false suggestion [imagination] and a true intuition:

"I [Dr. Tournier] am often asked what I think of the relation between sin and sickness. The following outline seems to me to give a clear picture of it:

> The son who loves his father is right and healthy.
>
> The son who hates his father is not right, but healthy.
>
> The son who loves and hates his father at the same time is neurotic. Neurosis rests upon an inner contradiction. This is what makes it possible for many doctors to say that the neurotic son will be cured if he frees himself from his moral scruples and hates his

154

father with all his heart. Other doctors, however, say
that he will never be able to stifle completely his ideal
of love [within his conscience] and can only be cured
by abandoning his hatred. (Tournier, *The Whole Person
in a Broken World,* p.12)

The Enneagram can help heal repressed memories **by bringing
them up to the conscious level**, so that we can name them, experience them, and then release them or let them go or abandon them. If
they keep coming back, that means the root causes have not been dealt
with. We become a compassionate witness of our behaviors without
judgment; we simply observe them and acknowledged them. Then, our
ego will gradually become powerless in making us angry, resentful, unforgiving, or fearful personalities.

Father Scanlon has experienced in his healing ministry people
whose hearts in various degrees appeared to be wounded, hardened,
or broken. (pp.58-61). The processes of healing of these hearts seem
to be different from those of the healing of memories. The conditions
of these people with wounded hearts are expressed in the Bible (James
4:1-10). The desires, directions, and attitudes at this level are wrongly
centered. They need drastic measures like a spiritual heart transplant
to replace a broken, wounded, hardened heart (Ezekiel 11:19-20). They
need a clean heart filled with the Spirit (Psalm 51:10; Galatians 4:6).
They need the Savior (Isaiah 61:1; Ephesians 3:17). Their prayers
become: "Lord Jesus Christ, Son of the living God, have mercy on me
a sinner."

As a teen-ager Helen observed the healing of her mother's broken,
loveless heart in a retreat setting. She told me (Cho-Kim): "I was responding to what the Lord is doing—the saving action of God at work."
When a case like this happens, there is a new openness, a new loving
affirmation, and a new peace. Helen said, "I had a new sense of identity
and resting in that identity, a new quiet call to holiness." At that crucial

moment, she was filled with the Holy Spirit and later on she became a "wounded healer" by preaching the gospel as a minister.

Cecil G. Osborne, a Psychotherapist, summarizes his work by writing:

> "Painful things do happen to nearly all of us early in life that get imprinted in our systems which carry the memory. They make our lives miserable by causing depression, phobias, panic and anxiety attacks and a whole host of symptoms. For inner healing we apply the "Primal Integration therapy," which brings painful memories to the *conscious level* from the *unconscious level* to feel them, to name them, and to release them in the Spirit of love...
>
> One might ask, since those things happened long ago, why dig them up and go through the pain of reliving them? The answer is that every experience, major or minor, has some effect upon the personality and the way we function. Childhood hurts [wounds], especially the deprivation of love, leave their mark. Some would unconsciously try to get their wife or husband to meet their unmet childhood needs. Their religious faith could not eradicate their childhood pain, any more than it would solve the problem of a diseased appendix." (Osborne, The Art of Becoming a Whole Person, pp. 54)

Inner healing can come when we give names to the sources of our pains and let them go or release them. When this takes place, we discover that we are opening up and letting go of years of the human bondage that we have been holding on to. When the light of Jesus Christ touches the darkness in us, they become doors through which His grace transforms our beings and uses us as the "wounded healer."

CONSCIOUS SELF-OBSERVER ("COMPASSIONATE WITNESS")

For the work of *self-realization* Riso emphasizes the importance of *dis-identifying with our personality* and its habitual responses: "Knowing our type helps us become more *conscious self-observers.* Learning how to observe ourselves prepares us to the possibility of *consciously* choosing our behavior. To do this, we must learn how *not to identify with our personality*—and this is where the Enneagram can be extremely valuable...When we learn to dis-identify with our personality, instead of feeling naked and deprived, we find that our personality is actually what has blocked us most of our lives." (Riso, *Enneagram Transformation*, pp. 3-4).

When we create a "gap" between our inner-observer and our personality, we catch a glimpse of a deeper, more essential self and the possibility of real freedom.

When we begin to step away and watch, we are no longer controlled by the physical events of our lives. For instance, when we experience anger, step back and observe it for a few moments. We will notice that we are liberated almost immediately from the pain associated with the anger. As we become less identified with our personality, it becomes a smaller part of the totality of who we are. The personality still exists, but there is a more active intelligence, a more active sensitivity, a Presence underlying it that uses the personality as a vehicle rather than being driven by it. As we identify more with our Essence, we see that we do not lose our identity—we actually find it."

157

SUPEREGO AS THE INNER CRITIC

The superego is the inner voice that is always putting us down for not living up to certain standards or rewards our ego when we fulfill its demands. Even the parts of the superego that may have been useful when we were two years old are probably not very useful to us today. Nonetheless, these voices are just as powerful now as they were then, but usually do more harm than good. This inner critic's voice keep drawing us back into identifying with our personality and acting out in self-defeating and defensive ways. We must recognize the irrelevance of these voices and successfully resist giving them energy._

If we feel anxious, depressed, lost, hopeless, fearful, wretched, or weak, we can be sure that our superego is on duty. Another way we can begin to free ourselves from our superego is by becoming more aware of our automatic reactions to problems or conflicts – and then contemplating on following "healing attitude" for our type.

HEALTHY ATTITUDES ACCORDING TO TYPES: (RISO AND HUDSON, *THE WISDOM OF THE ENNEAGRAM,* P. 355)

Type 1: Maybe others are right. Maybe someone else has a better idea. Maybe others will learn for themselves. Maybe I've done all that can be done.

Type 2: Maybe I could let someone else do this. Maybe this person is actually already showing me love in their own way. Maybe I could do something good for myself, too.

Type 3: Maybe I don't have to be the best. Maybe people will accept me just the way I am. Maybe others' opinions of me aren't so important.

Type 4: Maybe there's nothing wrong with me. Maybe others do understand me and are supporting me. Maybe I'm not the only one
who feels this way.

Type 5: Maybe I can trust people and let them know what I need. Maybe
I can live happily in the world. Maybe my future will be okay.

Type 6: Maybe this will work out fine. Maybe I don't have to foresee every
possible problem. Maybe I can trust my own judgments and myself.

Type 7: Maybe what I already have is enough. Maybe there's nowhere
else I need to be right now. Maybe I'm not missing out on anything worthwhile.

Type 8: Maybe this person isn't out to take advantage of me. Maybe I
can let down my guard a little more. Maybe I could let my heart
be touched more deeply.

Type 9: Maybe I can make a difference. Maybe I need to get energized
and be involved. Maybe I am more powerful than I realize.

THE CONTINUUM OF TRAITS

Riso discovered that within each personality type, there is an internal
structure. The continuum (with its Nine Levels of Development) forms
the backbone of each personality type. He taught that in understanding a person accurately, it is necessary to perceive where the person
lies within the Levels of his or her type: healthy, average, or unhealthy.
(Riso, Enneagram Transformation, p. 21)

He offers us how to move from the **"average type"** (**usual personality**) to the **"healthy type"** via a vertical upward movement within
our personality type. On the other hand, the "average type" can move
downward to the "unhealthy type." The Continuum for each of the
personality types is comprised of nine internal Levels of Development:
there are three Levels in the *healthy* range; three Levels of the *average*

range; three Levels of the *unhealthy* range. Through self-observation we know which actions and desires lead toward a healthy personality and which lead toward an unhealthy personality. Self–observation provides us with the wisdom to make the right choices on our path. Without it, we would be fragmented and neurotic.

CHART 1. THE CONTINUUM OF NINE BASIC PERSONALITY TYPES:

	TYPE TWO	TYPE THREE	TYPE FOUR
HEALTHY			
Level One	Disinterested Altruist	Authentic Person	Inspired Creator
Level Two	Caring Peron	Self-Assured	Self-Aware Intuitive
Level Three	Nurturing Helper	Outstanding Paragon	Self-Revealing Individual
LEVEL TWO	**CARING PERON**	**SELF-ASSURED**	**SELF-AWARE INTUITIVE**
Level Three	Nurturing Helper	Outstanding Paragon	Self-Revealing Individual
Average			
Level Four	Effusive Friend	Competitive Status-Seeker	Imaginative Aesthete
Level Five	Possessive Intimate	Image-Conscious Pragmatist	Self-Observed Romantic
Level Six	Self-Important "Saint"	Self-Promoting Narcissist	Self-Indulgent Exception
UNHEALTHY			
Level Seven	Self-Deceptive Manipulator	Dishonest Opportunist	Alienate Depressive
Level Eight	Coercive Dominator	Malicious Deceiver	Tormented Person
Level Nine	Psychosomatic Victim	Vindictive Psychopath	Self-Destructive

	TYPE FIVE	TYPE SIX	TYPE SEVEN
HEALTHY			
Level One	Pioneering Visionary	Valiant Hero	Ecstatic Appreciator
Level Two	Perceptive Observer	Engaging Friend	Free-Spirited Optimist
Level Three	Focused Innovator	Committed Worker	Accomplished Generalist

AVERAGE

Level Four	Studious Expert	Dutiful Loyalist	Exp. Sophisticate
Level Five	Intense Conceptualizer	Ambivalent Pessimist	Hyperactive Extrovert
Level Six	Provocative Cynic	Authoritarian Rebel	Excessive Hedonist

UNHEALTHY

Level Seven	Isolated Nihilist	Overreacting Dependent	Impulsive Escapist
Level Eight	Terrified "Alien"	Paranoid Hysteric	Manic Compulsive
Level Nine	Imploding Schizoid	Self-Defeating Masochist	Panicky "Hysteric"

	TYPE EIGHT	TYPE NINE	TYPE ONE

HEALTHY

Level One	Magnanimous Heart	Self-Possessed Guide	Wise Realist
Level Two	Self-Confident	Receptive Person	Reasonable Person
Level Three	Constructive Leader	Supportive Peacemaker	Principled Teacher

AVERAGE

Level Four	Enterprising Adventurer	Accommodating Role-Player	Idealistic Reformer
Level Five	Dominating Power-Broker	Disengaged Participant	Orderly Person
Level Six	Confrontational Adversary	Resigned Fatalist	Judgmental Perfectionist

UNHEALTHY

Level Seven	Ruthless Outlaw	Denying "Doormat"	Intolerant Misanthrope
Level Eight	Omnipotent Megalomaniac	Dissociating Automaton	Obsessive Hypocrite
Level Nine	Violent Destroyer	Abandoning Ghost	Punitive Avenger

The Continuum helps make sense of each personality type as a whole by providing a framework on which to place each of the healthy, average, and unhealthy traits, motivations, attitudes, and defense mechanisms.

According to Riso and Hudson we can enter <u>a portal or a point</u> on the Enneagram's circumference for each basic personality Type toward the self-development. (Riso and Hudson, *The Wisdom of the Enneagram*, pp. 76-77)

The healthy personality (in Level 1) becomes more transparent and flexible; we realize something powerful that frees us, rather than something negative that keeps us in bondage. There is no longer the manifestation of our old behaviors that used to overlook things, make mistakes, and create problems of all kinds. Instead, we experience moments of flowing and peak performance arising. That's when we are connected to the Essence and we have discovered our True Self. After the discovery of our True Self, we learn to become more <u>present</u> and we begin to experience the <u>positive</u> <u>qualities</u> of the next Type in our Direction of Integration naturally.

This is why self-observation is so vital: we must know which actions and desires are leading toward *wholeness* and which are leading toward *fragmentation*. self-observation guides us to make the right choices between the two paths.

BASIC OR IRRATIONAL FEARS

Jose Stevens calls irrational fears dragons: "The "seven dragons" are the main forms of unfounded fear, and to know them is the first step in eliminating fear. Without irrational fear, there is ultimately no human suffering." (Stevens, *Transforming Your Dragons,* p. 17)

He identifies irrational (basic) fears as dragons:

They are created by the illusion of separateness;

They are the illusion of the absence of love;

They are ignorant;

They are self-made;

They are blinders to vision;

They twist and distort reality;

They are painful and support all suffering;

They, if indulged, breed more of themselves;

They limit experience;

They paralyze;

They move in when love is forgotten.

He clarifies that all fears are negative: "There are legitimate forms of fear that help humans to survive. Fear of an avalanche causes you to avoid a dangerous area. This is not irrational fear but a real and positive form of fear. The dragons are about irrational fears, but they masquerade as sensible fears." (Ibid. p. 17)

THE RED FLAG FEAR

According to Riso and Hudson, before each Type moves into the unhealthy range, each Type encounters what they call the Red Flag Fear. If the Wake-up Call was an invitation to awaken before the person moved downward into the Average Levels and into fixation and increasing "sleep," the Red Flag is a far more serious alarm that signals an imminent crisis. If persons are shocked into awareness by their Red Flag fear, they may be able to stop acting out their behaviors and attitudes that have gotten them into their current perilous position. If they persist in their self-defeating attitudes and behaviors, they will fall into increasingly destructive states. (The Wisdom of Enneagram, pp. 80-84)

RED FLAG FEAR ACCORDING TO THE TYPES:

Type 1 -- They fear that their ideals are actually wrong and counter productive.

Type 2 -- They fear that they are driving away friends and loved ones.

Type 3 -- They fear that they are failing; that their claims are empty and fraudulent.

Type 4 -- They fear that they are ruining their lives and wasting their opportunities.

Type 5 -- They fear that they are never going to find a place in the world or with people.

Type 6 -- They fear that their own actions have harmed their security.

Type 7 -- They fear that their activities are bringing them pain and unhappiness.

Type 8 -- They fear that others are turning against them and will retaliate.

Type 9 -- They fear that they will be forced by reality to deal with their problems.

There are six fears that interfere with transformation: They are fear of failing; fear of disapproval, fear of suffering, fear of isolation, fear of looking foolish, and fear of success. When fear enters your personal life and you experience fear, gently allow it into your awareness. Feel it. Refuse to judge it. Deflect it. And "Get rid of it!" You know who walks beside you on your life journeys. Your faith in Christ can eliminate fear from your life.

Max Lucado suggests that we may get rid of fear by (1) examining fear; (2) exposing fear; (3) battling fear; (4) meditating several times a day on a single verse of Scripture from God's own mouth: "I will never leave you nor forsake you" (Hebrew 13:5). (Lucado, *Fearless,* pp. 216-217)

RELEASES AND AFFIRMATIONS TOWARD TRANSFORMATION

When we begin to understand that <u>we are not our personality,</u> we also begin to *realize* that we are spiritual beings who have a personality and who are manifesting our ego through our personality. When we stop identifying with our ego-driven personality and stop defending it, a miracle happens: we discover our Essential nature (*imago dei,* the image of God, is inherent worth and dignity) and spontaneously begin to arise to the Healthy Level 1. It's almost like an adult butterfly emerging from the chrysalis.

The Enneagram helps us strip off the false self and move toward developing the True Self. There are 16 releases and 9 affirmations for each personality type. For your own type, please consult Riso's book, Enneagram Transformation.

Following is sample statements of *the releases and affirmations* for *the Personality Type Six.* (Riso, Enneagram Transformations, pp. 76-84)

RESEASES:

1. I now release my fear of being abandoned and alone.

2. I now release my self-defeating, self-punishing tendencies.

3. I now release all feelings of dread about the future.

4. I now release feeling persecuted, trapped, and desperate.

5. I now release overreacting and exaggerating my problem.

6. I now release taking out my fears and anxieties on others.

7. I now release being suspicious of others and thinking the worst of them.

8. I now release feeling inferior and incapable of functioning on my own.

9. I now release feeling cowardly and unsure of myself.

10. I now release acting "tough" to disguise my insecurities.

11. I now release my fear and dislike of those who are different from me.

12. I now release blaming others for my own problems and mistakes.

13. I now release being evasive and defensive with those who need me.

14. I now release my tendency to be negative and complaining.

15. I now release my fear of taking responsibility for my mistakes.

16. I now release looking to others to make me feel secure.

AFFIRMATIONS:

1. I now affirm that I am independent and capable.

2. I now affirm that I can keep my own identity in groups and in relationships.

3. I now affirm that I have faith in my talents, my future, and myself.

4. I now affirm that I meet difficulties with calmness and confidence.

5. I now affirm that I am secure and ale to make the best of whatever comes my way.

6. I now affirm the kinship I have with every human being.

7. I now affirm that I am understanding and generous to all who need me.

8. I now affirm that I act courageously in all circumstances.

9. I now affirm that I find true authority within me.

The Releases and Affirmations help us "reprogram" our behavior by healing the way we think about ourselves. The Releases [letting go] allow us first to acknowledge the emotional problems under which we labor. They give us an opportunity to name the sources of pain in our lives and to work through our negative issues so that we can let them go. They take us inside our type to touch the pain that lies at the root of our problems, allowing us to overcome resistance, denial, and self-deception. Naturally, by acknowledging the negative aspects of our personality, we do not want to reinforce them in any way. But we do want to "make the unconscious conscious" by shining a light on our hidden conflicts and contradictions. Affirmations become prayers from the heart in which we finally do find healing to transformation and integration.

DIRECTION OF INTEGRATION AND DIRECTION OF DISINTEGRATION

The Enneagram corroborates the commonsense intuition that we must become healthy before we can integrate to next Type, just as we must become somewhat unhealthy range before we deteriorate into more negative and destructive states.

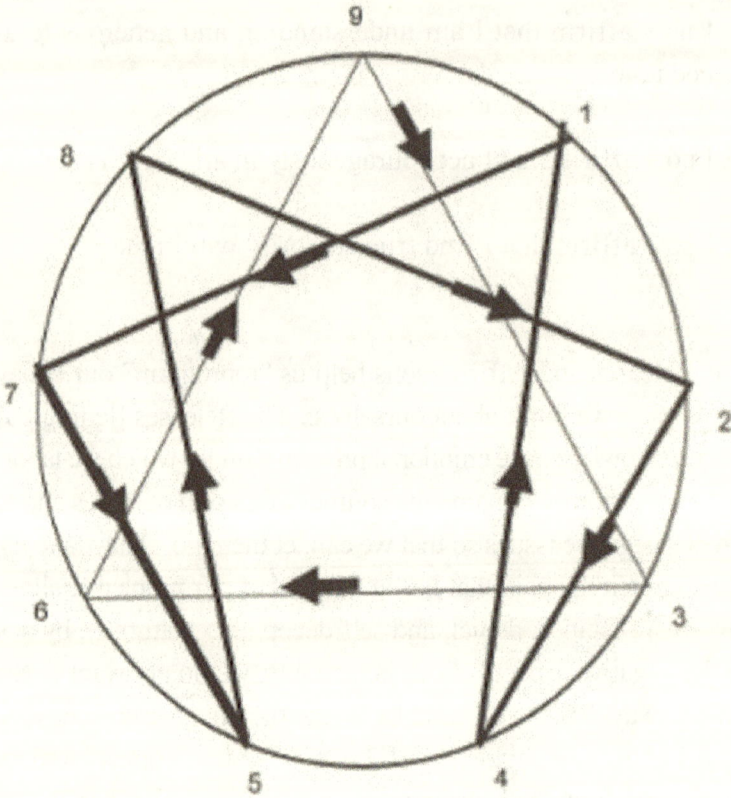

Figure 5. The Directions of Integration

*Arrows show the direction of movement.

It is in the healthy range in a Type can move on to the next Type according to our **Enneagram's Integration Directions** (Figure 5): arrows tracing the numbers 5 to 8 to 2 to 4 to 1 to 7 back to 5 according to the Enneagram's Hexad symbol AND arrows tracing the numbers 6 to 9 to 3, back to 6 according to the Enneagram's Triangle symbol.

The Direction of Disintegration is the opposite Direction of the Integration's Direction. We move from Type 5 to 7 to 1 to 4 to 2 to 8 to 5 in the Hexad symbol and Type 6 to 3 to 9 to 6 in the Triangle symbol.

168

In this Direction of Disintegration we gradually lose the possibility of actualizing the capacities of our Essence or True Self.

This is why self-observation is so vital: we must know which actions and desires are leading toward *wholeness* and which are leading toward *fragmentation*. Self-observation guides us to make the right choices between the two paths.

Riso and Hudson discovered that the healthy Levels, especially Level 1, we unconsciously know that what we need for our healing and wholeness. Even though we cannot yet fully integrate that quality into our personality structure. When we become healthier, we also begin to be in the position to access and claim our most needed qualities. For example, SEVENS need to learn the lessons of acceptance and self-discipline from ONES.

The healthy personality (in Level 1) becomes more transparent and flexible; we realize something powerful that frees us, rather than something negative that keeps us in bondage. There is no longer the manifestation of our old behaviors that used to overlook things, make mistakes, and create problems of all kinds. Instead, we experience moments of flowing and peak performance arising. That's when we are connected to the Essence and we have discovered our True Self. After the discovery of our True Self, we learn to become more present and we begin to experience the positive qualities of the next Type in our Direction of Integration naturally.

We must realize that the process of integration is not about what we should do—it is a process of consciously letting go (release) of the aspects of our personality Type that block us from becoming our True Self. When we stop holding on to defenses, attitudes, and fears AND we let go of our ego-propelled passions, we experience an organic unfolding and balancing as natural as the blossoming of a flower. As a healthy tree does not have to do anything for a bud to go to a flower then to a fruit: it is an organic, natural process, a healthy soul wants to unfold in the same way. The Enneagram describes this organic process (grow by itself) of each Type. The Type in the Direction of Integration gives us clues about when this is taking place and helps us understand and activate this process more easily.

Riso and Hudson emphasize that "while it remains true that everyone emerges from childhood as a unique member of only one basic personality type, it is equally true that as we develop over our lifetime, it is possible to integrate the healthy psychological aspects of the other types s we activate new capacities." It is possible that "we can move

beyond the type in our Direction of Integration to the next type and then to the next, around the Enneagram... suggesting that human nature is in process, always coming into being." (Understanding the Enneagram, pp. 29-30)

ATTENTION!

SCORING INSTRUCTIONS FOR THE APPENDIX III:

Count the number of *TRUE*'s circled.
If 20 or above—Splendid Integration;
If 15-19—Good Integration;
If 10-14—In need of additional growth;
If 1-9—Additional therapy indicated.

CHAPTER 6

SELF-TRANCENDENCE

TRANSFORMATION OF PERSONALITY

From Riso and Hudson we learn that we can enter a portal or a point on the Enneagram's circumference for each basic personality type toward personality transformation. (*The Wisdom of the Enneagram*, pp. 76-77)

- The angry, critical Type ONES become more spontaneous and joyful, like healthy SEVENS.

- Prideful, self-deceptive Type TWOS become more self-nurturing and emotionally aware, like healthy FOURS.

- Vain, deceitful Type THREES become more cooperative and committed to others, like healthy SIXES.

- Envious, emotionally turbulent Type Fours become more objective and principled, like healthy ONES.

- Avaricious (hoarding), detached Type FIVES becomes more self-confident and decisive, like healthy EIGHTS.

- Fearful, pessimistic Type SIXES become more relaxed and optimistic, like <u>healthy</u> NINES.

- Gluttonous, scattered Type SEVENS become more focused and profound, like <u>healthy</u> FIVES. Lustful, controlling Type EIGHTS become more open-hearted and caring, like <u>healthy</u> TWOS.

- Slothful, self-neglecting Type NINES become more self-developing an energetic, like <u>healthy</u> THREES.

THE INTERCONNECTED ENNEAGRAM

According to Riso and Hudson, the principle of the interconnected Enneagram warns us that each Type will eventually degenerate into its opposite <u>unless</u> it is counterbalanced by the strengths of the type in its Direction of Integration. (*Understanding the Enneagram*, pp. 325-326)

- Having a higher purpose in life, Type ONE degenerates into being led by rigid ideas and principles, unless we are open to a joyous acceptance of reality as Type SEVEN.

- Having a joyous acceptance of reality, Type SEVEN degenerates into a hunger for more experiences, unless we are open to the sacredness of each experience as Type FIVE.

- Having openness to the sacredness of each experience, Type FIVE degenerates into being led by elaborate and useless interpretations of reality, unless we are grounded in reality and committed to practical, constructive action as Type EIGHT.

- Being fully grounded and committed to practical, constructive action, Type EIGHT degenerates into an aggressive pursuit of control and self-importance, unless we are open to a devoted service to others, symbolized as Type TWO.

- Having a devoted service to others, Type TWO degenerates into manipulating others to fulfill one's own needs, unless we are open to being completely truthful about who we are and what we are doing, as Type FOUR.

- Being completely truthful about who we are and what we are doing, Type FOUR degenerates into being led by subjective states and emotional neediness, unless we are open to having a higher purpose in life as Type ONE.

- Having a humble self-love and esteem of one's true value, Type THREE degenerates into self-aggrandizement and ego glorification, unless we are open to commitment to others and the assumption of responsibility for our life as Type SIX.

- Being committed to others and taking responsibility for life, Type SIX degenerates into defending one's self from others and being fearful about one's own capacities, unless we are open to a complete trust in Being and a surrender to reality, symbolized as Type NINE.

- Having a complete trust in Being and surrender to reality, Type NINE degenerates into passivity and self-neglect, unless we are open to a humble self-love and esteem for our true value as Type THREE.

TRANSCENDING THE EGO

Wayne W. Dyer provides suggestions for transcending the ego (the false self). (Dyer, *Your Sacred Self,* pp.193-199)

1. You can tame your ego by your awareness. Ask yourself, "Am I listening to my false self or my True Self? If you are boasting to someone about yourself, or in any way feeling superior about your appearance, abilities or possessions, recognize that this is your ego at work trying to convince you of your separateness from God and of your superiority to other human beings. As you become aware of your ego, make a shift away from self-absorption into your awareness of the true self.

2. Start keeping track of how frequently you use the pronoun "I." Make a decision to take the focus off yourself by cutting back on the pronoun "I."

3. Begin to view your ego as an entity that sits on your shoulder with a purpose. The more you listen to this entity, the more you are off your sacred path.

4. Practice active listening to others and keeping the focus off yourself.

5. Actively resist the habit of letting your ego run rampant in your life. The more you resist allowing your ego to be authoritative, the sooner the day will come when your True Self fills the space previously occupied by the demands of your false self.

6. The more time you spend shutting down the inner dialogue, the more you come to realize that you are not separate from God nor any of the billions of souls that are extensions of the God's force.

7. Keep a journal.

8. Give more of yourself and ask less in return. This is a wonderful way to tame the ego.

9. Remind yourself every day that the highest worship of God is service to humankind and that it is through these acts that your true self will be realized.

10. Seek authentic freedom that needs nothing to prove its existence. Counterfeit freedom demands something in your hand to validate its existence.

THE LEADEN RULE

Riso and Hudson discovered the *Leaden Rule.* It is the opposite of the *Golden Rule, which* tells us, "In everything do to others as you would have them do to you." In another words, if you want to be forgiven, accepted, and loved by others, you would do that to others. In contrast, The Leaden Rule states, "Do unto others what you most fear having done unto you." In another words, you are inflicting others with your own basic fears, such as abuses and rejections.

The Leaden Rule points out: "Each personality type has its own special way of aggressively undermining others to bolster its own ego... Thus each type begins to inflict its own basic fear on others...

This occurs at the bottom of the average range." (*The Wisdom of the Enneagram*, pp. 82-83)

For instance, if the Type Fours fear that they have no identity or no personal significance of their own, they start threatening people by saying, 'you are nobodies and have no value, or significance.'

AUTHENTIC FREEDOM VS. COUNTERFEIT FREEDOM

Dr. Wayne Dyer described freedom as an unconcern about one's ego. According to him there are two kinds of freedom. *"Authentic freedom is detachment from self-absorption, from the ego. It is pure freedom that comes from transcending the ego and knowing God... Authentic freedom allows you the freedom to know and experience the love of God within you, and to share it in the physical world as an expression of that love rather than as an end unto itself.*

He teaches that the opposite of authentic freedom is *counterfeit freedom*. This is the freedom that the outside world tries to sell us. It is as much as an illusion as is the existence of ego as a separate entity. The idea is fed by the ego when it convinces you that to be truly free you must "get" something outside of yourself. The counterfeit freedom is the freedom that society offers and your ego seeks in order to strengthen the illusion and keep itself alive. To get to the joy of authentic freedom, you first have to examine the kind of freedom you have been pursuing. You need to see what kind of freedom you are continually being encouraged by your culture to pursue." (Dyer, *Your Sacred Self*, pp.188-189)

He presents three counterfeit freedoms that are being offered by society: chemical freedom; sexual freedom; financial freedom.

1. **Chemical Freedom**

The United States has been the most chemically dependent country in the history of the world. The search for freedom through chemicals has trapped users into lifestyle of never getting enough of what they don't want. The ego is telling the user, 'You'll be fee when you experience the fantastic high that comes with this chemical or this bottle of booze.' The idea that a chemical provides freedom is a counterfeit idea. All you will get from that counterfeit idea is a need for more of that chemical to boost your false self, your inflated ego.

2. **Sexual Freedom**

The pursuit of sexual freedom has resulted in shattered lives. Dr. Dyer points out that it is the work of your false self to convince you that this kind of sexual activity has something to do with freedom. Our pursuit of sexual freedom has brought the largest increase in sexually transmitted diseases in the history of humanity. Ego-inspired freedom is always based on a false sense of security.

3. **Financial Freedom**

The ego thrives on consumption. The false belief is that the more you will acquire the more freedom you will experience. Your ego says, 'You can buy freedom and you are free to spend the money you don't even have yet.' Ego insists that all you have to do is want it and that your specialness entitles you to have it.

This generally involves credit cards charging usurious interest rates. Objects cannot give you freedom. This is an ego-designed trap to keep you chasing and consuming, always feeding this false idea. Your ego insists that you will find freedom as long as you continue working toward increased financial success. (Ibid. pp. 190- 193)

In contrast to above-mentioned counterfeit freedoms, authentic freedom is not located in the physical world, but in the eternal, changeless world of God.

Thomas Oden enlightens us with the Christian perspective: "Since Christian teaching affirms the goodness and the wisdom of God in enabling and empowering human [authentic] freedom, it cannot be satisfied with a determinism that denies human freedom or asserts God's almighty power or influence in such a way as to eliminate all other influences or a view of chances that denies divine purposefulness; or a view of fate that denies divine benevolence." (Oden, *Living God*, p.278)

He proclaims that Christian teaching must also affirm "the sovereignty of God, the goodness of God, and the intelligence of God in balance" and that this God is involved in the world working simultaneously together with "human freedom and intelligibility of the natural order."

MOVING BEYOND THE DISCOVERY OF TRUE SELF

The Riso-Hudson's Enneagram is like a wise guide that points out to us our *individual direction, path*, and concrete *steps* toward the healing of the inner conflict, toward personal wellness, and toward personality transformation. In SECTION II we learned that the Enneagram is a valuable tool to discover our true self, but it cannot convert us into perfectly realized beings (whole persons). However, the discovery of our true self can motivate us to move forward into the deep spiritual journey because we realize that we may be free from inner conflict, the pain of the childhood, fears, ego-fixations, and the need of wearing our masks to defend our false self (ego-inflated personality).

However, learning how to transcend the ego is as hard as learning how to love others unconditionally. Many of us would rather continue the paths of self-deception (Type 2), malicious envy (Type 3), self-destructive subjectivity (Type 4), nihilism (Type 5), suspicion (Type 6), impulsiveness (Type 7), egocentricity (Type 8), complacency (Type 9), and inflexibility (Type 1). No matter how perfect the system is, it can't save our souls without the power of God's love and grace. Without this love and grace, we lose ourselves so easily in the many illusions that the ego sets before us.

Alan Watts points out the limit of the Enneagram as a psychological system:

> "Although we have applied all the psychological techniques at our disposal, we are still left unsatisfied because there remains a subtle, indefinable, and elusive inner discontent... This is truly a "divine discontent" for I believe it to be what the mystics describe as the yearning of the soul for God, as St. Augustine of Hippo says, "Thou hast made us for thyself, O Lord, and our heart is restless until it finds its rest in Thee." (Watts, *The Meaning of Happiness*, p. 120)

The Enneagram has been our guide in helping us to understand our behavior more objectively and in pointing the ways to personality transformation. But further growing toward the whole person requires a deeper journey of spiritual formation with practical disciplines. Therefore, we are continuously moving toward the spiritual journey. The Enneagram can still guide each transformed personality to grow and mature according to the individual's Direction of Integration. In our growing in the Spirit, transcending our egos is vital so that we maintain a stable, well integrated, tamed egos. Then, our transformative experiences in Section II will have a lasting effect on the Christian living in the Spirit and growing in maturity.

Riso and Hudson conclude that the Enneagram's transformational process is one of personality transformation with the inner healing—not one of self-improvement nor one of perfect salvation of the soul:

> "We are correcting a case of mistaken identity, not trying to "fix up" our false identity. In fact, when we discover our True Self, and recognize that we are *Essence,* we see that all of the noble qualities we have been seeking are already here—part of us…Our personalities are a response to the obscuration of the Virtues and Holy Ideas. When we correct our misperceptions, these qualities are rediscovered, and manifest freely again. Our *Essence* is always available because at our deepest level, it is what we are. The Enneagram reminds us again and again, that if we are on a spiritual path, we must begin to question our basic assumptions about our self and our identity. As awareness grows, we will open up to an expanded sense of self that includes more than the preoccupations of our personality; indeed, more than the personality can even imagine." (Riso and Hudson, http://www.enneagraminstitute.com/spirituality.asp, p.10)

INTEGRATING THE WISDOM OF ENNEAGRAM AND THE FAITH IN GOD

In the Chapter Three we learned that there are three factors blocking the psychological wellness. They were diagnosed by the Enneagram and healed by faith in the God of the Bible. It was suggested that three psychological factors, **anger (rage), shame (guilt), and fear** can be healed by **forgiveness, self-esteem, and providence**, respectively.

In Chapter Three we learned that the healing of these three factors can help us recover the original harmony and unity of human Essence in the Triads: the Thinking Center, the Feeling Center, the Instinctive [Doing] Center;

- Healing fears with trusting God's providence in <u>the thinking persons;</u>

- Healing anger with God's forgiveness in <u>the instinctive (doing) persons.</u>

- Healing shame (guilt) with God-given self-esteem in <u>the feeling persons;</u>

- In Chapter 8 we will discuss three essential life sources of the Christian living: faith, hope, and love.

CENTERING PRAYER

Centering prayer is distinctly different from practices of Eastern meditation that attempt to clear the mind of all thoughts. Centering prayer allows for the recognition of thoughts and then gently releases them into the hands of God. This form of prayer relies on the awareness that the Hoy Spirit resides in those who pray, connecting us heart to heart with God. In centering prayer, the goal is to so dwell in Christ that the fruit of this dwelling begins to show up in your life. Centering praying may "do" nothing at the moment. You sense no rapture, no mystical bliss. But later, as you move out into the busyness of life, you begin to notice that something has shifted. Your quiet center in Christ holds. Centering prayer is based on the trust that being with Jesus brings transformation. (Calhoun, *Spiritual Disciplines Handbook*, pp. 207-210)

A SHORT METHOD FOR CENTERING PRAYER
(Ibid. p.209)

1. Set aside a minimum of fifteen minutes (increase the time as you can. Set a timer if that helps you to be less concerned about when to stop.)

2. Settle into a comfortable position.

3. Intentionally place yourself in the presence of God, in the center of his love.

4. Choose a simple word, phrase or verse from Scripture that expresses your desire for God (e.g., love, peace, grace, Jesus, great Shepherd). Let this word guard your attention.

5. Take time to become quite. It is not unusual for the first minutes to be filled with many noisy thoughts. Don't worry about them or pay attention to them. Let them go. Gently return your attention to the center of God's presence and love by repeating

your word. When your thoughts wander, let them drop to the bottom of your mind. Don't go after them. Gently return to the presence of Christ through repeating your word. Let the word draw your attention back to Jesus. Be with Jesus. Listen. Be still. When distractions persist let one of the <u>following images</u> help you to return to Jesus.

6. Imagine that God's river of life runs through you. Deep down, the river is calm and slow. But on the surface there is rushing and debris. Imagine your distracting thoughts are part of the debris floating in the current. Don't try to capture these thoughts; release them and let the river of God's life carry them away.

7. Anytime you are distracted, let the distractions go with the river. Gently return to the presence of Christ with your prayer word.

8. Imagine that you are visiting a friend who lives on a busy city street. Because it is a warm day, the windows are open and all the noise and bustle of life float into the room through the window. At times you are conscious of sirens or people talking or children laughing, but your attention is devoted to your friend and you do not let your mind follow the sounds outside.

9. As you meet Jesus, acknowledge the noisy distractions that pull at your attention, but continually return to the moment with Jesus through your prayer word.

10. Rest in the center of God's love. Trust that the Holy Spirit who abides in the depths of your spirit will connect you with God.

11. Take several minutes to come out of prayer. Don't hurry. Breathe in the presence of Christ. Offer yourself to God for the tasks awaiting you (e.g., "I am yours," or "Remain with me." or "Grace upon grace." or "Peace upon peace").

LEARNING FROM THE METAPHOR OF BUTTERFLY'S LIFE CYCLE

The butterfly's life cycle is a teaching metaphor for the Enneagram's personality transformation and a Christian being born of the Spirit as the new self and the death of the old self (ego-driven self).

> "After each adult butterfly is mated; each fertilized egg is placed on a plant to be hatched; a caterpillar is formed and grows to its full size; it attaches to a branch or a blade. Now, the caterpillar, in a harder outer shell, trans- forms (*metamorphosis*) into a chrysalis (*pupa*) seem- ingly lifeless and inert. But inside this shell or cocoon, an amazing transformation is taking place. The tissues and structures of the caterpillar are being broken down and replaced with newly formed tissues and structures of the "adult" butterfly inside the cocoon (chrysalis). If transformation is proceeding without impediment, it takes one or two weeks. But if there is impediment, the chrysalis may enter a resting state for a few months, or even for the winter.

> Upon emergence (*eclosion*) the wings that are wrapped tightly around the butterfly's body are *unfurled* by fluid pumped through the veins of the wings. This is a very

vulnerable time in the life cycle of the butterfly as it
basks in the sunshine to harden and set its wings. Once
the adult butterfly emerges from the chrysalis it grows
no more in size." (Cho-Kim, God of Active Verbs. pp.
218-219)

In conclusion, we learn three important lessons:

- A crawling caterpillar from a fertilized egg can be compared to
an old self.

- Entering inside a cocoon can compare the conversion of a caterpillar into a chrysalis by entering inside a cocoon to the salvation
of a lost soul through the God's justifying grace. The growing as
a chrysalis inside of the dark, isolated cocoon can be compared
to the sanctification process through God's sanctifying grace.

- The emergence of an adult butterfly from the chrysalis (*pupa*)
can be compared to the spiritual birth of a new self.

ILLUSTRATIONS 9

Dr. Rooney introduces a woman named Joy to show us that humans
must discover True Self or New Self before we are ready to move forward to the next higher levels of joyful living in the Spirit. This is a
Joy's story in third person.

"With her last surge of energy Joy completed her struggle. Joy had been trying to break free for as long as she
could remember. As far into the past as her memory

would allow her to go, two specters had been there, the twin ghosts of prohibition and inhibition.

They were the *cant's* and *have to's*, the *should's* and *should not's*, the *ought to's*

and *ought not's* that Joy had been verbally bathed in every single day of her childhood. These linguistic limitations had doubtlessly been originated by people who loved her as a caring, guiding effort to steer her away from trouble and out of danger. As Joy had grown, however, they had become like a giant fist at her throat, slowly squeezing the creative life out of her, robbing her of hope, depriving her of the freedom to grow, to choose, to mature. Just as a collar that is not adjusted to its growth can slowly choke an animal, Joy realized that these overly severe restrictions on her creativity and freedom could be fatal for her spirit as well.

Then one day a wise counselor gave Joy some extremely valuable insights. He had said, 'Don't you now that these verbal prisons, imposed on you by others, cannot tell you where your world begins and ends? They only tell you how their worlds are limited. They cannot tell you about your reality, but only about their perceptions of reality. They cannot tell you about your tomorrows, but only about their yesterdays. They do not give you profound insights into the inner world of yourself; they do, however, give you penetrating glimpses into the pinched worlds of those who have sought to limit you to their own narrow horizons.'

Suddenly Joy was free! God saved her by using these words of wisdom at that moment. Joy released her hold on these linguistic boundaries of belief, these verbal killers of creativity these semantic assassins of the soul, they, in response, had released their hold on her. Escaping their grasp had not been as difficult as she had believed it would be. Since the days of her childhood, Joy had accepted others' decisions about her life, others' desires for her future, others' beliefs or lack of belief in her capabilities, and she had allowed their opinions about and assessments of her worth to function as if they were facts. And what was even worse, Joy had not even realized she was doing it. These perceptual mental prisons that had been fitted around her self-image had not been placed there to help her fulfill her own hopes and dreams, but rather they had been projected onto her to protect the others' fears and doubts about themselves.

Now Joy finally realized that her self-worth is from God's love, not from self-evaluation nor others' evaluation. To be sure, others had slowly slipped the nooses of their convoluted thinking around her spirit's neck and had expected her to live in the shadows of their own minds. But she let them do it. Like children often do, Joy had believed that all adults were kind and good and wise and always right. Now Joy could see that they had been doing the best they knew how, but there was so very, very much about her they did not know. Now that Joy was older, she could choose to cast off the narrowness of their thinking and could rid herself of the limitations of their restrictions, just as a trim, powerful schooner casts off the ropes that tie it to the dock, and sails into the open water to enjoy the beautiful seas and face the unknown oceans, according to the directions of the wind.

Joy's new, embryonic concepts of herself, who she was and what she could be, were now being conceived deep within her soul with God-intended potentiality. The mental limitations and emotional straightjackets of her childhood need no longer function as boundaries for her adulthood. Now they could be used as mere landmarks, guidelines and maps by which she could explore the territory of her life and become all she was designed and destined to be. Finally, Joy was free to allow her past to slip away and no longer imprison her. And Joy could do this without losing a part of herself or sacrificing something essential to her future. She realized now that what the caterpillar calls the end of the world, the rest of the world calls a butterfly (new self "born from above" in the Spirit). What Joy had been she would never be again, and what she would be was yet to *be discovered*." (Rooney, *Amphorae,* pp. 1-2)

St. John confidently encourages us with this vision of hope by saying:

"Beloved, we are God's children now; what we will be has not yet been revealed. What we do know is this: when he is revealed, we will be like him, for we will see him as he is. And all who have this hope in him purify themselves, just as he is pure" (1 John 3:2).

In the mean time, we shall grow toward the spiritual maturity through a life-long journey called sanctification in Christ. As we begin to move on toward the spiritual journey toward wholeness (holiness), we are reminded of the wise words of Ezra Taft Benson:

> "The Lord works from the inside out. The [secular] world works from the outside in. The world would take people out of the slums. Christ takes the slums out of people, and then they take themselves out of the slums. The world would mold men [humans] by changing their environment. Christ changes people, who then change their environment. The world would shape human behavior, but Christ can change human nature."

PART THREE

CHRISTIAN LIVING TOWARD
SPIRITUAL MATURITY

CHAPTER 7

SPIRITUAL FORMATION

A NEW LIFE WITH THE WINGS OF TRUST AND OBEDIENCE

We are no longer old selves like "crawling caterpillars." Like the newly transformed butterflies from the chrysalis, we are new selves who are born of the Spirit (*born from above*) (John 3:3). The spiritual birth is a beginning of the new life in Christ with the wings of *radical trust* and *joyful obedience*. The butterflies spread their wings of beautiful colors and patterns and they freely fly as they enjoy the enormity of the space around them; the beauty of the skies above them; and the power of the wind (the Spirit) beneath them lifting them up; they fly from flower to flower drinking life-sustaining nectar and they participate in a reproduction process by spreading pollen.

In similar ways, our new soaring life begins on the wings of radical trust in the God's provision and joyful obedience in following Jesus Christ. With the help of the uplifting Spirit (the Wind, *Ruah*) we fly freely and lightly by living the Spirit-filled life of abundance, promised by Jesus Christ (John 10:10). (Please reflect on the Appendix II). What we (as the old self) have been we should never be again, and we, as the new self, are *sent* to different places for many different ministries with our uniquely different Spiritual Gifts, so that we may participate in the divine ministries of compassion in the hurting world. As we carry on the blessings of discipleship, we learn and grow toward the spiritual maturity in the love and grace of God.

Let us celebrate our new spiritual journey by joyfully singing the Hymn,

"Spirit of God," written by Steve Garnaas-Holmes (*The Faith We Sing*, #2117):

"Spirit of God, bright Wind, breath that bids life begin,
Blow as you always do; create us anew.
Give us the breath to sing, lifted on soaring wings,
Held in your hands, borne on your wings.

Spirit of God, bright Dove, grant us your peace and love,
Healing upon your wings for all living things.
For when we live your peace, captives will find release,
Held in your hands, borne on your wings.

Spirit of God, bright Hands, even in far off lands,
You hold the entire human race in one warm embrace.
No matter where we go, you hold us together so,
Held in your hands, borne on your wings.

Spirit of God, bright Flame, send us in your holy name,
The power to heal, to share your love everywhere.
We cannot fail or fall, or know defeat at all,
Held in your hands, borne on your wings.

Spirit of God in all, we gladly hear your call,
The life in our hands that sings, the power of your wings.
Borne of your grace we rise, love shining in our eyes,
Held in your hands, borne on your wings."

DEFINITION OF SPIRITUAL FORMATION

I was introduced to the teaching of Dr. Robert M. Mulholland, the Professor of Ashbury Seminary, at a weekend retreat in 1996. It was there that I learned a definition of *spiritual formation* as "a process of being conformed to the image of Christ for the sake of others."

He explained that the spiritual formation is "a journey into becoming persons of compassion, persons who forgive, persons who are deeply caring for others and the world, persons who offer themselves to God to become agents of divine grace in the lives of others and their world—in brief, persons who love and serve as Jesus did." (Mulholland, *Invitation to a Journey*, pp. 20-44)

THE TWO DIMENSIONS OF SPIRITUAL FORMATION

Now, let us consider how to live our new life in Christ to the full harvest, i.e., growing toward spiritual maturity.

In my personal Bible study I discovered that each Gospel Writer has different emphasis on how we are to respond to God's actions of love and compassion.

First, in Mark 5:36, we are called "to believe" in Jesus of Nazareth as the Son of God.

Second, in Luke 1:4, we are called "to know" the saving truth about God and develop a loving union with God.

Third, in John 3:19, we are called "to choose" to become compassionate disciples who participate in Christ's ministry in a perilous world.

Fourth, in Matthew 25:35, 36, we are called "to be compassionate" and "to do acts of kindness" for final vindication in the Last Day. Thus, we inevitably participate in the coming of the kingdom of God.

Spiritual formation has two dimensions. The first and the second ("to believe" and "to know") are considered *a vertical dimension* of the journey inward, resulting in personal holiness. The third and the fourth ("to choose" and "to do") are considered *a horizontal dimension* of the journey outward, resulting in social holiness. In short, *the journey inward* is concerned about the nature and quality of our intimate relationship with God. We find joy of knowing and serving God. *The journey outward* is concerned with our harmonious relationships with others. The image or inner nature of Christ must be incarnate in our relationships with others both within the church and outside the church.

Dr. Mulholland further clarifies:

"There can be no true social holiness without personal holiness. The deep commitment of our beings toward God; the growing life of intimate relationship with God; the increasing work of God's transforming grace in our brokenness and bondage all lead us toward the wholeness of conformity to Christ. Such personal holiness, however, is conformity to the One whose life was given unconditionally for others." (Mulholland, *Invitation to a Journey*, p. 42)

Both dimensions—vertical and horizontal-- of spiritual formation emphasize our living for the glory of God as children of God and as disciples of Christ.

Mulholland also connects personal holiness with "corporate" spirituality:

"Such personal holiness is nurtured in the corporate community of faith. Without the nurturing growth and accountability of the community of faith, we will never have the clarity of discernment that will enable us to walk in Christ's way in the midst of a world that would try to bend us out of that way. Corporate spirituality [in the church] is the only hope for genuine social spirituality." (Ibid. p. 166)

Thomas Kelly who is in agreement with Dr. Mulholland, writes:

> "Our fellowship with God issues in world-concern. We cannot keep the love of God to ourselves. It spills over. It quickens us. It makes us see the world's needs anew. We love people and we grieve to see them blind when they might be seeing, asleep with all the world's comforts when they ought to be awake and living sacrificially, accepting the world's goods as their right when they really hold them only in temporary trust. Because we live a way of life "hidden with Christ in God" (Colossians 3:3), we re-love people; re-love our neighbors as ourselves; we are bestirred to be means of their awakening. The deepest need of men [human beings] is not food and clothing and shelter, important as they are. It is God" (*A Testament of Devotion*, pp. 98-99)

Kelly clarifies further:

> "We do help people because we genuinely love them, not because we feel sorry for them, and that the world needs something deeper than pity; it needs [compassionate] love. He encourages us to live a Christ-centered life that is a "heaven-directed life."...We live a life of unhurried peace, power, simple, amazing, triumphant, and radiant because Christ is at the helm. And when our little day is done, we lie down quietly in peace, for all is well." (Ibid. p.100)

As Andrew Purves expresses it well when he writes:

"Theology, spirituality, and ministry become the threads
of an emerging tapestry of faith and life." (Purves, *The
Search for Compassion*, p. 12).

THE MIND OF CHRIST

Spiritual formation is the experience of being *conformed* to the image
of Christ, not to the world. St. Paul admonishes us Christians, "Do not
be conformed to this world, but be transformed by the renewing of your
minds, so that you may discern what is the will of God- what is good and
acceptable and perfect" (Romans 12:2).

God is the initiator of our growth toward godliness (holiness) and
we are to be pliable clay in God's hand. But we resist God's shaping
touch, his changing grace and transforming love. We learn that spiritual
formation is not something that we do to ourselves or for ourselves, but
something we do in partnership with the Spirit by yielding ourselves to
the transforming work of grace. In order to be transformed, we are to
renew our minds by imitating the mind of Christ.

Apostle Paul gives us six qualities of the mind of Christ in his
prison letter to the Christians in Philippi:

"If then there is any encouragement in Christ, any con-
solation from love, any sharing in the Spirit, any compassion and sympathy, make my joy complete: be of the
same mind, having the same love, being in full accord
and of one mind. Do nothing from selfish ambition or
conceit, but in humility regard others as better than yourselves. Let each of you look not to your own interests, but

to the interests of others. Let the same mind be in you that was in Christ Jesus, who, though he was in the form of God, did not regard equality with God as something to be exploited, but emptied himself, took the form of a slave, being born in human likeness. And being found in human form, he humbled himself and became obedient to the point of death—even death on a cross. Therefore, God also highly exalted him and gave him the name that us above every name, so that at the name of Jesus every knee should bend, in heaven and on earth and under the earth, and every tongue should confess that Jesus Christ is Lord, to the glory of God the Father" (Philippians 2:1-11).

Six characteristics of the mind of Christ are:

First, the mind of Christ chooses to share his vision of the kingdom of God. We are to encourage sharing a common vision: Common purpose that reduces individualism and fosters shared mission; Commonplace that implies that we are to pursue spiritual community within our geographic community; Common possessions that combats consumerism and foster interdependence.

Second, the mind of Christ demonstrates mutual respect and deference (yielding). They are expressed in following ways: humility, regarding others as better than yourselves;

Look not to your own interest, but the interest of others.

But we all know that this is only possible when everyone in the community has the same mind of Christ and when everyone would be empowered and encouraged so that none of us would feel undermined, subservient or undervalued. When we lack these qualities we will end up inevitable conflicts.

Third, the mind of Christ chooses downward mobility. In this info-saturated, tech-driven culture, we are more tempted to have contemporary minds of upward mobility. People seek things bigger, better, faster, and we needed them yesterday. It's all about them—their improvement, advancement, and enhancement. But, our choosing downward mobility is anti-cultural.

Fourth, the mind of Christ chooses incarnating mission. When people are impacted by the life and work of Christ, they begin to ask him where they are to go and incarnate the love of God. His followers are to be Christ in the flesh to a world in need. Christ will lead us where to go and what to do, if we are willing to yield to his Spirit.
As John Wesley said, "Do all the good you can, by all the means you can, in all the ways you can, in all the places you can, at all the times you can, to all the people you can, as long as you can."

Fifth, the mind of Christ chooses exalting God. We may claim that we have bowed our knees to God here on earth. But all of us can point to patterns in our life where we are not reverencing Christ as we should. To have the mind of Christ means to look continually for areas that need to be brought into submission before God. The Westminster Catechism puts it this way. "The chief end [of human] is to glorify God and enjoy him forever." We glorify God by our lifestyle, worship, by making him famous, by surrendering to the Lordship of Christ.

Sixth, the mind of Christ chooses catalyzing your spiritual growth. In verses 12-13, "work out your own salvation with fear and trembling" is pointing out that we need to participate in our sanctification process. It is accomplished by "becoming participants of the divine nature" (2 Peter 1:4b). How to become participants of the divine nature is explored in "becoming a compassionate disciples" in Chapter 9.

We saturate our minds with the Word of God so that the teaching and the modeling of Christ *rule* our thinking, feeling, and doing;

We set our minds on godly things, not on worldly things;

We teach and admonish one another in all wisdom;

We clothe ourselves with compassion, kindness, humility, and patience. Above all, we clothe ourselves with love, which binds everything together;

We are grateful with singing hymns, psalms, and spiritual songs.

We learn to discern the will of God by sharpening the receptivity of our souls.

We may discern and understand the will of God—what is good, not bad, but acceptable to the godly perfect standard, not our ever-changing standard.

We are not to be conformed to worldly values and trends. That means we are set apart to follow Christ who revealed the God's attributes of holiness and just-love.

God is the initiator of our growth toward spiritual maturity and we are to be pliable clay in God's hand. We learn that "spiritual formation is not something that we do to ourselves or for ourselves, but something we allow God to do in us and for us as we yield ourselves to the work of God's transforming grace.

THE LIFE HIDDEN WITH CHRIST IN GOD

Christ came to offer salvation and abundant life to all by healing the sick, bringing sight to the blind, and by offering a new relationship with God, neighbors, and our new self. Sadly, not all receive his offer of salvation. Having a new identity after relinquishing old self, we begin the blessed spiritual journey as the new self in Christ (Colossians 3:3-17):

1. To become new self (true self) by "stripping off the old self (false self) with its practices;

2. To seek the things that are above, where Christ is;

3. To set your minds in things that are above us, not in things that are below.

4. The new self "is being renewed in knowledge according to the image of its creator" (v. 9).

5. Be hidden with Christ in God (v.3);

6. To put to death whatever in us is earthly.

7. To clothe ourselves with love that binds everything together in perfect harmony.

8. To let the peace of Christ rule in our heart.

9. To let the word of Christ dwell in us richly.

10. To teach and admonish one another in all wisdom;

11. To sing psalms, hymns, and spiritual songs with gratitude.

12. To do everything in the name of the Lord Jesus, giving thanks to God, the Father, through him.

John Calvin, the father of the Presbyterian Church, reflected on the text: "Our life is hidden with Christ in God" (Colossians 3:3). Then, Calvin said:

"Take courage, my friends. Even if we are nothing in our own hearts, something of us is safely hidden in the heart of God. What a touching, winsome, and assuring sentence for us all. It is indeed the foundation of the gospel message."

THE JESUS' *PARABLE OF THE VINE AND THE BRANCHES* (JOHN 15:1-8, THE MESSAGES)

This Parable illustrates the mystery of disciples' life being "hidden with Christ in God." Jesus says:

> "I am the real Vine and my Father is the Farmer. He cuts off every branch of me that doesn't bear grapes. And every branch that bears fruit, he prunes back so it will bear even more. You are already pruned back by the message I have spoken. Live in me.
>
> Make your home in me just as I do in you. In the same way that a branch can't bear grapes by itself but only by being joined to the vine, you can't bear fruit unless you are joined with me. I am the Vine and you are the branches. When you are joined with me and I with you, the relation intimate and organic, the harvest is sure to be abundant. Separated, you can't produce a thing. Anyone who separates from me is deadwood, gathered up and thrown on the bonfire.
>
> But if you make yourselves at home with me and my words are at home in you, you can be sure that whatever you ask will be listened to and acted upon. This is how my Father shows who his is—when you produce grapes, when you mature as my disciples."

It is Father, the farmer, who makes sure that branches are healthy and strong by pruning!" It is Christ, the Vine, who pulls up moisture and nutrients from the soil against the Law of Gravity and distributes them to its branches. It is the disciples, the Branches who bear sweet grapes without any efforts. The result is that all the people enjoy the grapes and God is glorified.

When I went to the Holy Land in 1986, Dr. Jim Fleming was our guide and Bible teacher for our group of fifty seminarians. According to him, young vines of Palestine are not allowed to produce grapes during their first three years. It is the vinedresser, God would cut their branches way back in order to develop healthy and strong branches.

Once branches are matured, however, the vinedresser knows which branches will develop into fruit-bearing branches and which ones will be fruitless. The vinedresser cuts the fruitless branches away drastically through the pruning process. By doing this, no nutrients are wasted and all effort goes to developing good-tasting, high-grade grapes.

I hope and pray that we are like fruit-bearing branches by abiding with Christ in God. This clearly illustrates: "our life is hidden with Christ in God." And the key for us is abiding with Christ as the Vine and its branches are so closely connected. Without being connected or "hidden with Christ in God," we cannot live the fruit-bearing life of pleasing God.

When the Prophet Micah asked God, "How can we please you?" God answered. "Do justice, love kindness, and walk humbly with God" (Micah 6:8).

THE DISCIPLES WHO "LIVE FREELY AND LIGHTLY"

Now, listen to the Jesus' invitation to the new relationship and new life in Christ:

> "Come to me and get away with me and you'll recover your life. "Are you tired? Worn out? Burned out on religion? I'll show you how to take a real rest. Walk with me

and work with me—watch how I do it. Learn the unforced rhythms of grace. I won't lay anything heavy or ill-fitting on you. Keep company with me and you'll learn to *live freely and lightly*" (Matthew 11:28-30, The Message).

Conversion to the new life in Christ occurs when we are *justified* to be righteous through faith in Jesus Christ. That's when each of us begins our spiritual journey as children of God toward spiritual maturity; as children of God by following Christ's teaching and examples.

Sadly, many are not responding to the invitation to be his disciple. Then, we must ask: "How come so many people are not responding to the Christ's invitation to *live freely and lightly?*"

A METAPHOR CALLED *PNEUMA*, THE WIND

Dr. Eugene Rooney answers our question in a metaphor called *Pneuma*, the Wind. (*Listening with the Mind's Inner Ear*, pp. 97-99)

> "In the beginning, birds could not fly. Or perhaps it would be more accurate simply to say that they did not fly. They had the capacity, but did not know how. In more practical terms, they didn't fly because they had never seen any-thing else fly, so they didn't think flight was possible. In fact, they didn't think about it at all. They were easily the clumsiest, ugliest, and weakest of all creatures.
>
> They had tried swimming, like the fish, the seals, the otters and turtles. But most of them almost drowned. A few of them got pretty good at it and grew webbed feet, but most of the birds hated the water.

They all had tried running, like the cats and dogs and horses, but for the most part they were terribly clumsy and ran very poorly. A few got to be pretty good runners, however, like the ostrich and emu, but most of them were so awful at running they never tried again.

They were better at hopping. They couldn't hop far or fast or well, but they could get around. So they settled for hopping. They were the laughingstock of all the other animals. Their legs were spindly. Their bodies were stubby. Their heads were too big, and those terrible lumps on either side of their body always got in the way and caused them to wobble off-balance.

Worst of all, birds were the natural prey of almost everything. Everything could chase them down. They easily fell victim to tooth and claw. Their only defense was climbing trees, but here again they were obviously not built for it. Slowly, laboriously they could make their way up a rough-barked tree, clumsily climbing, one little clawed foot at a time. But, in climbing, just as in hopping, the unsightly, ungainly lumps on each side of their bodies were always in the way.

Once in the tree they were more or less away from their ground enemies, but in the tree they were vulnerable to the worst enemy of all---the wind. They had named the feared wind, *pneuma*. They had learned to hold on with all their might until *pneuma* passed before hopping along the branch, looking for bugs under the bark. However, when the next puff of *pneuma* came along they would again grab onto the bark and cling for dear life, bitterly cursing their fate.

And so, the birds lived out their lives under the curse of being the ugliest, most miserable and defenseless of all God's creatures. "If ever God made a mistake," they thought, "we are it. We spend our whole lives clinging, grubbing for food, clinging, trying to survive, clinging, dodging our enemies and clinging."

One little bird, however, was very different from the rest. He loved the wind. He loved how it felt as it blew coolly over his face. He loved how it ruffled his feathers and occasionally brought food his way. In addition to loving the wind he hated clinging, which made him totally different from everyone else.

From time to time, he told the other birds that he was going to stop clinging and take his chances, but the others told him he was crazy. He said, "I am not crazy, but I am bored. I hate clinging. If I keep on clinging I shall die."

Each bird said, "Well, fool, if you let go you'll die a lot faster than boredom can kill you. The moment you let go that wind you think so much of will knock you off the branch and throw you to the hungry enemies below...

The little bird considered their warning very carefully. After all they were older and more numerous than he and that made them wiser, didn't it? He also remembered that once when he was a tiny little bird he had gotten careless and had fallen off a branch and hit his head. He had been dizzy for two days. So he held on tightly.

But one day, the bird couldn't take it any longer and decided to heed his friends no more...He waited until a strong gust of wind came and he let go. Sure enough, the wind blew him right off the branch, slammed him into the tree trunk, plummeting towards the ground, caroming off branches, twigs and the tree trunk as he went. He instinctively reached out to grab a limb with his wings. The wind lifted the feathers of his wings with great gusts of air. Free of the ground, the tree and clinging, the beautiful bird soared high above the ground, sailing along effortlessly. "Idiot," said all the other birds thinking he was being blown away. "There he goes." "We'll never see him again. Good riddance."

Miles from his home tree, the bird sailed along majestically. Birds clinging in the trees below, to which he was a total stranger, looked up and saw him. They were astounded, then afraid, then fascinated, then elated. "Look, look," they cried. "He looks like us, but he is not. He flies. He soars. He's free. He must be the One our legends speak of. He's the Messiah. He's come to save us all. He's come to carry us away."

But the bird high above heard them and said, "No. I did not come to carry you away. I did not come to save you. I only came to show you how to fly."

The birds below cried all the more, "Save us. Give us the gift of flight. Work a miracle for us."

Again the bird soaring high above said, "I cannot give you the gift of flight. You already have it. I only came to show you how to use it. Those lumps on your sides are wings. They can serve you as resources, not impediments. They are assets not liabilities. Concentrate on their lifting power, not their weight. They are a solution to your problem, not the problem. Spread them, rather than curse them. Let *Pneuma* use them. They were designed for *Pneuma*'s use. So, spread your wings and let go. The wind does all the work. All you must do is unlock your claws from the tree. It is the wind's good pleasure to bear you aloft. *Pneuma* is not your enemy. *Pneuma* is your friend."

Then suddenly a great gust of wind carried the bird away...The birds below clung to the branches even more tightly lest a great puff of *Pneuma* come along and blow them out of the tree and kill them..."

Let us let go of clinging and groundless fears. Let us spread our wings and let the Spirit lift us up to fly away from our clinging to the past memories and the fear of unknown. Then, we are no longer surviving in fear and cursing, but soaring in the freedom and joy of living as disciples of Christ in the power of the Spirit. Let us encourage one another: "It is Christ we proclaim, warning everyone and teaching everyone in all wisdom, so that we may present everyone mature in Christ" (Colossians 1:27, 28).

We used to be like crawling caterpillars. But now, we are like soaring butterflies!

A NEW IDENTITY IN CHRIST

The Spirit of God can help us in this process as the Spirit bears witness to the truth of our chosen-ness and our "Christ-in-me identity" or new self "hidden with Christ in God." This truth makes it possible to "strip off the old self and all its practices and we are clothed with the new self. This new identity is strengthened in knowledge according to the image of its creator" (Colossians 3:3, 8-10).

Spiritual birth means being born from above or being formed spiritually from above to a new self. And each of us begins a wonder-filled, glorious, spiritual life as "a new creation" (2 Corinthians 5:17). It is not an ending. With the God's promise of the resurrection power of the Spirit, each disciple is ushered into this new spiritual life with a new identity of a specific Fruit of the Spirit. The Fruit of the Spirit is "love, joy, peace, patience, kindness, generosity, faithfulness, gentleness, and self-control" (Galatians 5:22).

THE FRUIT OF THE SPIRIT

In Galatians Chapter 5, St. Paul admonishes us that we must not abuse our freedom of choice for the works of the flesh (vv. 19-21) and that we must live by the Spirit's leading and guiding because we have crucified the flesh with ego-driven passions and desires. We use our freedom as an opportunity to love our neighbors as we love ourselves.

While the works of the flesh in ego-propelled persons are demonstrated in the "Ichazo's Enneagram of passion" (Figure 6), the works of the Spirit in the maturing disciples are demonstrated in "Cho-Kim's Enneagram of the fruit of the Spirit" (Figure 7)

Becoming a disciple of Christ is the fruit (work) of the Spirit and each disciple is endowed with a spiritual quality listed above, so that he or she produces his or her own fruit *effortlessly* under the careful provision of the Holy Spirit.

It's like an apple tree producing many apples; an apricot tree producing many apricots, a banana tree producing many bananas, a cherry tree producing many cherries, an orange tree producing many oranges; a peach tree producing many peaches; a pear tree producing many pears; a plum tree producing many plums; a grape vine producing many grapes. Each tree produces its own fruit *naturally* under the careful eye of orchard's owner.

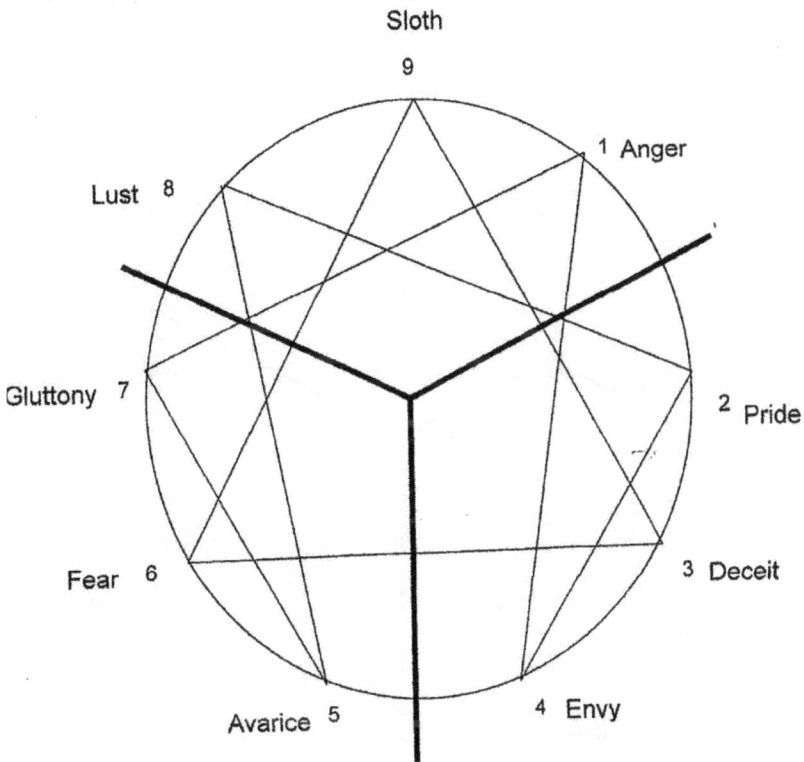

Figure 6. Ichazo's Enneagram of the Passion

At the altar of Coventry Cathedral, there is a prayer for forgiveness for following sins: The hatred which dives nation from nation, race from race, class from class;

The greed which exploits the labors of humans and lays waste to earth;

Our envy of the welfare and happiness of others;
Our indifference to the plight of the homeless and the refugee;
The lust which uses for ignoble ends, the bodies of men and women;
The pride which leads us to trust in ourselves and not in God.
Therefore, we all have sinned and come short of the glory of God.

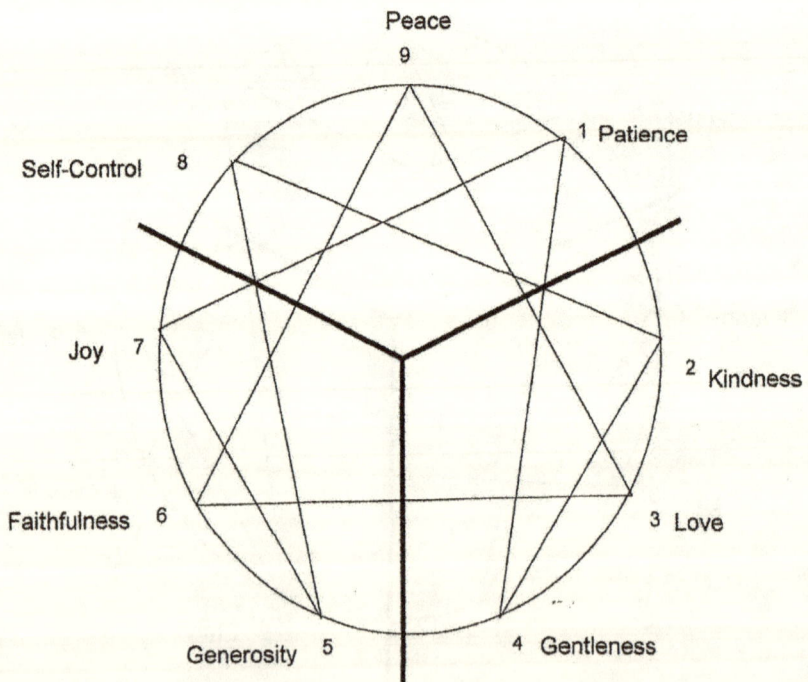

Figure 7. Cho-Kim's Enneagram of the Fruit of the Spirit

Good news is that the Holy Spirit has the power to transform the old-self bearing "flesh fruit" (sin) into the new-self bearing the fruit of the Spirit:

*The old Type 5 with ego-driven passion of avarice becomes the new Type 5 with spiritual fruit of generosity;

*The old Type 8 with ego-driven passion of lust becomes the new Type 8 with spiritual fruit of self-control;

*The old Type 2 with ego-driven passion of pride becomes the new Type 2 with spiritual fruit of kindness;

*The old Type 4 with ego-driven passion of envy becomes the new Type 4 with spiritual fruit of gentleness;

*The old Type 1 with ego-driven passion of anger becomes the new Type 1 with spiritual fruit of peace (serenity);

*The old Type 7 with ego-driven passion of gluttony becomes the new Type 7 with spiritual fruit of joy;

*The old Type 6 with ego-driven passion of fear becomes the new Type 6 with spiritual fruit of faithfulness;

*The old Type 9 with ego-driven passion of sloth becomes the new Type 9 with spiritual fruit of patience (enduring hope);

*The old Type 3 with ego-driven passion of deceit becomes the new Type 3 with spiritual fruit of love (mutual affection).

We are promised that the Spirit of Christ has given us the resurrection power for the spiritual *renewal* works that are necessary for each of us to bear spiritual fruit. We are growing toward our spiritual maturity so that we may be agents or instruments in God's "ministry of reconciliation" (2 Corinthians 5:18-21). Through spiritual formation and discipleship we are being conformed to become more like Jesus every day by moving in the *direction of integration* (See Figure 5)

For example, new Type 5 with the spiritual fruit of generosity moves to new Type 8 with fruit of self-control to new Type 2 with fruit of kindness to new Type 4 with fruit of gentleness to new Type

1 with fruit of <u>peace</u> (serenity) to new Type 7 with fruit of <u>joy,</u> back to Type 5, according to the Enneagram's Hexad. Similarly, new Type 6 with the spiritual fruit of <u>faithfulness</u> moving to fruit of new Type 9 with <u>patience </u>(enduring hope) to new Type 3 with fruit of <u>love,</u> back to Type 6, according to the Enneagram's <u>Triangle</u>. Thus, we are moving toward the perfect love that the Holy Spirit will help finish in us in the future.

SPIRITUAL DISCIPLINES (PRACTICES)

John Wesley, a discouraged Anglican priest, attended a meeting on Aldersgate Street in London. It was there while hearing the words read from Luther's Preface to the Book of Romans that he felt his heart "strangely warmed." This then changed the course of history—the beginning of Methodist movement in America.

If the Spirit of Methodism is losing its vitality, the spiritual revival must be found in the Word of God. We need to open the Bible, read it, pray over it, expound it in our preaching, and let the Holy Spirit unleash the power of God's Word. Then we may also feel our hearts "burn within us" thus reviving our souls and renewing our discipleship.

Adele Ahlberg Calhoun in her book, *Spiritual Disciplines Handbook: Practices that Transform Us,* writes:

"From its beginning the church linked the desire for more of God to intentional practices, relationships and experiences that gave people space in their lives to 'keep company" with Jesus. These intentional practices, relationships and experiences are known as *spiritual disciplines*...The desire to know and love [God] fueled these disciplines." (Calhoun, *Spiritual Disciplines Handbook,* p. 17)

Calhoun encourages us: "spiritual practices don't give us 'spiritual brownie points' or help us 'work the system' for a passing grade from God. They simply put us in a place where we can begin to *notice God* and respond to his Word to us."

Her work is the most comprehensive book on the Christian spiritual disciplines and consists of seven areas of disciplines using acronym, W.O.R.S.H.I.P:

W. for *worship*;
O. for *open* myself to God;
R. for *relinquish* the false self;
S. for *share* my life with others;
H. for *hear* God's Word;
I. for *incarnate* the love of Christ;
P. for *pray*.

Let us cultivate the wonders of God's creative power of love, which expand our awareness of divine presence. We are called to recognize and appreciate all the gifts of the earth and God's many good gifts that deepen our love of God.

- Let us stand in wonder and awe before the sunset, a rose garden, stars-filled the sky, the formation of clouds, stretch of beaches with tidal waves, and various shapes of snow crystals...

- Let us stand in wonder as we touch the little fingers and toes of a baby. Let us consider the wonder of human beings: "It was you who created my inmost self, and put me together in my mother's womb; for all these mysteries, I thank you: for wonder of my self; wonder of your works" (Psalm 139:13,14).

Let us cultivate wonders of God's on going labor in the world, which invites us to our radical trust in his providence. In everything we are called to rely on God "whose power, working in us, can do infinitely more than we can ask or imagine" (Ephesians 3:20).

- Let us acknowledge our powerlessness to make it on our own because I am not a "god."

- Let us surrender our lives to God's care with confidence that our help will come if we continue to do our responsible best.

- Let us pray without ceasing: "May you grant that we may be strengthened in our inner being with power through the Holy Spirit.

SPIRITUAL DISCIPLINES OF RELINQUISHING THE FALSE SELF

Spiritual disciplines help us relinquish our "false self", detaching us from our idols. When we recognize and name these idols [also known as dragons] that consume our energy, time, and other resources, we can ask God for the grace to "let go" or "release" and relinquish our dependence to these things. Through practices or disciplines of relinquishment we detach from idolatrous relationships and self-serving goals and agendas for success, money, power, ego, productivity and image to move with wholehearted attachment to and trust in God alone. The disciplines or the practices of *relinquishment* are "confession and self-examination, detachment, discernment, secrecy, silence, solitude, spiritual direction, and submission." (Calhoun, pp. 89-120)

216

THE DISCIPLINE OF CONFESSION AND SELF-EXAMINATION

We can practice the discipline of confession and self-examination by:

- Admitting to God the natural propensity to rationalize, deny, blame and self-obsess;

- Examining the "sin network" in your life as evidenced in presumptuous sin, besetting weaknesses, self-centered habits and broken relationships;

- Replacing sinful habits with healthy ones;

- Seeking God's grace to change;

- Confessing sins by examining your life in light of (1) the seven deadly sins, (2) the Ten Commandments, (3) prayer books or Scripture (Psalm 51), (4) life confession, journaling confessions and confessions made to others;

THE DISCIPLINE OF DETACHMENT

We can practice the discipline of detachment by:

- Naming and confessing our attachments that take priority over God;

- Allowing others to lead and win;

- Letting go of our need to manage our image;

- Letting go of notions that our money and possessions belong to us and make us who we are; living on less rather than more;

- Trusting outcomes to God rather than our own capabilities;

- Honoring the freedom of others; refusing to manipulate and control in order to get what we want.

THE DISCIPLINE OF DISCERNMENT

Practice includes:

- Taking time to listen to God; not hurrying to make a decision;

- Seeking to bring both head and heart into alignment with God's will;

- Asking for help, counsel and guidance;

- Going on a retreat to gain perspective and listen to God;

- Attending to the desires God has placed deeply inside you;

- Naming your addictions, predilections, prejudices, and unbelief and so on in order to understand how these play into making decisions.

THE DISCIPLINE OF SECRECY (ANONYMITY)

We can practice the discipline of secrecy (anonymity) by:

- Finding acts of service that we can render without letting anyone know what we have done or why we have done it;

- Holding confidences as secrets not to be shared;

- Reframing from the compulsion to tell all we know;

- Abstaining from reveling our good deeds, talent and qualities;

- Consecrating intimate moments of our walk with God to him alone; speaking of them with no one else;

- Being a safe place for others to share their secrets;

- Celebrating the achievements of others without having to bring up our own.

THE DISCIPLINE OF SILENCE

We can practice the discipline of silence by:

- Setting a period of time in which we don't speak but isolate ourselves from sounds (other than perhaps the sounds of nature);

- Driving or commuting without the radio or CD /DVD player turned on;

- Leaving the TV off; spending time in silence with God alone;

- Exercising without attending to noise; listening to God;

- Having personal retreats of silence.

THE DISCIPLINE OF SOLITUDE

We can practice the discipline of solitude by:

- Giving God time and space that is not in competition with social contact, noise or stimulation;

- Taking retreats;

- Observing Sabbath refreshment by abstaining from constant interaction with others, information and activities;

- Addressing our addiction to being seen;

- Communing with God alone wile we walk or run by ourselves;

- Practicing disciplines alone: study, prayer, examen, journaling and so forth.

THE DISCIPLINE OF SPIRITUAL DIRECTION

We can practice the discipline of spiritual direction by:

- Entering an intentional and regular relationship that fosters union with God;

- Opening our prayer life and experience of God to another for the sake of shred listening;

- Listening to our life and the desires God has placed in our heart;

- Letting the Spirit set the direction of the discussion;

- Living by what God is saying to us;

- Allowing another set of eyes and ears to help us interpret your experiences and the voice of God.

THE DISCIPLINE OF SUBMISSION

We can practice the discipline of submission by Practice includes:

- Seeking God's will (no mater where it leads) and doing it;

- Allowing others to mentor, disciple, teach, correct and guide us;

- Being a good follower;

- Laying aside the need to be in charge;

- Willing and eager obedience to God and those to whom we owe obedience;

- Being an eager learner, trainable and tractable.

According to Dallas Willard there are disciplines of abstinence and those of engagement. The disciplines of abstinence include solitude, silence fasting, frugality, chastity, and secrecy. The disciplines of engagement include study, worship, celebration, service, prayer, fellowship, confession, and submission. (Willard, *The Spirit of Disciplines*, p.158)

We may add to the above list: works of mercy, covenant group (including small groups), Holy Communion, fasting (from food and from anything that other distraction or encroachments on time with God).

Michael and Norrisey reported their research on small samples that there are applicable (not absolute) connections between temperament types (the Myers-Briggs Type Indicator, MBTI) and prayer forms. The MBTI was developed from Carl G. Jung's eight different psychological types (2x4) by positing two attitudes toward life (Extraversion and Introversion) and four operating functions (Sensation, Intuition, Thinking, and Feeling). They also suggest that temperament has affected Christian spirituality: the Trinitarian Spirituality, Spirituality of the Desert Fathers, Benedictine Spirituality, Augustinian Spirituality, Franciscan Spirituality, Thomistic Spirituality, Devotio Moderna, Ignatian Spirituality, and Teresian Spirituality. (Michael and Norrisey, *Prayer and Temperament Types,* pp. 7-9)

Thomas Keating provides us with a fresh insight:

"When we begin the spiritual journey in earnest with a program of centering prayer (see pp. 105-106) as a path to contemplation, we are initiating a dynamic that involves our personal responses to Christ and affects our whole lives... The commitment to contemplation is a new way of following Christ in our time. Just as the Spirit created a new way of following Christ at the close of the age of martyrdom by inspiring Anthony with his vision of the monastic lifestyle, so now the Holy Spirit is inviting lay persons and those in active ministries to become contemplatives where they are, to move beyond the restricted world of selfishness into service of their communities, and to join all others of goodwill in addressing the global problems of our time: poverty, hunger, oppression, violence, and above all the refusal to love." (Keating, Open Mind and Open Heart, p.138)

Three main *ends* (goals) of spiritual formation for the Christians are:

- Spiritual maturity as the beloved children of God;

- Spiritual union with God while experiencing God's presence and loving actions.

- In the ordinary labors and duties of life here and now, we practice the spiritual disciplines as the *means* of living for the glory of God and serving others in the world.

CONTINUING SANCTIFICATION

Through the voice of the Old Testament Prophet Jeremiah, the Lord says that there are two ways of living in the world. *The first way* is trusting our own resources and abilities by turning away from God and *the second way* is <u>radical trusting</u> in the God of provision:

> "Thus says the Lord: Cursed are those who trust in mere mortals and make mere flesh their strength, whose hearts turn away from the Lord...Blessed are those who trust in the Lord, whose trust is the Lord...I the Lord test the mind and the search the heart, to give to all according to their ways, according to the fruit of their doings" (Jeremiah 17:5-10).

*<u>The first way</u> is "like a shrub in the desert, and shall not see when relief comes. The people in the first way shall live in the patched places of the wilderness, in an uninhabited salt land."

*<u>The second way</u> is "like a tree planted by water, sending out its roots by the stream. The people in the second way shall not fear when heat comes, and the plant's leaves shall stay green; in the year of drought they are not anxious, and the plant does not cease to bear fruit."

> M. Robert Mulholland Jr. expounds the above text:
> "These two ways of being in the world are the "false self" and the "true self."...I realized for the first time that God's purpose for us was not simply to forgive sins but to transform our *false self*—to cleanse all its unrighteousness, to make us righteous, to transform us to our *true self*...I realized that I, as the false self, stood in the way of becoming the true self for which I had been created. I was a mud pie with thin layer of Christian frosting trying to pass myself off as an angel food cake, but the mud kept seeping through! I need God to take that mud and breathe into it the breath of life." (Mulholland, *The Deeper Journey*, pp. 23-24)

The Professor Mulholland introduces the reality of our "religious" false self:

> "We are slow to accept the fact that our false self is who we are all the way to the core of our being. We are profoundly habituated to a self-referenced way of being in the world. Jesus makes this unmistakably clear when he says, "If anyone would come after me, they must deny themselves," and, "Whoever loses their self for my sake will find it" (Matthew 16:24-25). Jesus is not talking about giving up candy for Lent. He is calling for the abandonment of our entire, pervasive, deeply entrenched matrix of self-referencing being [false self]." (Ibid. p.47)

Paul is calling for a spiritual life of radical abandonment to God in love and a decision to lose this worldly life for Christ's sake:

> "...I have been crucified with Christ; and it is no longer I who live, but it is Christ who lives in me. And the life I now live in the flesh, I live by faith in the Son of God, who loved me and gave himself for me" (Galatians 2:19-20).

We affirm that saving faith results in sanctification, the transformation of life in growing conformity to Christ through the power of the Holy Spirit. Sanctification means ongoing repentance, a life of turning from sin to serve Jesus Christ in grateful reliance on him as one's Lord and Master. This is an invitation to the way of *sanctification*—transformed, set-apart, radiant, and holy living for the glory of God. Thomas Kelly challenges us:

"We have too long been prim and restrained. The fires
of the love of God, of our love toward God, and of His
love toward us, are very hot. 'Thou shall love God
above all else in the world, with all your heart and soul
and mind and strength...And you shall love your neighbors as yourself.'" (Kelly, *A Testament of Devotion*, pp.
95-98)

For John Wesley, the Father of the Methodist movement in 19th century, "holiness [sanctification] is a process of becoming in reality what
already is ours in Christ through spiritual birth or regeneration through
justifying grace of the Spirit...Sanctification begins at the moment of
the spiritual birth [justification]; continuing sanctification is the process
of being *made perfect in love*. This experience of being made perfect in
love is humanly impossible to achieve except through faith as a gift of
God's grace...The tenor of Scripture throughout is that we are expected
to love God with our whole being! Surely St. John's comments, for
example, would suggest that some Christians are made perfect in love
while others may not be." (Ibid. p.99)

"There is no fear in love, but perfect love casts out fear;
for fear has to do with punishment, and whoever fears
has not reached perfection in love. We love because he
first loved us" (1 John 4:18-19).

In his writing on the Wesleyan view of Sanctification, Lawrence W.
Wood provides us with following summary:

• The sanctifying and purgative action of the Holy Spirit en-
ables the believer to be relieved and cleansed of these disor-
dered contents of the unconscious mind... There is no need

for pretentious behavior and perfectionistic attitudes, for we knowingly and willingly recognize that our sufficiency is totally in the relationship with God through Christ. This level of relationship to Christ means that whatever hurts, whatever maladjustments, and whatever sins that beset us, we are assured of Christ's forgiveness and cleansing through the power of his Spirit.

Genuine divine love, *agape* (1 Corinthians 13) is accepting and forgiving, not condemning and berating. Assured of Christ's love, we are assured of our spiritual identity even though our psychological identity is only gradually formed in the context of the Christian community of love.

- This concept of assurance is a distinctive emphasis of John Wesley. Whatever passing emotions they may feel threatened by, believers are possessed of an abiding conviction through the internal testimony of the Spirit that they are fully accepted of God in Christ. This acceptance means real "union with Christ through the Spirit; this acceptance is not a mere "as if" we are righteous; the believer really is righteous (1 John 4:12-13)...

- In Colossians 2:13, Paul speaks of our being "rescued from the power of darkness and have our being transferred into the kingdom of his beloved Son, in whom we have redemption, the forgiveness of sins."

- Bultmann argues persuasively that the Pauline emphasis is thus not on justification (*forgiveness of sins*) but rather on sanctification (*freedom from the power of the sin*).

(Lawrence W. Wood, in Donald Alexander's *Christian Spirituality: Five Views of Sanctification*, pp. 98-111).

MATURING CHILDREN OF GOD

All believers are thankful because "all who receive him [Jesus Christ], who believed in his name, are given power to *become* children of God" (John 1:12). From illustrations (#1 to #4) we realize that our "biological ages" have little to do with the "spiritual ages," and that all believers are in different stages of spiritual maturity.

St. Paul warns the "adult Christians" who behave in childish ways: "Do not be children in your thinking; rather, be infants in evil (meaning be innocent), but in thinking be adults" (1 Corinthians 14:20); "When I was a child, I spoke like a child, I thought like a child, I reasoned like a child; when I became an adult, I put an end to childish ways" (1 Corinthians 13:11).

In her devotional pamphlet, *Loved beyond Measure*. Jane L. Fryer inspires us in our growing toward full spiritual maturity.

> "Moms take great delight in watching their infants grow. Grandmas and aunts, too, note common growth milestones with great delight. Baby's first smile. Baby's first tooth. Baby's first steps. Baby's first sentence.
>
> Each of these milestones points forward toward future possibilities, more and greater achievements. Baby's first words today may one day become part of a peacemaking diplomat's dialog. The little girl who builds with blocks today may grow up to become tomorrow's Frank Lloyd Wright.

In a similar way, your heavenly Father delights in the spiritual milestones we reach. He smiles when he sees the children he has so loved from all eternity growing toward full spiritual maturity. Ephesians 4:14 describe one way of measuring that maturity.

As we grow up in Christ, the Bible says, we become steadier, more stable, more grounded in the truth:

"Then we will no longer be infants, tossed back and forth by the waves, and blown here and there by every wind of teaching and by the cunning and craftiness of people in their deceitful scheming" (Ephesians 4:14).

The Word of God is the bedrock that anchors us. We stand firmly on it. That truth keeps us from being blown back and forth by every new theory, every dubious promise made by every self-ordained prophet who claims to reveal some new, earth-shaking spiritual secret.

Instead, anchored in Christ and maturing in him, we take comfort in the promises of Scripture in days both fair and foul. Come what may, we find peace in Christ's immeasurable love. And we actively look for ways to share that love with others in the words we speak and the acts of kindness we do.

What creates this kind of spiritual maturity? The same Word of Christ that anchors us. Week by week, we soak up that Word. Day by day, minute-by-minute, we apply what we have learned to the choices of everyday living.

The Holy Spirit guides us into all truth, as he has promised, and we learn to rely on the Savior who has given that truth to us. 'Bring me to full maturity, Lord.'" (Fenton: CTA, Inc., 2014, pp. 56-57)

Growing toward spiritual maturity as the children of God naturally must lead to becoming faithful disciples who participate in the Christ's ministry of compassion in a hostile, hurting, hopeless world.

"It is he whom we proclaim, warning everyone and teaching everyone in all   wisdom, so that we may present everyone mature in Christ" (Colossians 1:28).

CHAPTER 8

THREE ESSENTIAL LIFE SOURCES

AN ABUNDANT LIFE IN ALL ITS DIMENSIONS

The Christian living in the Spirit is truly one that integrates more and more dimension of one's life into a united whole. Jesus told the crowd the good news: "The thief comes only to steal and kill and destroy. I come that "you may have life, and have it abundantly" (John 10:10). Please refer to Appendix II.

His coming was for us to have the abundant life in all its dimensions—physical, psychological, spiritual, vocational, relational, volitional, ethical, and aesthetic. Though we may think of the body, the mind, and the spirit as distinctive and separate, they are inseparably interrelated and an interdependent unity. Wellness in our outer lives reflects a cascade of healthy balance and harmony in our souls. This was presented previously in Chapter 2:

- Healing Anger with Forgiveness for the wellness in the Instinctive Doing Types;

- Healing Shame with Self-Worth for the wellness in <u>the Feeling Types</u>;

- Healing Fear with Trusting God's Providence in <u>the Thinking Types</u>.

When each one of us became a new self in the Spirit, we have more integrated thinking, feeling, and doing. The distinctiveness of Thinking, Feeling, Instinctive Intelligence Centers (the Triad or the Essence) of the old self (personality) are becoming more balanced and more harmonized. There is less conflict within the core Center and we remember our connection with the essential image of God.

A SOUL INVENTORY

Following is what can be used in a spiritual retreat to reflect on the degree of inner conflict within the Core Center by asking, "How is my soul?"

1. To what extent am I secure in my sense of self? Does the competence or the strength of others threaten me? Do I like being me? Do I project a shadow that inhibits the growth of those around?

2. How clearly can I define myself? Can I state clearly where I stand on controversial issues without being judgmental? Can I speak with authority?

3. Do I see life as a battleground? Must others lose in order for me to win? In the present conflict do I see a chance for a "win/

232

win" or must others lose in order for me to win? Can I practice solidarity?

4. How clear am I about my possibilities and my limitations? Does it feel like the outcome of this struggle is all up to me? Do I pray, in the words of the Serenity Prayer (written by Reinhold Niebuhr), "God, Grant me the serenity to accept the things I cannot change, the courage to change the thing I can, and the wisdom to distinguish the one form the other. Amen."

5. How grounded am I in the midst of ambiguity and conflict? Am I a conflict avoider? Am I a conflict solver? When the pressure is on, do I convey anxiety to others or do I convey that "inner peace that passes understanding," thereby encouraging others to be less fearful and more able to cope? How ready am I to "live into the pain" in order to learn from it?

6. Have I come to terms with my fear of death? How do I feel about risks that might shorten the length of my journey on earth? Risks that might result in personal rejection?

7. How liberated am I from the constraints of *careerism* and *consumerism*? Am I clear about the difference between the *Gospel of Grace* and the *gospel of success* or the *gospel of personal self-fulfillment*?

St. Paul considers faith, hope, and love is three essential life sources that abide forever: "And now faith, hope, and love bide, these three; and the greatest of these is love" (1 Corinthians 13:13). When these three are in harmony and an inter-connected one, our soul is well. Faith always accompanies hope and love; hope always accompanies love and faith;

and love always accompanies faith and hope. Each one will always include the other two within the realm of operation of the Essence in unity.

St. Paul praised God for the believers at Thessalonica for their faith, hope, and love by writing, "We always give thanks to God for all of you and mention you in our prayers, constantly remembering before our God and Father your work of faith and the labor of love and steadfastness of hope in our Lord Jesus Christ." (1 Thessalonians 1:3).

1. **Pursuing the "work of faith"** of deepening our radical trust in God, not trusting our human resources and abilities.

   "Let us approach with a true heart in full assurance of faith, with our hearts sprinkled clean from an evil conscience and our bodies washed with pure water (Hebrews 10:27).

   God's plan for us is good and purposeful. We, the thinking persons, do not make impossible demands upon God, but we rely more upon his providential wisdom. We choose to trust God who keeps his promises, because "faith is the assurance of things hoped for, the conviction of things not seen" (Hebrews 11:1).

   As we, the thinking persons, grow in the assurance of faith in God's providence, symptoms caused by the **paralysis of fears**, such as doubt, anxiety, ingratitude, and insecurity, will gradually disappear.

2. **Pursuing the "steadfastness of hope"** of anticipating the human's hopeful redemption through the in-breaking of the Kingdom of God.

Hope grows naturally out of the work of faith and it creates a responsible destiny.

"Let us hold fast to the confession of our hope without wavering, for he who has promised is faithful" (Hebrew 10:23).

God, the Architect, has a perfect plan for you and me so that it contributes meaningfully to its complete construction in the future. Like the farmers we can endure the present suffering because we understand the purpose of the seedtime when we have a vision of the good harvest.

St. Paul confessed his hope: "Now we see in a mirror, dimly, but then we will see face to face" (1 Corinthians 13:12). There is always a tomorrow and we have the steadfast hope that the sun will dispel the dark cloud. We anticipate the human's hopeful redemption through the in-breaking of the kingdom of God. Our experiences of God's unconditional forgiveness produce a healthful sense of forgiving others unconditionally. As we, the doing persons, grow in the forgiving Spirit, symptoms caused by **paralysis of anger and rage**, such as hostility, indifference, legalism, resentment, will gradually disappear.

3. **Pursuing the "Labor of love"** of doing justice and compassionate provision for those who are poor and in need.

Love (*agape*) knows that God accepts sincere repentance and offers unconditional forgiveness and acceptance. We are gifted with self-worth from God who says: you are "my beloved." Because of the loving relationship with God, we are empowered to cultivate other loving relationships—inner (with myself), intimate (with family and friends), infectious (with everyone).

"Let us consider how to provoke one another to love and good deeds, not neglecting to meet together... (Hebrew 10:24-25).

As we, the feeling persons, cultivate in God-given self-worth, the symptoms caused by the **paralysis of guilt or shame**, such as inferior complex, jealousy, loneliness, egotism, will gradually disappear.

WORK OF FAITH

If I were asked who I am, I would answer that I am a spiritually growing child of God and a faithful disciple of Jesus Christ. I have become who I am with the sustaining power of the Holy Spirit. But, it has been a very challenging work of faith. As disciples of Christ we are asked to rejoice when we are persecuted (Matthew 5:11-12); we are asked to turn the other cheek (vv. 38-39); we are asked to give freely to someone who wants to take from us (vv. 40-42); we are asked to love our enemies; we are asked to bless those who curse us, and to do good to those who hate us (vv. 43-44). According to the secular views this kind of lifestyle is for the losers. Sometimes, I felt that it seemed very upside down to me too. But, I have come to accept that Christ is not upside down – I am. That's why I must look forward for the eternal hope, the in-breaking of the Kingdom of God.

Before the Christ's coming to the world, human beings have all been born fallen and depraved. Being defective and broken by <u>original sin</u> (It means sin that we are born with, sin then is original to the human being), our first instincts are often wrong, which inevitably leave a big mess (Romans 5:12-14). The good news is that what was lost in the First Adam has been restored in Christ, the new Adam (vv. 15-17).

"For just as by the one man's disobedience the many were made sinners, so by the one man's obedience the many will be made righteous... so that, just as sin exercises dominion in death, so grace might also exercise dominion through justification leading to eternal life through Jesus Christ our Lord" (v. 21).

One of poisonous beliefs of toxic faith is that we can achieve salvation by works: the enmity between God and the humanity can be reconciled by human efforts. Just as there are those who think they can get God's love by being good, or those who think they can overcome some bad events in the past by working hard, there are those who believe heaven can be earned. They spend their lives in a working frenzy, trying to do more and more so God will look down, observe their fine works, and decide they are fit to enter heaven. It seems that most people, working so hard, have never resolved some tremendously debilitating issues from the past. If they could deal with those issues, perhaps they wouldn't need to punish themselves through all of the work they hope will be the key to eternal life. BUT, Christianity proclaims that we are not saved by any human moral or intellectual achievement, but by God's double graces--justifying and sanctifying graces (Romans 5:1-3; 6:14-18; 11:5, 6; Ephesians:2:8, 9).

Dr. Gerald D. May warns us that we must be not fall into the ego's ultimate ploy, spiritual narcissism. Dr. May reminds us of the *Pelagian heresy* in Christian history. He writes:

237

"The gentlest form of spiritual narcissism is the idea that one can accomplish one's own spiritual growth. Simply stated, spiritual narcissism is the unconscious use of spiritual practice, experience, and insight to increase rather than decrease self-importance... God created human beings to seek God, but the search is not ultimately ours...Our spirituality comes from God. In order for spiritual narcissism to work, it must make a possession of the entire spiritual process. I approach God or ultimate reality out of my own efforts and through my own desire. I make it happen.

But, before we say, I can do it; we must pray by saying, "I can not do it alone, Lord. Please help me." (May, Will and the Spirit, p. 115)

With this warning, let us consider how to live our new life in Christ to the full harvest, i.e., growing toward Christian maturity (Mark 4:26-28).

ACRONYM FOR G. R. O. W. T. H.

G Going to God to pray and meditate on the Word of God (Psalm 1) by opening our hearts to God to make room in a crowded life, and to notice and experience the mysterious workings of God's loving actions in the world.

R Renewing of our minds for personality transformation so that we "may discern what is good and acceptable and the perfect will of God... We do not conform to this world, but are to be transformed" (Romans 12:2).

238

The prerequisite to this personality transformation is a death to the old way of life in the flesh, and being alive to the new life in Christ (Galatians 2:20).

O   Obeying the Love Commandments: our loving devotion toward God—the Creator, the Redeemer, and the Sustainer—is expressed as our love of our neighbors as ourselves (Luke 10:27). The Jesus' Parable of "the Good Samaritan" (Luke 10:25-35) illustrates this wonderful principle of living for peace and harmony in the world. With resurrection power we are enabled to live a life pleasing to God: Do justice: love compassion; and walk humbly with God" (Micah 6:8).

W   Witnessing Christ to a broken and hostile world is demonstrating authentic Christian love among the followers of Christ and Christian unity in the Church using the spiritual gifts (1 Peter 4:10).

T   Together in the community of faith, we exhort one another so that all Christians "may have life, and have it abundantly" (John 10:10). The mission of the church is to make disciples by nurturing, outreaching, and witnessing. The author of "Purpose-Driven Life", Rick Warren insists: "We fellowship better together; We grow better together; We serve better together; We worship better together; We reach out better together."

H   Holy Spirit sustains us in the process of spiritual formation. It is the process of our involvement with the Spirit's work in personal holiness and social justice as an agent or instrument of the ministry of reconciliation between God and humanity.

In conclusion, there can be no wholeness in the image of Christ without incarnating in relationships with others, both in the Body of Christ (the Church) and in the world.

OVERCOMING THE TEMPTATIONS IN LIFE

The Spirit led Jesus into the desert for forty days. This must be an intentional parallel to the Hebrew's forty years of wilderness wondering after the Exodus. There, while physically hungry (he fasted 40 days) and vulnerable, and yet spiritually strong, he overcame three temptations by Satan. In that single illustration we see lifetime of the practical temptations that we all have to go through and overcome (Matthew 4:1-11; Luke 4:1-13).

Jesus is the Master Teacher in the way of life and his experiential knowledge of Satan and his tactics can instruct us how to overcome our temptations in life. Jesus, who represents the whole of humanity, was saying to us that he can help all of us who are tempted with three difficult temptations—possession (more prone to the Thinking persons), popularity (more prone to the Feeling persons), and power (more prone to the Instinctive/doing persons).

In the first temptation, the devil suggests that Jesus satisfy his hunger by turning stones into bread. This is the temptation of possession for the Thinking persons. The thinking people's weakness is insecurity. Therefore, they are easily tempted by the possession of security. Their worldview is based on a scarcity worldview (please refer to Appendix II). As Jesus rejects the temptation of possession by quoting the Scripture, "It is written, 'One does not live by bread alone, but by every Word that comes from the mouth of God.'"(Deuteronomy 8:3).

The second temptation is for Jesus to leap from the pinnacle of the Temple and have the angels catch him midair. This is the temptation of popularity and sensationalism for the Feeling persons. The feeling people's weakness is seeking attention from others and they are easily tempted by popularity and vainglory by forcing God on the spot to bail them out without their paying for the consequences of breaking the natural laws of the universe. Jesus rejects the temptation of popularity, by quoting the Scripture: "Again it is written, 'Do not put the Lord your God to the test.'" (Deuteronomy 6:16). Since we trust God in the daily routines of life, it is not our prerogative to put God to the test by requesting unnatural, special protection.

In the third temptation for power, Satan offers the earthly kingdoms and their splendor if Jesus would make Satan his god and worship him. This is the temptation of power for the instinctive (doing) people. The instinctive people's weakness is seeking autonomy and they are easily tempted by power because they feel that they can have autonomy by having domination and power over others. Jesus rejects the temptation of power, by rebuking the tempter, "Away with you, Satan! For it is written, 'Worship the Lord your God, and serve only him.'" (Deuteronomy 6:13).

Temptation in general has to do with being pushed to give up loving God. When we are seduced into believing that we can control life, when we think that we can live as if we don't need God's help; when we feel we don't want to love God above everything else, we are certain that we are in the throes (or struggle) of temptation and subsequent disaster, called detours in life. Ultimately, temptation is giving up our trust in God and relying on our power or on something or someone other than God.

If Jesus yielded to these temptations, Jesus would have been a very popular, powerful man over night in all Israel in human points of view. He would have established himself to be a most powerful earthly king beyond dispute. Imagine for a moment—stones turned to bread to feed the hungry, a spectacular fall from the pinnacle of the Temple as the crowds gasped in amazement and awe, political and military appeasement as the foundation of the kingdom program to deliver Israel from Roman occupation. Jesus restrained and resisted all three temptations. Finally, Jesus had to face

his last temptation. He could have walked away from the cruel death on
the cross, but he didn't. Before he was arrested, he prayed to his Father in
Gethsemane with sweat mingled with blood: "My Father, if it is possible,
let this cup pass from me; yet not what I want but what you want...For the
second time, he prayed, "My Father, if this cannot pass unless I drink it,
your will be done" (Matthew 26:39, 42). If he yielded to this temptation, we
would have a different human history. No salvation for humanity.

Let us begin by acknowledging the reality of temptations in our
lives. None of us is beyond temptation and we stumble and fall. The
Bible and Christian history are full of human failings. We all remember
Peter who betrayed his Master on the night Jesus was arrested. But after
experiencing the unconditional forgiveness of the risen Christ and after
he was filled with the Holy Spirit, he became the leader of the Way as a
commissioned Apostle.

St. Peter admonishes us that we "may escape from the corruption
that is in the world because of lust. Maintaining purity in the midst of a
sin-oriented culture is a challenge.

- How can we overcome temptation of corruption?

St. Peter's answer is that we must work on developing eight essential qualities of healthy disciples:

> "You must make every effort to support your *faith* with
> goodness, and *goodness* with knowledge, and *knowledge*
> with self-control, and *self-control* with endurance and
> *endurance* with godliness, and *godliness* with mutual af-
> fection, and *mutual affection* with *love*."

The above eight essential qualities of healthy disciples will be presented in Chapter 9.

- What can prevent us from being ineffective and unfruitful in the knowledge of our Lord Jesus Christ and we would not stumble?

St. Peter answers: "For anyone who lacks these things is nearsighted and blind, and is forgetful of the cleansing of past sins. Therefore, brothers and sisters, be all the more eager to *confirm your call and election*, for if you do this, you would *never stumble...*

For in this way, the entrance into the eternal kingdom of our Lord and Savior Jesus Christ will be richly provided for you" (2 Peter 1:5-11).

In conclusion, following principles are suggested for fighting evil temptations that are afflicting us internally, *whether* we choose to focus on battling substance abuse, racism, sexual addiction, domestic violence, *or* the disintegration of family system, school system, and/or political system:

1. We are to practice self-disciplines with the help of the indwelling Holy Spirit;

2. Our minds are to be transformed and be saturated with excellent thoughts. We try to find good report about others and avoid gossip. We learn to savor our life: do not complain; face the day with a smile.

3. We must rely on God's promises that we will never face a temptation we cannot resist. We need to let go of our fears, bitterness, and anger. Instead, we need to reaffirm our calling and election.

4. We celebrate the past, embrace the present, and anticipate the future. We share our struggles with others; confess to one another; pray for one another and be accountable.

5. We must recognize our weakness and bad habits. We also recognize that we are particularly exposed during vulnerable times such as traveling or working overtime.

6. We must cultivate a radical trust in the God of provision by "leaning on his everlasting arms." (The United Methodist Hymnal #133)

"O how sweet to walk in this pilgrim way,
Leaning on the everlasting arms,
O how bright the path grows from day to day,
Leaning on the everlasting arms.
Leaning, leaning, safe and secure from all alarms,
Leaning, leaning, leaning on the everlasting arms...
(second stanza)

What have I to dread, what have I to fear?
Leaning on the everlasting arms?
I have blessed peace with my Lord so near,
Leaning on the everlasting arms.
Leaning, leaning, safe and secure from all alarms,
Leaning, leaning, leaning on the everlasting arms. (third stanza).

RAHAB AS THE EXAMPLE OF A CONFIDENT FAITH

Faith is defined as "the assurance of things hoped for, the conviction of things not seen" (Hebrews 11:1). We may want to learn from J.P. Moreland and Klaus Issler that a confident faith takes risks when we have God-confidence. (Moreland and Issler, *In Search of a Confident Faith,* pp. 201-203)

In the following story Rahab, the prostitute, made "the Great Hall of Faith" (Hebrew 11:31 James 2:25) by following her deep passion to be receptive to God's guidance.

As the result of her radical trusting in God and courageously risking her interest, her reward was a joyful, abundant life. This is her story.

Joshua was God's choice after the death of Moses. He was to lead the Hebrew people into the "land of milk and honey, which God had promised to Abraham. Moses only led the people up to the Canaan border. Joshua was to lead them into Canaan. In the call, God gave Joshua full assurance, "As I was with Moses, so I will be with you; I will not fail you or forsake you" (Joshua 1:5).

The conquest of the Land of Canaan began with the crossing of the river Jordan; the first spot reached by the Hebrew people was Gilgal, East of Jericho (Joshua 4:19). The first thing Joshua faced was going into the land of Jericho. Joshua sent two spies to look over Jericho to insure his first victory (Joshua 2:1).

In this important juncture, the prostitute Rahab, a citizen of Jericho, played a vital role in bringing about a positive outcome for the Joshua's campaign. Joshua sent two spies to Jericho and they entered the house of Rahab (she was a common prostitute, who performed religious sexual acts with the priests of the fertility god, Baal).

If we put ourselves "back in the thirteenth century B.C., we might see that the Canaanite culture was a snake pit of child sacrifice and sacred prostitution, practices ruthlessly devoted to using the most innocent and vulnerable members of the community (babies and virgins) to manipulate their fertility gods for a good harvest.

As a common harlot she had to make living by prostituting with anyone, including strange travelers. Apparently through the travelers, she heard about Yahweh who delivered the Hebrew people from the mighty Pharaoh of Egypt and also who gave victories over two kings of Amorites (Joshua 2:10). Rahab confessed to the spies: "the Lord your

245

God is indeed God in heaven above and on earth below" (Joshua 2:11). She decided to hide the two enemy spies, risking her life and family because she believed Yahweh was the true God and she desired to please Yahweh, not her self-interest.

In Joshua 2:1-3 we read that the King of Jericho found out about coming of the spies and sent soldiers to Rahab's house to arrest them. But, Rahab already had decided to hide them, because she believed that God had promised the land to the Hebrews. In return she asked the Jewish spies to make a promise to Rahab by saying, "Our life for yours! If you do not tell this business of ours, then we will deal kindly and faithfully with you when the Lord gives us the land" (Joshua 2:14).

Rahab's desire to please God is remarkable for she risked putting herself and her family in danger. Her faith in God was so strong and she did not hesitate to help her country's enemies for their eventual victory. Her vision was much bigger than her nation's future. That is why Rahab along with Sarah are the only two women mentioned in the "Great Hall of Faith" in the Bible: "By faith Rahab, the prostitute, did not perish with those who were disobedient, because she had received the spies in peace" (Hebrew 11:31).

Rahab, as the mother of Boaz, and four other women are included in the Jesus' genealogy because of their special roles in the coming of the Messiah (Matthew 1:2-16). Can you believe that Rahab became the great-great-grandmother of the King David? (Please refer to the romantic story of Ruth and Boaz, in the Book of Ruth in the Hebrew Bible. Rahab was the mother of Boaz.

STEADFASTNESS OF HOPE

In the midst of pain and suffering in my life, I have been focusing on God's loving presence in my life as well as the eternal hope that gives me the reasons for my confidence in the Christian faith. The eternal hope sees beyond the present suffering, because it is not born from the absence of all that is harsh or sad, and it rises from the experience of both good and evil. This eternal hope sees what is possible even in the midst of what is undesirable human beings with deep-seated racism, sexism, abusive power, bitterness at systems that act like machines, resentments and cynicism, nihilism, self-hatred, despair, rage targeted at anyone, self-aggrandizement, and intolerance of anyone who is different from us.

LIVING HOPE

The eternal hope becomes living hope that heals our wounds with their pains of the past, such as childhood memories of abuse, abandonment, dysfunctional family issues, and lack of basic human needs. As a consequence, we suffer from anger (rage), shame (guilt), and fear of insecurity and uncertainty. With a genuine basis for healing hope we identify these negative emotions; we name their causes; our inner conflicts are healed by the grace of God--unconditional love and forgiveness-- for the anger/rage; God-given self-image and acceptance for shame/guilt; and the providence of God for the fear of insecurity and uncertainty.

The following illustration enlightens us that when we are healed and find wellness from God, we are forever changed: by receiving the ability to give up our dependency on others as well as blaming others for our misfortune; by willingly accepting the new abundant life that Jesus offers us.

ILLUSTRATION 10: AN EXAMPLE PREACHING ON HEALING

Lorraine Brugh preached at the Chapel of the Resurrection, Valparaiso University on **John 5:1-9**. She began her sermon by stating, "I don't think

Jesus' question to the invalid man in this passage was an idle one. Did you catch it? Jesus' question was "Do you want to be made well? The sick man answered him, "Sir, I have no one to put me into the pool when the water is stirred up; and while I am making my way, someone else steps down ahead of me." Jesus said to him, "Stand up, take your mat and walk." At once the man was made well, and he took up his mat and began to walk."

She continues, "At first glance it seems obvious. So why did Jesus bother to ask this invalid man who had been ill for 38 years? Anyone in that situation would want to be healed. Isn't it obvious?"

Then, she shared her personal experience of God's healing of depression from the loss of her beloved father...She felt unprotected by God who had always seemed as supportive as her father. She also felt that God seemed as remote to her as her father's physical presence. But, through the faithfulness of her loved ones (her husband, son, brother, and 2 friends) who stood by her during those lonely months, ever so slowly, she learned to see God's presence in places she had never noticed it before... And she accepted their faithfulness of her friends and family as tangible signs that God had not left her utterly alone. And, she said, "Ever so slowly, I accepted the healing that God was offering through these new and uncharted waters." After sharing her experience of God who made her whole, she went back to the text.

> "So it wouldn't have been an irrelevant question if Jesus would have asked me the question he asked the [sick] man in our story this morning. Sure, I would have wanted him to take away the pain of my grief and loss right away. But Jesus' healing also demanded a response on the man's part.
>
> In accepting Jesus' healing, the man simultaneously gave up his dependence on others to attend to him. Did you

notice that the healing which Jesus commanded included that the man picked up his own mat? So we, too, who know our own failings and infirmities might ask ourselves, "Are we ready to give up our dependencies in order to allow God to make us whole?" What would Jesus heal you from? What would you be living without if you accepted Jesus' healing?

Those little things we use to make ourselves feel better, seemingly harmless, may be the very things that block our healing. It might be a relationship from which we demand too much. It might be a pleasure we get from someone else's failure. It might be a right we reserve to feel critical of others. Or being good Lutherans, it might be the right to feel guilty if we want to. Whatever it is we use "to get through out day," these are the things that we must consider before we answer Jesus' question, "Do you want to be healed?"

Healing is gift, pure grace. But from it we are forever changed. Accepting our healing and taking our place in the Christian community is the follow-through in which we find ourselves. Whether we have been victim or perpetrator, violent or passively aggressive, mentally, emotionally or physically scarred, those no longer are our identity. Healing includes our willingness to leave those behind and accept the new creation Jesus gives us. It is no surprise that we often cling to our infirmities long after they have served their usefulness. So think twice as you bring your wish for healing to Jesus. Make sure you are <u>willing to take up your pallet and walk."</u>

A PARABLE OF A FALSE HOPE

Unfortunately, many people pursue false hope. The addict (to alcohol, illegal drugs, gambling, and sex) is someone who says, "My addiction has cost me my job, my family, my friends, my marriage, my health, my house; yet I think I'll give it one more try." As long as there is false hope, the adult children of the alcoholic will continue to seek love from the rejecting parent(s). The attached and hurting child who cannot mature says, "I've waited for my father's acceptance for 40 years. I've refused to believe that anyone else loves me until he comes through my door with affection. It has ruined my marriage and estranged me from my own children. Although he's now dead, I think I'll wait for him another 10 years.

Frank Kafka describes this false hope in his parable called "the Trial."

> "Before the door of the promised palace stands a doorkeeper. To this doorkeeper there comes a man from the country that begs for admittance. But the doorkeeper says he cannot admit the man at the moment. The man asks if he will be allowed to enter later. 'It is possible,' answers the doorkeeper, but not at this moment.' 'If you are so strongly tempted, try to get in without my permission. But notice that I am strong and powerful, and I'm only the lowest doorkeeper. From hall to hall, guards stand at every door, one more powerful than the other.'
>
> The man looks closely at doorkeeper in his furred robe, with his huge pointed nose and long thin 'Tartar' beard, he decided that he'd better wait until he gets permission to enter. The doorkeeper gives him a stool and lets him sit

down at the side of the door. There, he sits and waits for days and years. As he grows old, he mutters to himself, he begs even the fleas in the doorkeeper's fur collar to help him persuade the doorkeeper to have a change of mind.

Now his life is drawing to a close. Before he dies, all he has experienced condenses into one question. 'How does it come about then, that in all these years, no one has come seeking admittance but me?' The doorkeeper replies: 'No one but you could gain admittance through this door, since this door was intended just for you. I am now going to shut it.'"

The man spent his entire life outside the door of the Promised Palace with the passive hope of entering the Palace, never recognizing that the hope must arise from within. Passive waiting is hopelessness disguised as the virtue of hope; impotence or inaction masked as endurance. He needed more than this passive waiting hope. He could have entered the Promised Palace if he gathered **courage** and **confidence**. He needed the courage to disregard the legalistic, bureaucratic doorkeeper; he also needed a confident faith and healing hope to enter the door into the Promised Palace.

What do we learn from this parable?

Purves enlightens us that "the true Christian hope is related directly to the resurrection of the body, and therefore to the coming future of the kingdom of God which is promised, announced, and anticipated." But, he cautions us about the possible danger of our living in the "other worldliness," not living in the here and now:

"It [the Christian theology of hope] will function as premature and inappropriate access point to heaven, allowing us to flee the earth while we still have work here to do...For true Christian hope sends us back into the world...The theology of hope leads to a prophetic energizing and criticizing of that which is not yet the kingdom, of those structures and conditions in society which lead to numbness, despair, and death. Hope also means that evil, suffering, and death do not have the last word." (Purves, *The Search of Compassion*, p. 100)

SPIRITUAL SOJOURNERS

In most journeys it is good to have companionship. When we travel with another, we share more of the trip's delight. We can help one another in case of trouble: "If they fall, one will lift up the other; but woe to one who is alone and falls and does not have another to help" (Ecclesiastes 4:10). On our spiritual journey Jesus promises to be with us. When we share the table of Holy Communion, Jesus is present. Jesus promises: "Where two or three are gathered in my name, I am there among them" (Mathew 18:20).

A key word is "gathered." The Christian living is not a solitary journey. Even though we can pray, meditate and commune with God in private, we are called to gather. Whether for worship, fellowship, study, or service, gathering is an important part of the Judeo-Christian heritage. Another key is the phrase "in my name." When we intentionally expect the presence of Christ, that presence is guaranteed.

A familiar story tells of the little boy who was frightened by a thunderstorm one night. He came to his mother's bedroom door and said, "Mom, I want be with you." The mother seeking to teach him self-reliance and independence, responded, "It's alright son. You go back to your room. Just remember that Jesus is with you." He went back to his room. After another loud clap of thunder, he returned with a sense of panic and said, "Mom, I know Jesus is with me, but right now I want somebody with skin on."

If we confess Jesus as the Son of God and we believe in Jesus as the God with human skin on, we truly can be the sojourners in our faith journey together. And when we gather in his name, Christ is there, and he will be with us through the journey we call life.

In Hebrew 10:23, the writer encourages us: "Let us hold fast to the confession of our hope without wavering, for he who has promised is faithful." This hope is naturally flowing out of faith in Christ. Faith in Christ led Paul to become a man of hope from a man of despair. Through Jesus Christ all humans may have the gift of eternal life. These hopeful words can sustain us through so many perplexities and setbacks in life.

In his letters to the early churches the Apostle Paul sounds everywhere a note of expectance, of assurance of better things to come: "We know that all things work together for good to them that love God, to them who are called according to his purpose" (Romans 8:28).

He had the conviction that life has a goal and that, despite inevitable reverses, all things tend toward perfection in the ultimate purposes of God for his children. His attitude toward such setbacks and reverses may be summed up in his declaration, "We also boast in our sufferings, knowing that suffering produces endurance, and endurance produces character, and character produces hope." (Romans 5:3, 4)

THE LABOR OF LOVE

We affirm that our work of faith and our steadfastness of hope naturally lead us to our labor of love of doing justice and compassionate provision for those who are poor and in need.

There may be some Christians in the church who enjoy a reputa-tion of spirituality because no one has ever put their claims to the test. If someone can annoy our self-preservation, it shows our old nature is still within. If we cannot take insult and critical words from others, we must learn that all things shall be judged by the measure of self-giving love that is in us.

It is so easy to do unloving things and not realize it in our zeal for doing what is right for each of us. The temptation is to sacrifice love for the sake of some minor virtue. And thus we have the sorry sight of Christians disputing with other Christians, each of holding some petty beliefs or ideas as paramount.

There is no place for divisive differences among the disciples of Christ. We need to cultivate honest conversation, patience, loving ac-ceptance, and mutual agreement. Every disciple willingly practices two dimensions of spiritual formation: the inward journey of becoming the image of Christ; the outward journey of living for the sake of others with a labor of love. We willingly commit ourselves to Christ by following his direction–for each of us has unique ministry in accordance with his or her spiritual gifts.

Hagberg and Guelich have constructed a *six-stage framework* to help us understand our spiritual growth and development. Although they do not offer exactly how or when we need to move along in our personal pilgrimages, nor offer formulas for spiritual growth, we are interested in *characteristics* of their stage 6 called *the life of love*. According to them this stage is characterized by Christ-like living and total obedience; wisdom gained from life's struggles; compassionate living for others; de-tachment from things and stress; life underneath or on top; life abandoned. Concerning "compassionate living for others" they write:

> At stage 6 we can reach far beyond or our own capacity
> and love our fellow human being with deep compassion,

because we know that all come from and are loved by God. As Jesus was compassionate even in Gethsemane, at his trial, and on the cross, so we are compassionate under extreme hardship...

Compassion does not mean to be lacking convictions or the absence of [righteous] anger. It means that, in the midst of anger, we are still willing to love, help, and be there for others." (Hagberg and Guelich, *The Critical Journey*, pp. 154-155, 159)

DEFINITION OF LOVE

The subject of love (several different meanings of love) has stimulated more songs than any other subject. In English this one word, love, must express all varieties of love. But there has never been a greater song on love than that written by St. Paul in 1 Corinthian 13. St. Paul is not talking about physical love (*eros*), nor love between parents and children (*storge*), nor friendly love (*philia*). He chooses the one word, *agape* that means self-giving love. It is primarily God's own love, manifested in the life of the Son of Man who came to seek and to save that which was lost, above all in his death on the cross.

Greek New Testament Scholar, Spiros Zodhiates, writes a book on First Corinthians 13, the love chapter, to help us learn from the Greek writing:

"Only through [hu]man's appropriation of God's con-descension and love can [hu]man really experience the divine feeling called *agape*-love. The love of the Christian for his [or her] neighbor is shown by St. Paul to be simply

God's own agape-love active in the human heart, that is, through the indwelling Holy Spirit." (Zodhiates, *To Love Is To Live*, pp.7-8)

When we trust in the all-embracing God with our whole being and when we do not rely on our limited human effort, we become God's children whose "ethos" is *agape-* love. The word *ethos* means "distinguishing character, sentiment, moral nature, guiding principles of a person, group, an institution or a society." Therefore, I consider *agape*-love is the ethos of Christianity.

Agape-love involves the will of the person—perfect good will toward the other person; and desire to do what is best for that person unconditionally. *Agape*-love is not a state of feeling or a state of being. Rather, it is an action. We need to insert the mental image of Jesus dying for us on the cross. That action is what *agape-* love is all about. Therefore, the cross is the ultimate symbol of God's love in action.

St. Paul insists that agape love is the most excellent way of living because "love is patient; love is kind; love rejoices in the truth; it bears all things, believes all things, and endures all things." These characteristics capture the fresh, unpolluted love of a trusting person who embodies the perfect love of Christ.

When we capture the meaning of the cross of Christ, we can comprehend the meaning of embodying or incarnating love. We feel the highs and lows of the Disciples; we are shocked by the malevolent resolution of the religious leaders (members of Sanhedrin) to kill Jesus; shocked by the selfish envy of the high priests; shocked by the casual cruelty of those fickle crowds; shocked by the calculated injustice committed by Pilate. We feel Jesus' physical torture, social rejection and humiliation as well as the total brokenness of Jesus who felt his Father's total abandonment.

The cross symbolizes Christ's sacrificial self-giving *agape*-love:

When we incarnate this love in the spirit of a dedicated servant, there is filling up of our hearts with the Spirit of Christ. St. John admonishes us: "Beloved, let us love one another, because love is from God; everyone who loves is born of God and knows God" (1 John 4:7).

THE LOVE COMMANDMENTS

The Jesus' Love Commandments (combination of Deuteronomy 6:5 and Leviticus 19:18) simply express the heart of the Law and puts well-known precepts together in a new way. "The first is, Hear, O Israel: The Lord our God is one Lord; and you shall love the Lord your God with all your heart, with all your soul, with all your mind, and with all your strength. The second is this; you shall love your neighbor as yourself. There is no greater commandment than these" (Matthew 22:37-40).

Acceptance of ourselves as children of God is basic to any acceptance of reality. And reality exists in our relationship to God and to our neighbors who are created in "the image of God." The knowledge of our being precious and unique in God's sight empowers us to love God with our whole being-- body, mind, and spirit-- and to love our neighbors as ourselves. Who is our neighbor? They are those who are in need-- "hungry, thirsty, a stranger, naked, sick, in prison" (Matthew 25:35, 36). We find them in our families, in the church, in our community, in our country, and in the global community.

Moses' Ten Commandments given by YHWH (*Yahweh*) contain our relationships with God (the first four commands) and with all human beings (the second six commands). By Jesus' time, the religious leaders of Judaism expanded the Ten Commandments to 613 laws and prohibitions, thus making them dogmatic and oppressive Laws because they missed the truth that the Ten Commandments are about "how to nurture" our relationships with God and with our neighbors as we love ourselves.

We are only just beginning to realize that we have vastly underestimated the power of loving ourselves. Modern psychology has been helpful here, pointing out the pitfalls of trying to love God and others, when we do not love and accept ourselves. Such a loving becomes a desire for external recognition and acceptance. Inevitably it becomes the only way we know how to feel worthwhile—loving others conditionally in order to feel loved and valued ourselves.

Jesus did not say "love God first, others second, and yourself last." He valued all three-love relationships as equally important and interdependent. When we love and value ourselves, as God does, we are genuinely able to respond in love to both God and our neighbors who are created in the image of God.

Love knows that God accepts sincere repentance and offers forgiveness. It cultivates love relationships—inner (with oneself), intimate (with family and friends), infectious (with everyone). In Hebrew 10:24, the Author encourages us: "Let us consider how to provoke one another to love and good deeds…" It must be borne in mind that repentance and confession are the catharsis that produces a healthy sense of being forgiven.

Christ's new commandment, "Love one another as I have loved you" (John 15:12) is much more demanding than the love commandment to love your neighbor as yourself. Loving your neighbor is to respect the image of God in every human being with all the rights, which that dignity and sacredness confers. However, to love one another as Jesus loves us is to love one another in the faith community with mutual affection in our humanness—in our individuality and divisiveness in personality conflicts and in unbearable situation. It is to continue to show love, no matter what the provocation may be to act otherwise.

A HIGHWAY TOWARD BLISS

How does our common description of *the blessed* or *happy,* compare with those listed in the *Jesus' Sermon on the Beatitudes* (Matthew 5:1-12)?

Jesus' teaching words are anti-cultural: "Blessed are...those who are the poor in spirit; those who mourn; the meek; those who hunger and thirst for righteousness; the merciful; the pure in heart; the peacemakers; those who are persecuted for righteousness' sake; those who are despised."

His teaching is not an *interim ethic*; it is not a banner for the *social gospel*; it is not *legalism*; it is not impractical *idealism*; it is not *reserved for the future age.* The sermon addresses people who live in our kind of world. The sermon is *a call for new birth in the Spirit*; it is *a call to new life in Christ*; it is *a call to a blessed highway* that leads to the *eternal happiness.*

1. "Blessed are the poor in spirit, for theirs is the kingdom of heaven" (Matthew 5:3).

    God takes up his reign in those who acknowledge their poverty. The moment you humble yourself and pour out your heart to God and recognize that you are spiritually bankrupt and receive him into your life, the King of kings comes and sets up his throne in your heart. You are blessed if you put your trust in God rather than in possessions or other symbols of security.

2. "Blessed are those who mourn, for they shall be comforted" (Matthew 5:4).

We mourn for personal loss and personal sin. When we mourn, we shall be comforted. What does it mean to be comforted? The word comfort means to strengthen and encourage.

After Jesus was crucified and buried, two lonely disciples were trudging home to Emmaus seven miles out of Jerusalem (Luke 24:15-16). They were discouraged, dejected, and defeated. The dreams and expectations about their Messiah were dashed upon the beams of an ugly Roman cross. Their hope was shattered. When we let go of some person, place, or thing that we love, we automatically enter a period of mourning. In the midst of their sadness, Jesus appeared. Does it not still happen? This reminds us the beatitude we have read so often, "Blessed are those who mourn."

The Savior often finds our readiness to respond within us when we are on the road to "Emmaus." Jesus, man of sorrows and acquainted with grief, breaks in upon us, turning our sadness to joy, our darkness to light. How comforting that is. With gentle chiding, Jesus noticed their ignorance of Scripture. How often our lack of knowing the Scripture leads us to defeat and confusion. Amidst all of our sadness and disappointment, we need to seek the Word of God and find comfort from the presence of risen Christ.

3. "Blessed are the meek, for they will inherit the earth" (Matthew 5:5).

A meek person is one who has power, who has strength, but is self-controlled and channels his or her power usefully rather than being destructive. Meekness is strength; it is power under control. A meek person is one who has yielded himself or herself and is obedient and trusts in the Lord. They have no drive for power. They do not want to control situations, people, or their own life. The promise for the meek person is they will inherit the earth. It means they are at peace with their world. Also there is assurance of a future inheritance that God will provide eternally and abundantly.

4. "Blessed are those who hunger and thirst for righteousness, for they shall be   satisfied" (Matthew 5:6).

Jesus is saying, "Just as food and water are basic to the physical life, righteousness is basic to the spiritual life. What is true in our physical bodies is also true spiritually. Unless there is a craving after righteousness, you will perish spiritually. It is basic—it is not a luxury. The loss of appetite is one of the first symptoms of diminishing health. Righteousness is not something that comes from within—it is a gift from God. It is God's life imparted to us. It is God's life given to those who hunger and thirst. It's having one's ground for justice. When we hunger and thirst for righteousness, God will make us satisfied for we will be filled with joy.

5. "Blessed are the merciful, for they shall receive mercy" (Matthew 5:7)

Mercy is an attribute of God. His love is an expression of his mercy.

Truth is an attribute of God. His faithfulness is an expression of his truth.

Holiness is an attribute of God. His justice is an expression of his holiness. Grace for our sin; grace cleanses and reinstates, while mercy relieves; it helps and cures. Mercy comes out of the heart to remove pain and hurt with power, then our pity, and participation. When we give mercy to others, we receive mercy from God and from others, so that we are channels through whom God's mercy can flow continuously.

6. Blessed are the pure in heart, for they shall see God" (Matthew 5:8).

We can blame people or circumstances for all our troubles, but the Bible blames the heart. In Bible language, the heart is the very core of our inner being that consists of our intelligence, our emotion, and our will. The Enneagram calls it the "Triad Center." Jesus' whole problem with the Pharisees was that they had focused upon the externals of religious life. Jesus was more concerned about the purity of the heart--the very control center of their beings. When Jesus says the pure in heart shall see God, he is saying that our hearts need to be purified and cleansed by God himself. It's the cleansing of sin. And removing impurity (dross) from ore makes pure silver. They will see God with the eyes of the spirit purified by faith.

7. "Blessed are the peacemakers, for they will be called children of God" (Matthew 5:9).

There are four general areas where the peacemaker becomes involved in conflict: in the community; at work; at church; at home. The peacemakers are blessed because "they shall be called children of God. God is the source of peace. God is the author of peace. God is the giver of peace. So when we are the peacemakers, we act as God does. And we are called the children of God. The peace that Jesus offers is the great gift of the resurrection and is not sentimental. This peace transcends joy and sorrow, hope and despair.

8. "Blessed are those who are persecuted for righteousness's sake, for theirs is the kingdom of heaven. Blessed are you when people revile you and persecute you and utter all kinds of evil against you falsely on my account. Rejoice and be glad, for your reward is great in heaven" (Matthew 5:10-12).

The verb "to persecute" means to put to fight, to drive away, to pursue. The word *persecute* means to *pursue* to give you trouble; to *oppress* you; to *vex* you because of your faith. You are not persecuted when you pay ticket for speeding. That's punishment for breaking a law. But when you stand up for God and you are oppressed, that's persecution. The Christian church has a long history of being persecuted. This beatitude is the wisdom that finds happiness in persecution. Those who have experienced this beatitude have moved beyond self-interest and entered into the peace of Christ. They become sources of the divine life and peace for others. Through them God is pouring divine light, life, and love into the human family.

As the late John Stott said, "Persecution is simply the clash of two irreconcilable value systems." We are strangers and pilgrims and aliens in this secular world, and most people don't put out a welcome mat for aliens. We are to rejoice and be glad because there is the promise of eternal happiness.

The good news is this. All human beings are invited to prepare the way of the Lord so that he can enter "straight" into every [repented] heart: "Every valley shall be filled, and every mountain and hill shall be made low, and the crooked shall be made straight, and the rough ways made smooth; and all flesh [repented sinners] shall see the salvation of God" (Luke 3:4-6, quoted from Isaiah 40:3).

We are blessed when we invite him into our hearts; we are blessed when we are chosen to hear the voice of Christ: "Listen! I am standing at the door knocking; if you hear my voice and open the door, I will come into you and eat with you, and you with me" (Revelation 3:20).

BEING THE SALT OF THE EARTH AND THE LIGHT OF THE WORLD FOR THE SAKE OF OTHERS

After the sermon on the Beatitudes, Jesus said: "You are the salt of the earth...You are the light of the world...Let your light shine before others, so that they may see your good works and give glory to your Father in heaven" (Matthew 5:13-16).

We are to be distinct but not isolated; we are to be involved with the world, salting it and shedding light in it. We are salt and light. There are two ways in which Christians influence the world: (1) in a subtle way, as salt and (2) in an obvious way, as light. The *subtle* Christian influence is the salt of the earth. How is salt used? Salt, to have any effect at all, must be mixed in with the substance, which needs salt. Nobody but a collector sets up fancy saltshakers and admires them.

Salt produces thirst; Salt provides flavor; Salt preserves food.

A Christian influence makes people thirsty for God;

A Christian adds flavors to bring zest in life.

A Christian preserves and prevents decay.

The Christian needs to penetrate the world to stop the process of decay.

The obvious Christian influence is the light of the world. How is light used? Light is most effective in a dark place. Light is obvious. It's difficult to hide light.

Light has two qualities: it illumines and it reflects.

Light illumines; it dispels darkness and it shows us truth. As light we are in the world to share the truth that Jesus Christ can free those who are in bondage, and that they can live a liberated life in freedom by the grace of God.

Light reflects: The Christians can only reflect the light of Jesus. We cannot shine on our own. Jesus is the light. The reason the world is still in darkness is because we don't always reflect the light of Jesus very well.

ILLUSTRATION 11

John came to see his pastor Paul and ask him to pray that he would find different job. "The place I work is so rotten you wouldn't believe it," John said. "I hear nothing but foul language and dirty jokes, and there's not one other Christian there as far as I can tell."

Paul said, "I can't pray for you to get a different job. Why would I pray for you to take the only source of light out of dark place? He continued: "Here is what I will do." Paul said, "I will join in prayer with you. I want you to call me every morning before you go to work and we'll pray together that God will keep your light shining down there."

For two weeks John called Pastor Paul and they prayed together every morning. Then John stopped calling. A week later when Paul saw John, he said, "I am missing my wake-up call." John replied, "Listen, since we started praying, three of guys at work have come to know Christ and I go down early so we can have a Bible study together before work.

Paul joyfully responded, "OK, now you'll probably get your new job. God has a core of light there now and I wouldn't be surprised if you get transferred to another place that's just as rotten as this one was when you started.

That's what the collective gathering of the Body of Christ (the Church) is for—to restore and strengthen one another. We want each member to come to wholeness; be released into the world to minister.

Christ is calling you and me to be the salt of the earth and the light of the world so that we may continue the ministry of reconciliation through the incarnate, crucified, and resurrected Christ.

THE MEANING OF TAKING UP OUR CROSS

Learning and growing in *agape*-love rooted in faith in Jesus Christ is the ultimate mark of mature Christians and actively growing disciples. Jesus gave the patterns that his disciples are to emulate, by saying:

> "If any want to become my followers, let them deny themselves and take up their cross and follow me. For those who want to save their life will lose it, and those who lose their life for my sake, and for the sake of the gospel, will save it." (Mark 8:34-35)

We follow Jesus who called himself the Son of Man. We may see him operating with the special advantage of knowing everything, and he knew his life was prefigured in the O.T. as the suffering servant rather than a conquering king. He foreknew he would be rejected by the religious authorities, his family, and his disciples.

On the night before his death, Jesus prayed for his Father to provide another way, but only if it was his will. But Jesus understood that this was his mission-- reconciling God and humanity. As Jesus was compassionate even at Gethsemane, at his "monkey" trial, on the road of Via Dolorosa, and on the cross, so we are called to be compassionate under extreme hardship with the power of *agape*-love that comes from the above. A disciple is one who responds to God's loving actions in his or her life by following the way of Jesus Christ by denying oneself and taking up one's cross and following him.

Jesus clearly warns us that following him is difficult and costly, but our reward is becoming participants of the divine nature:

1) Denying ourselves;

2) Taking up our cross;

3) Following Jesus Christ while allowing him to come alive in us.

4) Saving our lives by losing our life for Christ's sake and for the gospel.

There are many mistaken ideas about what it means to take up the cross daily. A man said to his friend, "I have a bad temper, but I suppose that is my cross to bear." His friend replied, "No, that is not your cross. That's your wife's cross.

In life we are faced with many burdens, things like chronic debilitating disease, natural disasters, accidents, and foreclosure... Burdens are not crosses because we have no choice on that matter. I affirm that "the cross we carry is taking on somebody's burden willingly as the compassionate Jesus has willingly chosen to carry the cross for our sake."

ILLUSTRATION 12

This is a story about what it really means *to take up your cross daily.* One year after my retirement from the ordained ministry as a pastor, I was diagnosed with last-stage kidney disease. About that time I had already made a plan to go to San Diego for the winter months to enjoy the wonderful weather there. But my doctor made me cancel the trip to prepare me for kidney dialysis. Then, it became my routine to go to the dialysis center three times a week, five hours a day to be connected to a blood cleaning machine to keep me alive. Also, I was put on a long waiting list for a matching cadaver kidney.

One day, a close friend of mine from my previous charge (the church) sent an e-mail inquiring about my blood type. We shared the information that we had a same blood type. A week later she called me and said: "After my sincere prayers to God and my heart-felt conversations with my husband and children, I am compelled to give you my kidney." I could not comprehend what I was hearing at that moment. I had an overwhelming feeling to know that someone loves me enough to give me her vital organ so willingly. This was the first time in my life that I had ever experienced this kind of self-giving love from any person. Following her decision she met for seven-months with a kidney transplant team. During those waiting months, I communicated with her to make certain that she was sure of her decision. I told her that it warmed my heart just knowing her willingness to go through this for me. I also told her that she was free to change her mind... Her determination to give up her kidney for me was her way of bearing her cross for others voluntarily when she does not have to. In fact, she was participating in the ultimate divine nature of agape-love.

It has been less than two years since I received a kidney from Judi. The kidney transplant surgery was very successful. My quick recovery surprised my doctors and nurses on the transplant team. I thank God that Judi is doing very well too. We, both the donor and the receiver, affirm that God is the orchestrator who planned and carried out the whole process of this kidney transplant surgery. And there were many Christians who lifted us up through their intercessory prayers and personal encouragement.

A REFLECTION FROM MY KIDNEY DONOR

Upon my request, Judi sent me her reflection on "My Lessons Learned from the Kidney Donation." She writes: "Well, these are the immediate things I wanted to share with you and your readers:

1. The Lord drives out fear. Any time I felt fear I cried out to my Lord and he instantly soothed me. Eventually he took away all fear and even I was amazed at the calmness and confidence I felt. Psalm 34:4 became my prayer and Proverbs 3:27-28 became my courage.

2. God can use each of us differently if we let him. I always felt like I wasn't measuring up to some standard of faith. I would compare myself to other believers and their spiritual journeys. I learned that God made me to be me and I don't have to be like anyone else. All I have to do is go where he leads me.

3. The little world we live in is a mission field. So many people, including doctors, didn't understand why I was donating my kidney. They would look at me and then each other with looks that said I was foolish. Part of me dreaded telling people in anticipation of their response. I learned to take the opportunity to explain I am a Christian.

4. I learned there is still a lot of loving people in the world. My paths crossed with other donors who reached out to strengthen me, a total stranger.

5. I learned God is with us even when we can't or don't reach out to him. The doctors kept telling me to expect a lot of pain after the surgery. I fully planned on praying my way through it. However, after surgery I was too weak to even think straight. I laid and looked out the window and could only whisper "God..." Yet He never left me. I felt him surrounding me.

6. I learned what true love looks like. My husband's and my grown children's reactions to the news that I was donating was one of total love and support...though I learned later how frightened they were. They gave me nothing but love and support. I wondered if I would have reacted the same or in fear?

7. I learned that God puts each one of us in someone's path. We had to leave our former church as it was more secular than Bible based. This was very disturbing to us. However, it's what brought us back to the same church, which we left, and put me in Cho-Kim's path. I now thank God for the twists and turns that brought us together.

8. I learned that someone may look fine on the outside but be struggling on the inside. After the surgery, on my first outing, I was walking ridiculously slow to get to my car. A car had stopped and was waiting for me. Inside I was saying, "I'm walking as fast as I can." It made me realize that I may make similar judgments about people. Someone may look healthy but you don't know their story.

9. I realized that most of my memories of acute happiness came after a period of pain or struggle. This was no exception.

10. I learned that others prayers can carry you when you're too weak to carry yourself.

11. While in my stay at Boston Medical, I realized firsthand there is so much pain in this world and it comes in all different forms. I could hear moans and cries during the night. It drove home the point that we need to help someone if it's in our power to do so."

CHAPTER 9

BECOMING COMPASSIONATE DISCIPLES

THE ROLE OF THE CHURCH

How do you look upon any church? Do you see the Church as a means
or an end? Is it God's desire to bring as many people as possible into
the church, equating church membership with an end of God's purpose?
Or, do you understand the Church as God's people, called, recruited, and
equipped, as participants with God in his ministry of reconciliation and
compassion for the hurting world? A group discussing these questions
concluded that the danger of the Church as an end will cause the Church
to be committed only for quantity to get people into the church and equate
the Church with the kingdom of God. Once a person is "in" or a member,
they are safe and saved and can now consider themselves "Christians."

On the other hand, understanding the Church as a means will
cause the Church to be committed for quality, i.e., making compassionate disciples. Those who are called to follow Christ are concerned for
the people in the hurting world, seeing the local church as the means

272

for recruitment, equipping, and training Christians who may become participants of divine nature and the ministry of compassion.

Christ desires us to become actively growing disciples who encourage one another to grow toward wholeness by demonstrating holy (*set apart*) living for the glory of God; by establishing the loving union with God; by doing the compassionate love to those who are suffering in the hurting world. Christ asks us *to strive* to be disciples by entering the narrow gate (Luke 13:22-30).

Greg Ogden objectively analyzes the gap between the biblical standard and the reality of the church to explain why the church has failed in making disciples. (Ogden, *Transforming Discipleship*, pp. 24-38)

Ogden gives us seven gaps between the biblical mandates of the church and its current reality:

1. The Scripture picture the church has full of ministers according to 'the priesthood of all believer,' and yet the reality is that a majority of so-called Christians are mere names on a membership roll.

2. The Scriptures picture followers of Jesus as engaged in a disciplined way of life, and yet the reality is that a small percentage of believers invest in spiritual disciplines.

3. The Scripture picture discipleship as affecting all spheres of life, and yet the reality is that many believers have relegated faith to the personal, private realm.

4. The Scriptures picture the church as a counter-cultural force, and yet the reality is that we see isolated individuals (church members) whose lifestyle and values are not much different from those of the un-churched.

5. The Scriptures picture the church as an essential, chosen organism called the body of Christ, and yet the reality is that people view the church as an organized institution.

6. The Scriptures picture all believes as biblically informed people whose lives are founded on the Word of God—the revealed truth, and yet the reality is that most believers are biblically ignorant people whose lives are a syncretistic compromise.

7. The Scripture picture all believes as those who share God's grace and life in Christ with others, and yet the reality is that we shrink from personal witness in our words and deeds.

Bishop David J. Lawson approaches the same problem using an analogy of his old shoes. He shared in a workshop that he did not want to let go of his *old shoes* because they were *comfortable*. He said that same way "many of us want to belong to *old shoe congregations* because they have been good places to find our sustaining faith, comfort, friends, and in a deep and satisfying way, to be in touch with the presence of God. Just being with the congregation is important enough to bring us back each week.

He elaborates further by commenting:

> "The old shoe congregations have some major disadvantages. The very comfort that we value frequently blinds us to new challenges and certain shortcomings.

Some major disadvantages are:

1. Insensitivity or indifference to persons with different needs or problem by insulating ourselves from human suffering;

2. Our stewardship tends to become *just enough but not too much*;

3. We resist any new way of worshipping or doing mission and refuse to any change or to run risk, thus making comfortable old shoe congregations to become our *spiritual prison*;

4. We refuse to participate in the Christian-forward-movement according to what God is seeking from the church. The people, who are suffering from the *old shoe syndrome*, are influenced by *fortress mentality*.

5. We need more faithful disciples of Christ with imagination and courage to respond to God's nudging into *new shoes*."

Now it is our turn to close the gap between the biblical standard and the reality of the church so that the mission of the church is "making disciples" who are freely yielding increasing portions of our life to the influence of Christ's teaching and examples.

Each local church must "transform believers by helping them become both disciples (who know and follow Christ) as well as apostles (who are sent into the world to minister to the hurting people with the Good News). Therefore, the mission of the church is empowering the laity to become disciples who participate in God's mission of reconciling the world as apostles.

Our mission is to point out what the compassionate God is doing in the hurting world. Because the world is the arena of God's compassion, we, the disciples, are called to take the world seriously and to ask ourselves in what way we can witness meaningfully and relevantly to what God has done; what God is doing; What God will do.

We no longer want to remain as nominal and passive Christians, but 'disciple-making disciples" who help others to grow together toward maturity in Christ, demonstrating wholeness (holy living), Christ-likeness, fruit-bearing, and Christian unity.

As Greg Ogden put it so well, "a disciple is one who responds in faith and obedience to the glorious call of Jesus Christ. Being a disciple is a lifelong process of dying to [old] self, while allowing Jesus Christ to come live in us." (Ogden, *Disciples Essentials,* p.24)

As actively growing disciples we want "to know Jesus clearly; to love him deeply, to follow him nearly." Then, we must constantly engage in the practice of deep sustained reading of the Hebrew Bible (the Old Testament) as well as the New Testament, particularly the four Canonical Gospels. From study we realize that this Jesus is not dead, but he lives... Jesus can be known not only as a figure of the historical past, but as the living Lord of the Church and of the World. His living presence can be experienced in the community of his people, the body of Christ. This is the main reason why we go to church to participate in a lifelong process of discipleship in the Spirit.

Some regular practices can help us each day to stay connected to the source of life. The following "simple" practices are suggested.

- Read the Bible daily for inspiration and understanding by meditation.

- Set aside a regular time for two-way communication with God in prayer.

- Seek to know God's love and justice for this day.

- Pray without ceasing for needs in our community. Pray for the hurts and wounds of the world. Pray with news headlines as our guide.

276

- Worship and Bible study with a community of believers and your colleagues.

- Participate in a small group to be accountable as an actively growing disciple.

- Share your insights and reflections from meditations on the scripture and inspirational readings with the group.

- Witness to others by sharing your story and allow them to share theirs .

- Practice gratitude. Count blessings, not troubles.

CHURCH MEMBER'S SELF-EXAMINATION:

The following questions may wake up some *church members* who do not wish to become a disciple. They may want to pay attention to the warning: "How can we escape [a just penalty] if we neglect so great a salvation?" (Hebrew 2:2-3).

___ What kind of church would my church be if every person were just like me?

___ How many worship services would we have had this year if everyone had stayed   away from the church when I did?

___ How many times would evening programs, such as small groups, have been omitted if no one had gone except when I was there?

___ How many times would the Pastor's Bible study have met if they had met only when I attended?

___ How much Christian instruction would the children of our community receive if everyone showed as much interest in it as I do?

___ How many of my neighbors would have been invited to worship or welcomed into the church if everyone invited as many as I have?

___ How many prayers would have been offered for my pastor, the church staff, my neighbors, my church and those who are hurting?

___ How many words of faith would have been shared with others over a lunch or a cup of coffee?

___ How much money would my church have to be in ministry if every person gave what I give?

___ How many genuine Christians would my church have if every person were just like me?

THE CORE PROCESS OF FAITH DEVELOPMENT

THE FOUR PRIMARY DIMENSIONS OF THE CHURCH:

There are four dimension of the Church that came from the Jesus' public ministry as the incarnate Son of God:

--Community (*koinonia*)—the depth of caring relationship

--Proclamation (*kerygma*)—message of free grace and inclusive love

--Education (*didache*) and/or discipleship (*paideia*)—for the public or the private

--Service *(diakonia)*—incarnational ministry of compassion.

THE TWELVE MINISTRIES OF THE CHURCH:

1. *Reaching and Receiving and Returning*:

   The Ministry of Small Groups (the Cure of Souls)

The Ministry of Fellowship;
The Ministry of Worship (Praising God and Preaching
the Gospel

2. *Relating to God and others:*

The Ministry of Teaching and Training
The Ministry of Hospitality (Mutual affection)
The Ministry of Spiritual formation (Prayer)

3. *Equipping:*

The Ministry of Gift-oriented Discipleship
The Ministry of Leadership
The Ministry of Service

4. *Sending* and back to returning for evaluation

The Ministry of Compassion
The Ministry of World Mission
The Ministry of Witnessing (Need-based Evangelism).

PORTRAITS OF CHRISTIAN FAITH DEVELOPMENT

Let us imagine portraits of Christian faith development. A Christian
friend invites you to her church and you feel accepted by the gathered
people in the church. As a seeker you begin to hear the message (*kerygma*) of God's good news in Jesus Christ, the story of his life, death
and resurrection. The experience of the gospel gradually draws you into
the fellowship community (*koinonia*) where you may learn (*didache*)

how to share mutual affection. In the context of this new faith community, you learn (*didache*) of Christ through Bible study and you receive training (*paideia*) that is necessary for you to be nourished and grow in your faith. As all other Christians, you find your ultimate purpose in the incarnational ministry of servanthood (*diakonia*), modeled after that of Christ combining works of *piety and mercy*. As you carry on the privilege of discipleship, you learn and grow toward spiritual maturity, while sharing your faith, hope, and love to those in need by using your unique spiritual gifts.

THE APOSTOLIC CHURCH

Traditionally, the Church has been given four characteristics or marks that distinguish the Church of Jesus Christ from other religious organizations: it is *the One, Holy, Catholic (universal), and Apostolic Church*. The church's oneness, holiness, and catholicity must be apostolic if they are to be authentic.

Hans Kung expresses it well when he writes, "In our search for unity in diversity, catholicity in identity, holiness in sinfulness, "How far can the Church be one, holy, and catholic?" is expressed in the fourth attribute of the Church: an apostolic Church." (Hans Kung. *The Church*, p. 344)

Hopefully you will want to learn more about the theology of the church for your further study by reading *Paradigm Shift in the Church*, written by Christian A. Schwarz who is the author of *the Natural Church Development*. Schwarz challenges anyone who is deeply concern about the future church by asking theological questions: "What is the effect of the underlying paradigm on the discussion about baptism and communion, on church tradition, and on the question of church planting and ecumenism? He is waiting to engage your mind through his book

(*Paradigm Shift in the Church: How Natural Church Development Can Transform Theological Thinking,* St. Charles, IL: Church Smart Resources, 1999).

Avery Dulles evaluates five models of many traditions of the church: "the church as institution, the church as mystical communion, the church as sacrament, the church as herald, and the church as servant." His thesis is that the church must express the apostolic nature of the church precisely: "by looking to Jesus, the Servant Lord; by subjecting itself to the Word of the gospel; and by serving humankind in a hurting world." He concludes: "only by acknowledging the sovereignty of God's Word can the church avoid an uncritical and unhealthy complacency." (*Dulles, Models of the Church*, pp. 197-210).

Every church must strive to be *apostolic*, so that disciples are <u>sent into the world</u> and work with the goodness in the created order, even if the order has gone awry. There is no room for complacency, but a zealous, and yet a humble service.

As Carnegie S. Calian emphasizes that *"the priesthood of all believer* demands our willingness to be incarnate witnesses at work and play." He writes:

> "Unless the homemaker and the breadwinner are willing to expose themselves and their faith in some tangible way, there is little hope that the priesthood of all believers will become anything more than a paper theology. Mission is not simply a programmed and systematic enterprise carried on by the institutional church. Mission depends upon persons. Mission begins whenever and wherever individuals take it upon themselves to raise questions of life and death with their neighbors in the name of Jesus Christ. Frankly, this implies overcoming the gap that currently exists between private and public

existence. It happens when clergy invite laity to truly
serve with them as co-pastors." (Calian, *Today's Pastor
in Tomorrow's World*, p. 101)

We need to have a shift in paradigm—laity truly seeing themselves as the people (*laos*) of God and as ministers ordained in their
baptism to a life of witness, whatever their secular occupation may
be. The pastor-people ministry team carries out the ministry of the
church, which belongs to the whole people of God. Every believer,
as the people of God, is called into service (*diakonia*), to a diversity of duties and opportunities using the different gifts of the Spirit.
(Romans 12:6; 1 Peter 4:10, 11)

THE CHURCH AS THE PEOPLE OF GOD

In my doctoral paper I included *biblical and theological foundation
of the church*. (Cho-Kim, *A Family Systems Approach to the Small
Membership Church*, pp. 12-32) The following is its *brief summary* so
that we Christians understand "the church as the people of God."
    The term *ecclesia* means "a called out assembly or congregation."
The 'congregation' (assembly) in the desert' for Israel (Acts 7:38) makes
us understand that the church of Jesus Christ is dependent upon its continuity with the Israelites of the Old Testament (the Old Covenant).
    As Alston gives insight as to how the church fits into God's whole
scheme of the things:
    "In Christianity, God opened the [New] Covenant to the human-
kind without supplanting the Old Covenant with the Jews. The task of
the Jew is to witness to God's activity through the Old Covenant into
which the Jew entered by [physical] *birth*. The task of the Christian is

to 'go therefore and make disciples of all nations' and bring others into New Covenant by *adoption.*'" (Alston, The Church, p.22)

Therefore, the church must proclaim the mystery of the cross, i.e. on the cross God in Christ paid the painful price for the sin of humanity. In some mysterious but real way, Christ stood our stead, suffered the consequences of our sin, paid the wages that we owe, and became the instrument of our forgiveness. We must proclaim that 'God was in Christ reconciling the world to himself' (2 Corinthians 5:19).

Christians need to learn from Jewish people that the tie that binds God's people to their Lord binds them also to one another. The bond of Israel's nationhood was not ethnic but *religious.* It was the Covenant at Sinai that forged Israel into unique nationhood. It was tragic that those who once were the people of God have become 'no people' (Hosea 1:9) because of their rebellion. But by the grace of God in Christ, all people, both the Jews and the Gentiles have been made the people of God.

In Christ, the New Testament Church is the *new Israel,* one with the Old Testament saints in the spiritual ethnicity that defines the people of God in all ages (1 Peter 1:1; Ephesians 2:12). To be separate from Christ is to be outside the commonwealth of Israel and strangers to God's covenant. But Christ has broken down the middle wall of partition that preserved the distinctiveness of the circumcised (Israelites).

In conclusion, the church is 'a new nation under God', and the bonds that unite it are God-given. The quest for holiness for the New Israel is both individual and corporate. Not only must each Christian pursue holiness (wholeness), the church must grow together in the image of Christ. The overflowing love and grace of God radically renew the assembly of the New Covenant. The church that has been purchased with Christ's blood cannot ask, "Who is my neighbor?" with a view of limiting the circle of those to whom the ministry of compassion must be shown.

The church is a gathered people. "Where two or three are gathered in my name," said Jesus, "there am I in the midst of them" (Matthew 18:20). The church, by the virtue of its being the sign of Christ, is not primarily an institutional reality; it is a sacramental reality--worshipping the transcendent glory of God.

Most people have mixed feelings about our experiences in local congregations and institutional aspects of the church. Hunter and Johnson give an affirmative and encouraging statement concerning the church:

> "The Lord of the church does not leave us to our own devices. Still he visits his people as that disturbing and beckoning presence. His way of death and resurrection still stands as the paradigm for our way of thinking and imagining, as well as for our way of doing and living. We are free to think new thoughts and search for new ways of service in the church, to strike out on new and uncertain journeys. Christ still appears between us on the journey. People can affect structures. Where two or three are gathered in his name, there is still the power of his presence." (*The human Church in the Presence of Christ*, p.13)

CHURCH AS THE BODY OF CHRIST

Many images are used for the church in the New Testament. It is pictured as a bride, a flock, a vine, a field, and a temple. But, St. Paul emphasized that the church is the body of Christ. Evidently he is not simply saying that the church is a Christian corporation. Every image for the church is intimately related to Christ. If the church is a bride, Christ is the bridegroom; if the church is a flock, Christ is the shepherd;

284

if the church is a temple, Christ is the builder; if the church is the branch, Christ is the vine.

THE NATURAL CHURCH DEVELOPMENT

Christian A. Schwarz has written a book called, *Natural Church Development*, which revolutionizes the way we think about the church and its ministry. (Schwarz, Natural Church Development, pp. 16-48) Following is the summary of the content.

He defines the natural church development as "releasing [not making] the *growth automatisms* (*all-by-itself* principle) by which God himself builds his church. In the Jesus' parable we find the mysterious description of the earth producing fruit *all by itself* (Mark 4:26-29). 'The earth produces crops by itself: first the blade, then the head, and then the mature grain in the head...The farmers sow and harvest, but they cannot bring forth the fruit.'"

The church as the body of Christ emphasizes each body part's interdependent relationships to one another and their relationships to Christ, the head of the body.

The image of Jesus' washing his disciples' feet after the Last Supper reminds us of the communion of the saints and the disciple's serving one another.

The church as the body of Christ is also the fellowship of the Holy Spirit. Apart from the Spirit, the church can be only an institutional sepulcher, organizing the bones of dead humans. The Spirit is the life source for the mission of the church. The body functions according to the God's biotic (life) principles: interdependence, multiplication, energy transformation, multi-usage, symbiosis, and functionality. All parts equipped with different spiritual gifts function as a balanced, harmonious unity for being the church and doing the ministries of the church.

Christian A. Schwarz attempts to link the discussion between church development and systematic theology by presenting the bipolar model of the church-- the static pole on the right and the dynamic pole on the left. Following is the summary. (Natural Church Development, pp. 82-102)

The static pole in on the right stimulates the dynamic pole in on the left, which in turn *produces* the static pole. For instance, in the body of Christ as a bipolar model, dynamic pole is *organism* and static pole is *organization*. The static pole *stimulates* the dynamic pole and in turn it *produces* the static pole, having a circulating reciprocal relationship. God helps us keep the circulation going, thus empowering the process of the *growth automatisms* ("all-by-itself" principle).

The problem is that in most churches the circulation cycle has broken down, resulting in dangers to the far right or to the far left. The danger to the right is monistic thinking that treats both poles as one, while the danger to the left is dualistic thinking that disconnects them. A monistic thinking that leads easily to a technocratic paradigm, while a dualistic thinking that leads easily to an anti-institutional spiritualism.

The static pole consists of doctrine, biblical canon, ethics, sacraments, tradition, cooperation, offices, order, and proclamation (preaching).

The dynamic pole consists of faith, word of God, love, fellowship, change, multiplication, spiritual gifts, incarnational ministry of compassion, social justice, and evangelical outreach.

In conclusion,

- The church emphasizes the Lordship of Christ who is the common ground for the oneness of the church.

- The bipolar church concept: both *organism* (the left dynamic pole) and *organization* (the right static pole). They are interrelated and interacting: The dynamic pole (organic) produces the static pole (technical), which stimulates the dynamic pole.

- We see bipolar thinking of the church in the Bible: "living stone" (1 Peter 2:5); "growth of temple" (Ephesians 2:21). "Living" is dynamic and organic, while "stone" is static and technical. "Growth" is organic and dynamic, while "temple" is static and technical.

- The life source of an organism is six biotic principles: interdependence, multiplication, energy transformation, multi-usage, symbiosis, and functionality.

- The church needs the spiritual gifts of all Christians—the clergy and the laity;

- Natural Church Development insists that healthy churches must have a high level of eight essential qualities, each containing both the static pole (such as *ministry* and *structure*) and the dynamic pole (such as *passionate* and *inspiring*). They are:

Empowering leadership; *Gift-oriented* ministry; *Passionate* spirituality; *Functional* structures; *Inspiring* worship service; *Holistic* small groups; *Need-oriented* evangelism; *Loving* relationships.

Today, as we live in this post-modern era, all Christians must grow in the Spirit so that "we may become participants of the divine nature" and we may participate in the God's mission of completing the divine act of redemption of all God's creation. And with confidence of children of God, we pray the Lord's Prayer without ceasing:

"Our Father in heaven, hallowed be your name, your kingdom come, your will be done, on earth as in heaven. Give us today our daily bread. Forgive us our sins as we forgive those who sin against us. Save us from the time of trial, and deliver us from evil. For the kingdom, the power, and the glory are yours now and forever. Amen."

IMITATION IS THE KEY TO DISCIPLESHIP

JESUS' EXAMPLE OF SERVING ONE ANOTHER

When Jesus knew that the time had come to leave this world to go to the Father, he taught his disciples how to serve one another by washing his disciples' feet. The Gospel of John describes the scene in detail so that we can follow his example:

> "He got up from the table, took off his outer robe, and tied a towel around himself. Then he poured water into a basin and began to wash his disciples' feet and to wipe them with the towel that was tied around him…After he had washed their feet and had put on his robe and had returned to the table, he said to them, "Do you know what I have done to you? You call me Teacher and Lord—and you are right, for that is what I am. So if I, your Lord and Teacher, have washed your feet, you also ought to wash one another's feet. For I have set you an *example that* you also should do as I have done to you. Very truly, I tell you, servants are not greater than their master, nor are messengers greater than the one who sent them. If

you know these things, you are blessed if you do them."
(John13: 3-17).

We serve one another by using our whole body-- the heart, the
head, and the hand.

1. **<u>The heart matters:</u>**

Servants don't fill up their time with other pursuits that
could limit their availability.
Servants are always on the lookout for ways to help
others with compassion.
Servants don't make excuses, procrastinate or wait for
better circumstances.
Whatever they do, servants do it with their whole heart.
Servants don't leave a job undone, and they don't quit
when they get discouraged.
Servants don't promote or call attention to themselves.

2. **<u>The head matters:</u>**

Servants focus on others, not on themselves.
Servants understand they are the stewards of God's cre-
ation and all things in it.
Servants don't criticize, compare or compete with other
servants.
Servants put God's will before ours; "Your will be done."
Servants serve willingly for the glory of God.
According to Rick Warren's book, "The Purpose Driven Life,"
we are *shaped* for serving God (pp. 227-8). The eleven servant

characteristics mentioned <u>above</u> are relating to the heart and the head. To the list I would add three more servant characteristics using the *hand*.

3. **<u>The hand matters:</u>**

> Servants use hands to anoint/bless and to prepare and serve meals.
> Servants touch to mend and heal (with a surgeon's knife), not to hurt.
> Servants use hands to give generously and to hold other's hands to show support and solidarity.

Albert Schweitzer once told his listeners his words of wisdom: "I know not what your destiny will be, but one thing I know is this: 'The only ones among you who will be truly happy are those who have sought and found how to serve.'"

"HOW WELL DO I KNOW JESUS?"

If we claim to be Christians and we want to follow this Jesus of Nazareth by imitation, then we must ask, "How well do I know Jesus?" We know Jesus by reading the Scripture. His identity is forever bound up with God's people of ancient Israel. It is highly significant that his first followers acclaimed Jesus as the Christ: the Messiah of Israel promised by the Scripture, by which they mean Israel's sacred writings: the law, the prophets and the Psalms (see Luke 24:44; 1 Corinthians 15:3-5). Do you love him enough to follow him?

The late Eugene H. Peterson, best known for *the Message,* his 12-year project of translating the Bible into *contemporary language*, insisted:

"Scripture is about God, not about us. God has revealed God's self to us in scripture so that we might know and respond to God, understand where we are in God's creation, what it mean to be called into a life of God's salvation.

When we read scripture, we are listening to God revealing God the Father, the Son and the Holy Spirit. We do, in fact, find ourselves included. We are addressed, we are invited, we are commanded, we are promised, and we are immersed in a world where God rules and saves and blesses—us. But there are no secrets here on how we can rule and save and bless. We are not the subject and we do not supply the action.

So, what is the way in regard to the Scripture? How do we receive the Word of God? Here's how: by listening and responding and submitting. "Let it be to me according to your Word" is the way I read this text. Our reading of this text is a personal listening to a personal God. We listen to God speak our lives into being. We listen to the story that provides a narrative of shape and meaning to a life of following Jesus in the conditions of the world. It is a prayerful, relational, obedient listening." (Peterson, *Contemplative Christian: Transparent Live,* p.25)

This way of reading the Scripture results in our *becoming less* and Jesus *becoming more.* This is the way to develop a contemplative life, a life in which Jesus' way and the Jesus' truth are congruent.

Peterson's concluding remark was:

> "We cannot participate in God's work when we insist on doing it in our own way. We cannot participate in building God's kingdom when we use the devil's tools and nails. Christ is the way as well as the truth and the life. When we don't do it his way, we mess up the truth and we miss out on the life. Only when we live Jesus' truth in Jesus' way do we get Jesus' life. Such congruence is not easily achieved. It arises from long, patient work. In the deepest sense, however, it is not our work at all, but God's work in us." (Ibid. p.26)

BEING IMITATORS

As St. Paul defines this life of discipleship, "I want to know Christ and the power of his resurrection and share his sufferings by becoming like him in his death, if somehow I may attain the resurrection from the death" (Philippians 3:10).

Also, he gives a loving but firm command to be imitators (1 Corinthians 4:16) so that "we lead a life worthy of God, who calls you into his own kingdom and glory" (1 Thessalonians 2:12).

This idea that imitation is the key to the discipleship begs a few questions.

First, Christ does not call us to literal imitation. It would be presumptuous to want to imitate him literally. He calls for personal discipleship; each of us has his or her own path to follow.

Second, Who are you imitating? From whom are you learning what it means to live as a disciple in this messed-up world? Is it your Spirit-filled spouse or a mature Christian friend or a faith-filled parent or a pastor? In Philippians 3:17,

292

St. Paul boldly says, "Join in imitating me."

Third, who is imitating you? Your children? But your sphere of influence extends beyond the home. Who in your life knows that you are a Christian and, who is influenced by your words, your actions, and your attitude? Are you living as a contemplative Christian? Are you congruent? Are you transparent? Who is learning from you? That's a scary one to wrestle with. Isn't it?

The bottom line is that if there is no one for you to follow, then there is a void of influence in your life that must be filled. Likewise, if there is something going on that leaves you feeling completely unworthy of having any kind of following, that's an issue that needs to be addressed with some wise and mature spiritual leaders.

When we imitate the faith and the life of a person like St. Paul or St. Peter or St. Apollo or our Christian brothers and sisters around us, the end result is not going to be a bunch of little Christian clones, but a community of believers who are becoming healthy disciples of Jesus Christ.

In his incarnation and earthly ministry, Jesus of Nazareth took on the role of our Savior by taking our sin as his own on the cross and defeating the power of death in his resurrection. Also, in his living and breathing, in his walking and talking and eating, in his healing and loving and perfect commandment-keeping, he became our Master Mentor and Model. The God-man Jesus Christ demonstrated for the world what it means to be fully human as well as to be right with God the Father. He was filled with the Holy Spirit and completely in step with the rhythms and patterns of life in our created world. We also have embarked on a lifelong journey of being "conformed to the image of his Son (Romans 8:29). That is, we will slowly but surely start thinking like him, talking like him, loving like him, forgiving like him, and doing things like him. Someday, we will resemble Jesus Christ. Knowing this, let's embrace the instruction found in 3 John: "Dear friend, do not imitate what is evil but what is good" (v.11).

THEOLOGY OF COMPASSION

Christians grow toward spiritual maturity as the children of God by following the incarnate, crucified, resurrected Christ who is the way to God the Father. Our life's journey toward spiritual maturity begins with our faith in the triune God who reveals himself in three different ways.

> "Experiencing God in three different ways links together in unity the non-negotiable *persona* (*forms*) in the Christian understanding of One God in three Persons known as God the Father, the Son and the Holy Spirit:

> • The transcendent God exists beyond the world as its source of the Creator—God the Father who is above us;

> • The human face of God revealed in the person of Jesus Christ, the Redeemer—God the Son who is among us;

> • The immanent God who is present and active throughout the world as the Sustainer—God the Spirit who is within us.

> This means that Jesus of Nazareth was a mortal person, *within* natural conditions and a historical time and place. According to the Prologue of the Gospel of John (1:1-18) the Word (*logos*)—the God's own loving design for humanity—actually became flesh and dwelt among us. For that reason, Christians believe all that has been foretold in the Old Testament concerning the coming of the Messiah was fulfilled in Jesus Christ." (Cho-Kim, *God of Active Verbs*, pp. ix-x)

We began our spiritual journey as children of God by believing in Jesus as the long-awaited Messiah and we were given "power to become [maturing] children of God, who were born, not of blood or of the will of the flesh or of the will of man but of God" (John 1:12, 13).

The Holy Spirit nurtures us to establish our faith by deepening our human "response-ability" (responsibility) to God's loving actions in our lives (Please reflect on the Appendix I). Therefore, we can define faith as human responses to the loving action of the compassionate God. For example, "God blesses you, so that you are enabled to bless others; God forgives your sins, so that you are enabled to forgive those who sin against you; God accepts you unconditionally, so that you are enabled to accept others unconditionally…"

Andrew Purves proclaims that God's compassion helps us to understand the internal relations within the triune God:

> "It is vital to the integrity and rationality of Christian faith that we assert that God was fully and personally present in human history in all aspects of the life and death of Jesus of Nazareth. The suffering and death of Jesus mean then that God (the Father and the Creator) has taken suffering and death into God's own experience. If this were not the case, the passion was a fraud, a superficial event in which God was not really involved but remained an unaffected spectator. But because the Christ event was a God event, it is now a part of the history of God, a part of God's Trinitarian life. In other words, the incarnation and the cross force us to think about the internal relations within God: that is, about the doctrine of the Trinity…This liberates the concept of God from speculative theism and leads to a revolution

in the concept of God...God will be compassionate in
the future as God has been compassionate in the past."
(Purves, *The Search for Compassion*, pp. 74-77)

Compassion (the opposite of apathy) is used as a verb in the
Gospels; it is not mercy, empathy, sympathy, or pity. The spirituality of
compassion then becomes *a process* of our responding to the "works of
mercy" attributed to the triune God as --the Creator, the Redeemer, and
the Sustainer. In the Hebrew Bible (the Old Testament) we find fourteen
works of mercy: feeding, clothing, sheltering, setting people free, giving
drink, visiting, burying, educating, counseling, admonishing, bearing
wrongs, forgiving, comforting, and praying. In the New Testament we
can identify the six corporate works of mercy taught by Jesus, explicitly
showing that God is to be loved through the relief of the pain and suffering of others who are hungry, thirsty, a stranger, naked, sick, and in
prison (Matthew 25:34-46).

JESUS' MINISTRY OF COMPASSION

Jesus' compassion could not be separated from his ministry. His "having compassion" always moved him to works of mercy: healing, teaching, feeding, and raising the dead. The suffering people moved him to
perform compassionate actions, because he felt their deep pain and sorrow with all his intimate sensibilities. In him all suffering was felt with
an intense sensitivity.

The verb "to have compassion"—*splanchzomai* in the Greek New
Testament-- means a *gut-wrenching* experience. It is used nine times in
reference to Jesus in the Gospels:

Healing of the two blind men (Matthew 20:29-34);
Exorcising demons (Mark 1:25; 9:25, Matthew 15:22-28);

296

Healing of the lepers (Mark 1:40-45);

The healing of the epileptic youth (Mark 9:14-29);

Teaching the crowd (Mark 6:34);

Raising the dead (Luke 7:11-17);

Feeding the hungry (Matthew 14:14-21; Mark 8:1-10).

Jesus also used compassion as a verb in three parables: Matthew 18:23-35, the *parable of the unforgiving debtor;* Luke 15:11-32, the *parable of the prodigal son*; Luke 10:30-37, the *parable of the Good Samaritan* to indicate the quality of God's concern for the hurting world. The *parable of the Good Samaritan* is presented at the end this book.

Jesus uses his parables as teaching tools to enlighten his hearers (including us) concerning deep theological insights of Christ's ministry of compassion. For instance, the above-mentioned parables help us to understand God's compassion for pleading sinners, the unconditional acceptance of the prodigal son(s) and his compassionate ministry toward a just-love society. Jesus taught with many parables.

THE PARABLE OF THE UNFORGIVING DEBTOR (MATTHEW 18:23-35, THE MESSAGE)

Peter asked Jesus, "Master, how many times do I forgive a brother or sister who hurts me? Seven?" Jesus replied, "Seven! Hardly. Try seventy times seven." Jesus answered with following story:

"The kingdom of God is like a king who decided to square accounts with his servants. As he got under way, one servant was brought before him who had run up a debt of a hundred thousand dollars. He couldn't pay up, so the king ordered the man, along with his wife, children, and goods, to be auctioned off at the slave market."

"The poor wretch threw himself at the king's feet and begged, 'Give me a chance and I'll pay it all back.' Touched by his plea, the king let him off, erasing the debt.

"The servant was no sooner out of the room when he came upon one of his fellow servants who owed him ten dollars. He seized him by the throat and demanded, 'Pay up. Now!'

"The poor wretched man threw himself down and begged, 'Give me a chance and I'll pay it all back.' But he wouldn't do it. He had him arrested and put in jail until the debt was paid. When the other servants saw this going on, they were outraged and brought a detailed report to the king.

"The king summoned the man and said, 'You evil servant! I forgave your entire debt when you begged me for mercy. Shouldn't you be compelled to be merciful to your fellow servant who asked you for mercy?'

The king was furious and put the screws to the man until he paid back his entire debt. And that's exactly what my Father in heaven is going to do to each one of you who doesn't forgive unconditionally anyone who asks for mercy."

The lesson of the Parable is:

The king expected the servant to extend the compassion that had shown to him. God expects the forgiven sinner to do the same.

THE PARABLE OF THE PRODIGAL SON
(LUKE 15:11-32, THE MESSAGE)

"There was once a man who had two sons. The younger said to his father, 'Father, I want right now what's coming to me when you pass away.'

"So the father divided the property between them. It wasn't long before the younger son packed his bags and left for a distant country. There, undisciplined and dissipated, he wasted everything he had. After he had gone through all his money, there was a bad famine all through that country and he began to hurt. He signed on with a citizen there who assigned him to his fields to slop the pigs. He was so hungry he would have eaten the corncobs in the pig slop, but no one would give him any.

"That brought him to his senses (being awaken from his spiritual amnesia). He said [to himself], 'All those farmhands working for my father sit down to three meals a day, and here I am starving to death. I'm going back to my father. I'll say to him, Father I've sinned against God, I've sinned before you: I don't deserve to be called your son. Take me on as a hired hand.' He got right up and went home to his father.

When he was still a long way off, his father saw him. His heart pounding, he ran out, embraced him, and kissed him. The son started his speech: Father, I've sinned against God, I've sinned before you; I don't deserve to be called your son ever again. 'But the father wasn't listening. He was calling to the servants, "Quick. Bring a clean set of clothes and dress him. Put the family ring on his finger and sandals on his feet.

Then get a grain-fed heifer and roast it. We're going to feast! We're going to have a party! My son is here—given up for dead and now alive! Given up for lost and now found!" And they began to have a wonderful time.

"All this time his old son was out in the field. When the day's work was done he came toward home. As he approached the house, he heard the music and dancing. Calling over to one of the servants, he asked what was going on. He told him, 'Your brother came home.' Your father has ordered a feast—a barbecued beef! Because he has come home safe and sound."

"The older brother stalked off in an angry sulk and refused to join in. His father came out and tried to talk to him, but he wouldn't listen. The son said, 'Look! How many years I've stayed here serving you, never giving you one moment of grief, but have you ever thrown a party for me and my friends? Then this son of yours who has thrown away your money on whores, shows up and you go all out with a feast?'"

"His father said, 'Son, you don't understand. You're with me all the time, and everything that is mine is yours—but this is a wonderful occasion, and we had to celebrate. This brother of yours was dead, and he's alive! He was lost, and he's found!'"

The important point of the parable is God's forgiving love toward a sinner who repents. The father celebrates the return of the young son by fully accepting him as his son. The father could have refused to grant the request of the younger son. But he let him go, though it broke his heart. The elder brother refused to come in and participate in the festivities. Leaving the story unfinished, Jesus indicated that the door stood wide open. Jesus portrayed the love of the father for his two sons in order to make abundantly clear that God's love is unconditional.

THE JESUS' PARABLE OF THE GOOD SAMARITAN (LUKE 10:25-37)

The parable is fully presented at the end of this book.

This *parable of the good Samaritan* is the best illustration of our becoming participants in the Christ's ministry of compassion, motivated and propelled by agape-love. As the Samaritan (despised by the Jews) ministered to the wounded person (possibly a Jewish man), we, as Christians, are called upon to help **all** who are suffering as neighbors, loving them as we love ourselves.

THE COMPASSIONATE GOD, REVEALED BY JESUS

We can conclude that the God, whom we have seen to be a suffering and compassionate God in dealings with Israel people, is the God now fully and uniquely revealed in Jesus, the Lamb of God. As we have seen,

Jesus was a compassionate person. Compassion marked his ministry in a unique way. The compassion of Jesus tells us something about God and about how God deals with us in our sufferings today.

Also, he challenges the disciples to be compassionate by saying "go and do likewise" (Luke 10:37).

The greatest obstacle to the Christian mission in the [post]-modern era is our lack of love for the crucified Christ and our lack of proper balance between humility and humanity:

> 'There is a great need for a healthy fusion of humility and humanity in our reliance on the power of the Holy Spirit. We need the *humility* to let God be God, acknowledging that God alone can give sight to the blind and life to the dead, and the *humanity* to be ourselves as God has made us, not suppressing our true-self, but exercising our God-given gifts and offering ourselves to God as instruments of peace, compassion, and righteousness in God's hands...The verbal witness of the church must be extended by the witness of the life of the believing community." (Cho-Kim, *A Family System's Approach,* p.32)

PETER'S TRANSFORMATION

Peter's life may best illustrate how crisis throws everything out of kilter. He had left family, home, and business to follow Jesus (Mark 1:16-18; 10:28). In front of Jesus and all his friends, he came with assurance to confess Jesus to be the expected Messiah (Mark 8:29). He witnessed that Jesus, the Nazarene, was indeed a prophet mighty in deed and word in the sight of God and all the people. So certain had he and his friends been of who Jesus was and they were forewarned what Jesus was to do in Jerusalem. And yet they could not comprehend those warnings Jesus foretold about pending disaster.

The arrest of Jesus placed in jeopardy all of Peter's beliefs about what God was doing in Jesus. Disappointed, confused, and maybe even feelings of failure and death, Peter abandoned his Master and then denied any knowledge of Jesus (Mark 14:66-72). His tears reflected his brokenness. But, later Peter reemerged after encountering the risen Lord by the Sea of Tiberius (or the Sea of Galilee) as a different Peter from the man for whom the cock had crowed. When the guilt-ridden Peter met the risen Christ, he was given a second chance and commissioned to be an Apostle by the risen Christ. (John 21:15-19) Peter was a failed Disciple as Judas, but he became a compassionate Apostle, because he encountered the risen Lord.

On the day of Pentecost, one hundred twenty followers of Jesus were gathered at the Upper Room to pray as instructed by the risen Christ before his ascension. And all of them experienced the coming of the Holy Spirit and they were filled with the power of the Holy Spirit. When the Spirit-filled Peter preached in Aramaic language to the Jewish people who came from many different countries to celebrate the Pentecost festival, they heard his powerful sermon in their own languages. On that day about three thousand persons became converted believers of the Way (Acts 2:14- 42).

<u>PETER'S TEACHING ON CHRISTIAN DISCIPLESHIP</u>

The Spirit-filled Apostle Peter admonishes future disciples by writing the most inspirational Word of God on Christian discipleship:

"His divine power has given us everything needed for
life and godliness, through the knowledge of him who

called us by his own glory and goodness. Thus he has given us, through these things, his precious and very great promises, so that through them you may escape from the corruption that is in the world because of lust, and you may *become participants of the divine nature.* For this reason, you must make every effort to *support* your faith with goodness, and goodness with knowledge, and knowledge with self-control, and self-control with endurance, and endurance with godliness, and godliness with mutual affection, and mutual affection with love.

If these things are yours and are increasing among you, they keep you from being ineffective and unfruitful in the knowledge of our Lord Jesus Christ. For anyone who lacks these things is *nearsighted* and *blind,* and is *forgetful* of the cleansing of past sins. Therefore, brothers and sisters, be all the more eager to *confirm* your **call** and **election,** for if you do this, you will never *stumble.* For in this way, an entry into the eternal kingdom of our Lord and Savior Jesus Christ will be richly *provided* for you." (2 Peter 1:3-11)

The above text may be summarized as follows:

1. The Spirit forms disciples. Eight essential qualities are established in each disciple's life in the Spirit and he or she becomes more and more participant in the divine nature and the ministry of compassion.

2. When we have these essential qualities we will discern what's right and wrong.

3. When these essential qualities are established in us, the way to the eternal kingdom is wide open to us.

4. When we lack these qualities, we are *nearsighted* and *blind*, and are *forgetful* of the cleansing of past sins. These spiritual symptoms of **myopia**, **lack of vision**, and **amnesia** of shriveled souls causes disciples to stumble and make them ineffective and fruitless. The above-mentioned manifestation of spiritual symptoms must be treated with reaffirmation of each believer's calling and election.

5. We are not carrying out the divine ministry of compassion ourselves! I affirm that becoming the healthy disciples with the eight essential qualities, we *are established* in the Spirit so that we may *participate* in Christ's ongoing ministry of compassion for the hurting world today.

BECOMING PARTICIPANTS OF THE DIVINE NATURE

We may have some difficulty in understanding the concept of our *becoming participants in the divine nature* of compassion. It is clear that I am *not* in control in Christ's ministry of compassion and I am not doing it my way! I am simply participating in it as though I am *riding a tandem bike with Christ* and I am *in the back helping him with pedal.* I hope you come to the same understanding as you enjoy the Tim Hansel's poem, called "the road of life," from *Holy Sweat*:

At first, I saw God as my observer, my judge,
Keeping track of the things I did wrong,

So as to know whether I merited heaven or hell when I die.
He was out there sort of like a president.
I recognized His picture when I saw it, but I really didn't know Him.
But later on when I met Christ,
It seemed as though life were rather like a bike ride.
But it s a *tandem bike*,
And I noticed that Christ was in the back helping me pedal.
I don't know just when it was that He suggested we change places,
But life has not been the same since.
When I had control, I knew the way. It was rather boring,
But predictable… it was the shortest distance between two points.
But when He took the lead, He knew delightful long cuts,
Up mountains, and through rocky places at breakneck speeds—
All I could do was to hang on!
Even though it looked like madness, He said, "Pedal!"
I worried and was anxious and asked,
"Where are you taking me?"
He laughed and didn't answer, and I started to learn to trust.
I forgot my boring life and entered into the adventure.
And when I'd say, "I'm scared," he'd lean back and touch my hand.
He took me to people with gifts that I needed,
Gifts of healing, acceptance, and joy.
They gave me gifts to take on my journey, my Lord's and mine.
And we were off again.
He said, "Give the gifts away. They're extra baggage.
Too much weight."
So I did, to the people we met.
And I found that in giving I received.
And still our burden was light.
I did not trust Him, at first, in control of my life.

I thought He'd wreck it; but He knows bike secrets.
Knows how to make it bend to take sharp corners.
Knows how to jump to clear high rocks.
Knows how to fly to shorten scary passages.
And I am learning to shut up and pedal
In the strangest places.
And I'm beginning to enjoy the view
And the cool breeze on my face
With my delightful constant companion, Jesus Christ.
And when I'm sure I just can't do any more,
He just smiles and says… "Pedal!"

EIGHT ESSENTIAL QUALITIES OF COMPASSIONATE DISCIPLES

In 2 Peter 1:4b-7 the Apostle Peter admonishes disciples that we need to establish **eight essential qualities** so that we my become participants in the divine nature:

> "You [we] may become participants of the divine nature. For this reason, you [we] must make every effort to support faith with goodness, and goodness with knowledge, and knowledge with self-control, and self-control with endurance [enduring hope], and endurance with godliness, and godliness with mutual affection, and mutual affection with love" (2 Peter 1:4b-7).

In short, faith, goodness, knowledge, self-control, endurance, godliness, mutual affection, and agape-love are eight essential qualities of actively growing disciples. These essential qualities are inter-connected as the helix (spiral) way, and linking faith (as the *root*) and love (as the *roof*).

These eight essential qualities include the three essential life sources--faith, hope, and love--discussed in Chapter 8.

1. <u>FAITH SUPPORTED WITH GOODNESS</u>

The Inter Varsity Christian Fellowship by expanding the Fuller Statement of Faith adopted a new faith statement as recently as 2000. (J.I. Packer and Thomas C. Oden, *One Faith,* pp.21-22)

<u>WE BELIEVE IN:</u>

    a. The only true God, the almighty Creator of all things, existing eternally in three   persons—Father, Son, and Holy Spirit—full of love and glory.

    b. The unique divine inspiration, entire trustworthiness and authority of the Bible.

    c. The value and dignity of all people; created in God's image to live in love and holiness, but alienated from God and each other because of our sin and guilt, and justly subjected to God's wrath.

    d. Jesus Christ, fully human and fully divine, who lived as a perfect example, who assumed the judgment due sinners by dying in our place, and who was bodily raised from the dead and ascended as Savior and Lord.

e. Justification by God's grace to all who repent and put their faith in Jesus Christ alone for salvation.

f. The indwelling presence and transforming power of the Holy Spirit, who gives to all believers a new life and a new calling to obedient service.

g. The unity of all believes in Jesus Christ, manifest in worshiping and witnessing churches making disciples throughout the world.

h. The victorious reign and future personal return of Jesus Christ, who will judge all people with justice and mercy, giving over the unrepentant to eternal condemnation but receiving the redeemed into eternal life.

NOW, let us consider what happens when we *believe* Jesus Christ as our Lord and Savior:

- We are spiritually "born from above" (John 3:3);

- We are given the power to become children of God (John 1:12);

- Through the basic faith in God's grace, not the result of works, we have been saved for good works, which God prepared beforehand to be our way of life (Ephesians 2:8-10);

- We have new life in Christ (Revelation 3:20, Colossians 1:27);

- We are forgiven sinners (Colossians 1:14);

- We receive the promise of eternal life (John 5:24);

- We begin the wonderful spiritual journey of becoming the image of Christ, for which God created us to become (2 Corinthians 5:17, 1 Thessalonians 5:18).

A national study of Protestant Congregations by Peter L. Benson and Carolyn H, Elkin has come up with eight core dimensions to determine *mature faith*:

- Trusts in God's saving grace and believes firmly in the humanity and divinity of Jesus;

- Experiences a sense of personal well-being, security, and peace;

- Integrates faith and life, seeing work, family, social relationships, and political choices as part of one's religious life;

- Seeks spiritual growth through study, reflection, prayer, and discussion with others;

- Seeks to be part of community of believers in which people give witness to their faith and support and nourish one another; responsibility for the welfare of others;

- Advocates social and global change to bring about greater social justice;

- Serves humanity, consistently and passionately, through compassionate acts of love and justice.

- The development of faith must be supported with goodness (good works).

THE TENSION BETWEEN GRACE AND WORKS OR FAITH AND LOVE

The Apostle James, the brother of Jesus, has written in the Book of James that faith without work is dead:

> "Religion that is pure and undefiled before God, the Father, is this: to care for orphans and widows in their distress and to keep oneself unstained by the world." (James 1:27);

> "…If a brother or sister is naked and lacks daily food, and one of you says to them, 'Go in peace; keep warm and eat your fill', and yet you do not supply their bodily needs, what is the good of that? So faith by itself, if it has no works, is dead." (James 2:14-17)

There is dynamic tension between grace and works or faith and love:

FAITH (JUSTIFICATION)	and	WORKS (SANCTIFICATION)
Salvation by faith alone	and	Salvation by Holy living
Foundation	and	Goal
Beginning of faith	and	Fullness of faith
Forgiveness of sin	and	Power of love
Pardon (relative change)	and	New birth (real change)
What God does for us	and	What God does in us
Faith is the means	and	Love is the end
Ephesians 2:8-9 (Paul)	and	James 2:14, 17 (James)
Reformed theology	and	Roman Catholic Theology

The Wesleyan theology considers the salvation as <u>both</u> the Paul's "faith alone" <u>and</u> the James' "holy living." We may consider it as two sides of the same coin called salvation.

It is easy to view the Christian life simply as a matter of forgiveness of sin, on one side, or of cheap triumphalism—victory without sacrifice—on

310

the other. The gospel message is one of both death and life, sacrifice and victory, both weakness and power. Freedom from guilt is joined to empowerment for holy living. Therefore, faith must be supported with goodness. Please refer to Chapter 8 for further insight.

2. <u>GOODNESS SUPPORTED WITH KNOWLEDGE</u>

We believe in the indwelling presence and resurrection power of the Holy Spirit, who gives to believer's spiritual gifts to equip them for obedient service of offering Christ to the world. The spiritual gifts are divine, supernatural abilities to be used as special tools for ministries according to each believer's calling. They are specifically Christian in origin, and are unique endowments from the Holy Spirit, to be shared within the Body of Christ for the servant ministry of compassion in the church and the world. A process of discovering, nurturing, and applying the varied gifts of Spirit is a way of good living as effective and fruitful disciples.

The Holy Spirit sovereignty bestows and distributes the spiritual gifts within the Church. The gift of the Spirit is distributed to all believers (1 Corinthians 12:29-30). Individual members of the church receive gift of the Spirit according to the purpose of ministry and the building of the Church. Sample lists of some of the gifts are listed in Romans 12:6-8 and 1 Corinthians 12:8-10. Men and women of God thus gifted by the Spirit (apostles, prophets, evangelists, pastors, and teachers are named) become God's gifts to the Church (Ephesians 4:11). The Holy Spirit gives detailed restrictions for the use of only one gift—speaking in tongues (1 Corinthians 12-13).

The Holy Spirit convicts the world, to regenerate and indwell those who trust in Christ, to baptize them into the Body of Christ, to seal them for the final day of redemption, to guide them into truth, to fill them for a life of holiness and victory and to empower them for witness and service. The Holy Spirit gives spiritual gifts to believers for the proper functioning of the Body of Christ, which is the Church.

To be sure, different ones of us minister [disciple] in different ways, according to our spiritual gifts; but all of us come to think together through holy conferencing for discernment of God's will for action plans according to each person's gift. Our offering Christ, appeals to some people who are spiritually thirsty, but not all will believe us if we give no evidence of knowing the living God ourselves or if our public worship (witness) or goodness lacks reality and relevance. The goodness must be supported with spiritual knowledge and godly wisdom from above.

3. <u>KNOWLEDGE SUPPORTED WITH SELF-CONTROL</u>

Let us consider knowledge or spiritual understanding or knowledge of the basic Christian faith.

Do you know what it means to be a Christian and a disciple?
A Christian is the one who personally answers the Jesus' question: "Who do you say that I am?" as Peter did: "You are the Son of God." A Christian is a believer in God, the Creator, who is enabled by the Holy Spirit to submit to Jesus Christ as Lord and Savior. Christians are called to follow Jesus Christ as the disciples and to live the life of God's kingdom. The disciples seek to become actively growing in Christ, so that we become participants in Christ's ministry of compassion for the hurting world.

Do you know what it meant by the gospel?
The gospel is the good news of the Creator's eternal plan to share his life and love with fallen human beings though the sending of his son Jesus Christ as the Savior of the world. The gospel centers on the life, death,

resurrection and return of Jesus and leads to a life of holiness, growth in grace and hope-filled, though costly, discipleship in the fellowship of the church. The gospel includes the announcement of Jesus' triumph over the powers of darkness and of his supreme lordship over the universe.

Do you know what is meant by salvation?
This word means rescue from guilt, defilement, spiritual blindness and deadness, alienation from God. This deliverance involves present justification, reconciliation to God and adoption into his family, with regeneration and the sanctifying gift of the Holy Spirit leading to discipleship and works of righteousness and service here and now, and a promise of full glorification in fellowship with God in the future. This involves in the present life joy, peace, freedom and the transformation of character and relationships and the guarantee of complete healing [wholeness] at the future resurrection of the body. We are saved by faith through the justifying grace and are spiritually growing toward wholeness or holiness through the help of the sanctifying grace for glory of God alone.

Do you know what is meant by growing toward spiritual maturity?
Believers are regenerated and spiritually born from above and become children of God and begin to live a new life in Christ toward spiritual maturity. As we are led by the Spirit, we grow in the knowledge of the Lord, freely keeping his commandments and endeavoring so to live in the world that all may see our good works and glorify our father who is in heaven.

Do you know what is meant by the kingdom of God?
The kingdom of God is his gracious rule through Jesus Christ over human lives, the course of history, and all reality. Jesus is Lord of past, present, and future, and Sovereign ruler of everything. The salvation Jesus brings and the community of faith he calls forth are signs of his

kingdom's presence here and now, though we wait for its complete ful-fillment when he comes again in glory. In the meantime, wherever Christ's standards of peace and justice are observed to any degree, to that degree the kingdom is anticipated, and to that extent God's ideal for human society is displayed.

Finally, ***Do you know about the consequences of knowledge without agape-love?***
St. Paul insists that knowledge should be wedded to agape-love: "And if I have prophetic powers, and understand all mysteries and all knowl-edge...but do not have love, I am nothing" (1 Corinthians 13:2).

The wonderful understanding of the above mentioned spiritual truth must be balanced with experiencing God's loving actions as I have emphasized in the book, "God of Active Verbs, A to Z." When we expe-rience God's love, we no longer search to find out "who am I?" Because we already have the answer: "I am *a beloved* child of God who frees me from my sense of shame and guilt by uplifting my self-worth."

When knowledge (Peterson interprets knowledge as "spiritual un-derstanding" in "the Message,") is married to agape-love in harmony, we have an unshakable foundation upon which we rest our Christian identity that nothing can shake. But if knowledge and love are divorced, knowledge cannot stand alone. Those who have the gift of knowledge, "but do not have love," must admit that "I am nothing."

Knowledge without agape-love makes the young conceited and the aged dictatorial. Knowledge without love makes skeptics, agnostics, and pessimists. Knowledge without love makes people hard, cold, proud, presumptuous, arrogant, self-conceited, self-centered, dogmatic, legal-istic, unapproachable, and incomplete. Loveless knowledge never con-verted anybody; never attracted anybody, and never comforted anybody.

It is unfortunate that our schools are not teaching moral values and character development. The children are exposed to casual sex and violence. There are hardly any good stories on television to teach young minds about the importance of mutual friendship and self-giving love. They lack the knowledge of how to resist the temptation of seeking material wealth, popularity, and power. Instead of the church's challenging the prevailing culture, the church has less and less impact on the world. We are deeply ashamed of the times when, both as individuals and in our faith communities, the Church, we have affirmed Christ in word only and denied him in deed. That's living a life lacking relevance and congruence.

Spiritual understanding and knowledge must be supported with self-control.

4. <u>SELF-CONTROL SUPPORTED WITH ENDURANCE</u>

We have experienced that we are profoundly habituated to a self-referenced way of being in the world. As long as we live in this fallen world and we allow the old habits of letting our ego run rampant in our lives, our behavior will never become complete. The inflated ego that used to develop psychologically repressed complexes (and not necessarily a sinful heart) is often the sources of misconduct and hypocritical behaviors of the false self. Therefore, we must tame our egos and we must control them, through the sanctifying grace of the Spirit, so that we may keep on moving toward the Christ-centered way of being in the world.

Self-control is required for moral formation; it is working those areas in which we still fall far short of what we know to be God's will for us. Self-control is about deepening our commitment to God in every aspect of our lives. It is not about the mindless observance of rules; it is about trusting God enough to purify us to become moral agents and instruments of God's activity in the world.

The Bishop Timothy W. Whitaker challenges the church by saying, "In our current era characterized by the violence of war and abortion, consumerism and economic exploitation, sexual abuse and permissiveness, and incivility, and hate crimes, the church has a responsibility and an opportunity to form Christian moral character and practices that save human lives from destruction and offer an alternative vision of what the world can become." (*The Church's Task of Moral Formation,* in Circuit Rider, 2005, 29(4): 4-5)

As John B. Cobb Jr. states, "The church emphasizes in helping people to feel good, but is the church effective in empowering people to be good moral agents?" St. Paul reminds us: "Work out [not work for] your own salvation with fear and trembling, for it is God who is at work in you, enabling you both to will and to work for his good pleasure." (*Grace and Responsibility: A Wesleyan Theology for Today,* p. 124)

Our challenge to others to deny themselves, take up their cross and follow Christ will be plausible only if we ourselves have evidently died to selfish ambition, dishonesty, and covetousness, and are living a godly life of simplicity, contentment, and generosity. We can overcome the bondage of sins and ego-driven passions and we can face the futility of life and fear of death because of the resurrection hope and eternal life.

Therefore, in addition to justification by faith in Christ, salvation also includes a gradual (not instant) process of sanctification that is our work of resisting the ego's influence in our life.

Self-control must be supported with endurance.

6. <u>ENDURANCE (ENDURING HOPE) SUPPORTED WITH GODLINESS</u>

Please refer to Chapter 8 for further insight on enduring hope.
In the midst of the pain and suffering in life, we endure because we believe in the "blessed hope of the glorious appearing of our great God and Savior, Jesus Christ" (Titus 2:13).

Enduring hope is born not from the absence of all that is harsh or sad, and it rises from the experience of both good and evil. We endure suffering and pain because they are limited on this side of grave. In that sense, all our sufferings are temporary. Pain, grief, tears, and death will not touch us on the other side of the grave.

Here is a story about a deceitful scorpion and a foolish turtle from *Sparkling Illustrations*. (Gaukroger and Mercer, p.43)

"A deceitful scorpion, being a poor swimmer, asked a foolish turtle to carry him on his back across a river. "Are you mad?" exclaimed the turtle. "You'll sting me while I'm swimming and I'll drown!" "My dear turtle," laughed the scorpion, "if I were to sting you, you would drown and I would go down with you! Now, where is the logic in that?" "You're right!" cried the turtle. "Hop on!" The scorpion climbed aboard and halfway cross the river he gave the turtle a mighty sting. As they both sank to the bottom, the turtle resignedly said, "Do you mind if I ask you something? You said there would be no logic in your stinging me. Why did you do it?"

"It had nothing to do with logic," the drowning scorpion replied, sadly. "It's just my character."

While the character of the scorpion caused its death along with that of the unwise turtle, the Christian character produces living hope of eternal life. In general character has nothing to do with logic: positive thinking will not change our character.

We are thankful for "God's love that has been poured into our hearts; for the hope of sharing the glory of God; for the knowledge that "*suffering* produces *endurance*, and endurance produces *character*, and character produce *hope*." As Paul assures us, this is a wonderful benefit for being a Christian.

"Therefore, since we have peace with God through our Lord Jesus Christ, through whom we have obtained access to this grace in which we stand; and we boast in our hope of sharing the glory of

God. And not only that, but we also boast in our sufferings, knowing that, and hope does not disappoint us, because God's love has been poured into our hearts through the Holy Spirit that has been given to us." (Romans 5:1-5).

We believe in the present ministry of the Holy Spirit by whose indwelling power the Christian is enabled to endure suffering because of the resurrection hope.

We must be prepared for many kinds of suffering, "for our struggle is not against enemies of blood and flesh, but against the rulers, against the rulers, against the authorities, against the cosmic powers of this present darkness, against the spiritual forces of evil in the heavenly places" (Ephesians 6:12). We need both watchfulness and discernment to safeguard the biblical Truth. We acknowledge that we ourselves are not immune to worldliness of thought and action, that is, sometimes we are tempted to be influenced by secular values of possession, popularity, and power. We have compromised our message, manipulated our hearers through the "prosperity gospel" and we have unduly preoccupied with statistics or even dishonest in our use of them. We are not of the world, but we are in the world, living as "the salt of the earth and the light of the world."

The risen Lord told his eleven disciples before his ascension: "Go therefore to make disciples of all nations, baptizing them in the name of the Father and of the Son and of the Holy Spirit, and teaching them to obey everything that I have commanded you. And remember, I am with you always, to the end of the age." (Matthew 28:19-20) So the Christian mission is an urgent one. We do not know how long we have. We certainly have no time to waste.

We can overcome the bondage of sins and ego-driven passions and we can face the futility of life and fear of death because of the resurrection hope and eternal life.

Our enduring hope must be supported with godliness or godly living. Please refer to Chapter 8.

6. GODLINESS SUPPORTED WITH MUTUAL AFFECTION

We are charged to behave in a manner that is worthy of the gospel of Christ, and even to "adorn" it, enhancing its beauty by holy lives. For the watching world rightly seeks evidence to substantiate the claims which Christ's disciples make for him, i.e., our caring affection for one another.

The sanctifying grace of the Spirit works within us through faith, renewing our fallen nature and leading us to spiritual maturity, that measure of development, which is meant by "the fullness of Christ" (Ephesians 4:13). We believe in the present and continuing ministry of sanctification by the Holy Spirit by whose infilling the committed Christians are cleansed and empowered for a life of holiness and service. The gospel calls us to live as obedient servants of Christ and as his emissaries (ambassadors) in the world, doing justice, loving kindness [compassion], and helping all in need, thus seeking to bear witness for the kingdom of Christ.

Nothing commends the gospel more eloquently than a transformed godly life, and nothing brings it into disrepute so much as personal inconsistency and in-congruency. Recently, the word *contemplative* entered my vocabulary, giving shape to the way I wanted to live my life. I used to be apprehensive with the word because I associated it with the kind of living in monasteries or in mountain retreats or in desert caves.

Then, I came across an article, *The Contemplative Christian: Transparent Lives,* written by Eugene H. Peterson, the author of the Message, a contemporary version of the Bible. That article inspired me that an authentic Christian life is one in which there is congruence between the truths asserted and the life lived, and congruence between ends and means. This is counter to most things the contemporary culture stand for. For instance, the situation ethic of "the ends justifies the means" or the post-modern philosophy of "anything goes."

The late Eugene H. Peterson wrote:

> "If there's a single word to identify the contemplative life, it is *congruence*—congruence between what we do and the way we do it…It is easier to talk about what Christians do, life performance, behavior appropriate to followers of Jesus codified in moral commandments and formulated in vision statements and mission strategies…It has always been more difficult to come to terms with Jesus as *the way* than with Jesus as *the truth*, more difficult to realize the ways our thinking and behavior get fused into a life of relational love and adoration with neighbor and God, God and neighbor…A contemplative life is the Christian life maturely lived, life in which Jesus is taken seriously as the way to live and truth to be lived by (John 14:6)." (Christian Century, November 29, 2003, pp. 20-27)

Godliness must be supported with mutual affection of "loving one another."

7. <u>MUTUAL AFFECTION SUPPORTED WITH</u> <u>*AGAPE*-LOVE</u>

We believe that God expects every believer to live a life of obedience, in which every area of our living is brought under the Lordship of Jesus Christ so that the indwelling Holy Spirit becomes increasingly evident in our Christian living. The goal of the Christian life is to be conformed to the image of Christ and to become actively growing disciples of Christ, who is the compassionate One. The Christian way of life according to compassion must be noticeably distinct from the worldly way of life according to competition. A wise person has said: "A friend is one who knows you as you are; one who understands where you have been; one who accepts who you have become and still invites you to grow."

Our commitment to the mutual affection of friendship must be: "I want to lead a life worthy of the calling to which I have been called, with all humility and gentleness, with patience, bearing one another in love, making every effort to maintain the unity of the Spirit in a bond of peace (Ephesians 4:1-3).

In a mature view of life, security and inner peace are grounded in the most important reality that we are "the beloved" through faith in Christ. As the beloved children of God, we have an authentic sense of self-worth by accepting God's valuation of us in place of the self-valuation, or the social-worth valuations of our culture or of others. God-given self-esteem liberates us *from* being a thing with relative values *to* a person with eternal value and infinite worth. It is based on our innate sacredness as human beings. We are God's image-bearers. Nothing in the world can ever make us question our self-esteem because nothing in the world can give it to us. It is created within us, an innate gift, and a permanent sacredness. This truth leads us to self-love with humility and humanity. Genuine love of self that is rooted in God's affirmation—God's prior love- must find expression in love of others. The two must be held together.

Jesus Christ who is the Rock of our faith gives a new commandment by saying,

> "I give you a new commandment, that you love one another. Just as I have loved you, you also should love one another. By this everyone will know that you are my disciples, if you have love for one another" (John 13:34-35).

This new commandment is different from the Ten Commandments where the first four commands are related to our loving relationships with God and the second six commands are related to our loving relationships with all human beings. The religious leaders of Judaism expanded the Ten Commandments to 613 laws and prohibitions, thus making them dogmatic and legalistic. I affirm that the Ten Commandments are about how to nurture our relationships with the God of the Bible and with our neighbors with innate sacredness.

The well-known *Parable of Good Samaritan* (Luke 10:25-35) illustrates God's wonderful principle of our living together with all human beings in peace and harmony in a hurting world. Because of his reverence and love toward God who created all human beings in God's own image, the Good Samaritan demonstrates the risk-taking, self-giving love for an unknown victim of a violent society.

By combining Deuteronomy 6:5 and Leviticus 19:18, Jesus puts this matter of our loving relationships with all God's created beings in another love commandment, a condensed version of the Ten Commandments: "You shall love the Lord your God with all your heart and with all your soul, and with all your strength, and with all your mind; and love your neighbor as yourself" (Luke 10:27).

This *love commandment* includes our love toward God with our whole being and our love toward the neighbors as we love ourselves. As mentioned earlier, our *self-love* is grounded in the God's valuation of us as the beloved children of God. Our love toward our neighbors is grounded in their innate sacredness of being created in God's image. Our love toward God is grounded in the truth that God proved his love by sending his only Son into the world as the Savior of the world. How do we love God?

We love God through worshipping and praising, trusting and obeying, pleasing and glorifying. The Prophet Micah expresses it so well when he writes, "Do justice; love kindness (or compassion); walk humbly with God" (Micah 6:8).

At the close of his ministry, Jesus considered his future death on
the cross. In his final hour, Jesus prepared his disciples for what was to
come. It was here that he made clear what would be the distinguishing
mark of the disciples.

> "Little children, I am with you only a little longer. You
> will look for me; and as I said to the Jews so now I say
> to you, where I am going, you cannot come. I give you
> a new commandment, that you love one another. Just as
> I have loved you, you also should love one another. By
> this everyone will know that you are my disciples, if you
> have love for one another" (John 13:33-35).

Francis A. Schaeffer comments on the above text:

> "This passage reveals the mark that Jesus gives to label a
> Christian not just in one era or in one locality, but at all
> times and in all places until Jesus returns...The condition-
> al clause, 'if you have love for one another,' is involved.
> If you obey, you will wear the badge Christ gives. But,
> since this is a command, it can be violated. The point is
> that it is possible to be a Christian without showing the
> mark, but if we expect non-Christians to know that we
> are Christians, we must show the mark." (Ibid, pp. 14-15)
> Schaeffer calls for the unity of the church:

> "The church is to be a loving church in a dying cul-
> ture. How, then, is the dying culture going to consider
> us? Jesus says, 'By this everyone will know that you
> are my disciples, if you love one another.' In the midst
> of the world, in the midst of our present dying culture,

Jesus gives the world the right to judge a Christian on the basis of the love we show to all other true Christians... Too often we have failed to show the beauty of authentic Christian love in unity. And the world has disregarded Christianity as a result...In his high priestly prayer to the Father (John 17:21) Jesus prays: 'They may be all in one...so that the world may believe that you have sent me.'... This Christian love and the unity it attests to, is the *mark of the Christian* to wear before the world so that the world may know and believe that Jesus was indeed sent by the Father." (Francis A. Schaeffer, *The Mark of the Christian,* pp. 22-25, 59)

The witness of every Christian is put in the context of mutual caring:

As Dietrich Bonheoffer, a theologian and a martyr of the Nazi, told us so many years ago: "In the presence of a psychiatrist I can only be a sick man [to be treated with empathy]; in the presence of a Christian [with mutual affection] I can dare to be a sinner...It is not lack of psychological knowledge but lack of love for the crucified Christ that makes us so poor and inefficient in brotherly confession."

In the new love commandment of "loving one another" is about mutual loving relationship among Christians even in the midst of our differences.

"For God so loved the world that he gave his only Son, so that everyone who believes in him may not perish but may have eternal life" (John 3:16).

Christian mutual love and unity must be supported with agape-love of God.

8 AGAPE-LOVE SUPPORTED WITH COMPASSION

Please refer to Chapter 8 for further insight on agape-love.

St. Paul defines: "agape-love is patient; love is kind; love is not envious or boastful or arrogant or rude. It does not insist on its own way; it is not irritable or resentful; it does not rejoice in wrongdoing, but rejoices in the truth. It bears all things, believes all things, hopes all things, and endures all things" (1 Corinthians 13:4-7).

There is an old story about a certain rich disciple who approached his Master, asking "How can I rightly related to God?"

The Master took the rich man before a **window**, "Look out this window," the Master instructed.

"What do you see?"

"I see the world," the rich man replied.

"What is it like?" the Master queried.

"I see people: a single mom working two jobs in order to feed her tiny child; an old man struggling with depression; a pregnant teenager confused and frightened about the future. And many others who have great need," the rich man replied.

The Master then instructed the rich man to turn around and face a **mirror** in the room.

"What do you see?" The Master again asked.

"A mirror," was the response.

"What does it show?"

"I see only myself," the rich man answered.

The Master concluded, "There are two kinds of windows we look through. When the window is clear, we see the world with all its suffering and needs. When silver is added to the glass of the window, it becomes mirror, and we see only ourselves. If we are to be rightly related to God, we must not let your vision of the world be obstructed by the wealth we possess."

A rich ruler came to see Jesus and asked him: "What must I do to inherit eternal life?" Jesus asked him to keep the commandments. The rich ruler told Jesus that he kept them since his youth. "When Jesus heard this, he said to him, 'There is one thing lacking, Sell all that you own and distribute the money to the poor, and you will have treasure in heaven, then come, follow me.' But when he heard this, he became sad; for he was very rich. Jesus looked at him and said, 'How hard it is for those who have wealth to enter the kingdom of God!'" (Luke 18:18-24)

Indeed, wealth, power, prestige, and high positions can be added to the windows of life that reflect only our self-interest and self-reliance, **not** other's suffering pain in the hurting world. The rich ruler was too rich to follow Jesus. If we want to be his disciple, our windows must be clear, so that we can see the suffering and needy people outside. Then we may become the disciples who participate in the Christ's ministry of compassion.

Our ministries of compassion rise out of our intimate relationship with Jesus Christ who alone is the compassionate One. We who have our identity "in Christ," will discover that *agape-love* is the gift of Christ who urges us to participate in his ministry of compassion.

THE PARABLE OF THE GOOD SAMARITAN

The Jesus' *parable of the Good Samaritan* (Luke 10:25-37) is the best illustration of our becoming participants in the Christ's ministry of compassion, motivated and propelled by agape-love. As the Samaritan ministered to the wounded person (possibly a Jewish man), we as Christians are called upon all who are suffering as neighbors, loving them as we love ourselves.

According to the story Jesus told, a man was going down the Jericho road. Whether he was a rich man or a poor man is not said. He was robbed and, because he resisted, he was beaten. Stripped of his clothes, he was left half dead alongside the road. Soon after the crime was committed, a priest came by on his way home to Jericho from Jerusalem. He took one look at the victim, and passed by on the other side. If he were riding a donkey, he did not even bother to get off. He denied the victim any help or hope. A little later, a Levite did exactly the same thing—one look and he went on.

Along came a merchant, whose clothes identified him as a Samaritan. He stopped and looked at the victim, helpless and laying in his own blood. The Samaritan was filled with compassion. If he had been in the victim's place, he too would have expected relief. He approached, and gently lifted the wounded man. He tore some linen into strips, applied oil and wine, and cleansed and bound up the man's wounds.

Then the Samaritan went the second mile, so to speak. He placed the man on his own donkey and, steadying him, brought him to the nearest inn. There he nursed him for the rest of night. With business pressing, he had to leave the wounded man the following day; but first he paid the innkeeper two silver coins and gave instructions to look after him. He told the innkeeper if more money was needed, he could simply charge it to the Samaritan, who would pay him on his return trip.

Jesus ended the story by asking, "Which of these three do you think was a neighbor to the man who fell into the hands of robbers?" The lawyer had to say, "the one who had mercy on him." In other words, the Samaritan proved to be brother to the wounded man. With the admonition, "Go and do likewise," Jesus dismissed the lawyer.

EXAMPLES OF BEING COMPASSIONATE

Following illustrations (#13 to #17) will provide us with practical ideas of "How one can be compassionate as the Good Samaritan.

ILLUSTRATION 13

There is a beautiful story about a young man in Milwaukee named Manuel Garcia. He had cancer, and the chemotherapy treatments caused his hair to fall out in patches. The patterns of fall-out were so strange and ugly that he decided just to shave his entire head. But he began to worrying and brooding over how he would look to his friends and others. When his brother Julio learned how upset Manuel was about his appearance, Julio shaved his own head and then enlisted the support of fifty friends and relatives who did the same thing. Soon, Manuel's hospital room looked like a convention suite for bald headed people. Those bald headed people understood "the Word (*logos*) became flesh and lived among us, and we have seen his glory, the glory as of a father's only son, full of grace and truth" (John 1:14).

ILLUSTRATION 14

The biblical scholar Carl Howie tells about an incident that took place in a New York
Subway. It was winter, and an especially cold and bitter night. Very few people were on the subway at that hour. At each station, the train would screech to a halt, open its doors, allowing a few people to come and go. At one station, a woman got on. Her clothes were ragged and dirty. She was either extremely tired or drunk. As the train lurched

forward, she stumbled and fell into a seat and went fast asleep. She was wearing two worn-out gloves with full of holes. Few people in the train could take their eyes off this homeless woman, asleep on the subway with her hands wearing gloves with holes.

Then, a strange thing happened. A young man got up to get off the train as it slowed to a stop. He could have gone out the exit closest to him, but he went by the sleeping woman instead. He paused by her for a few moments, removed his gloves, laid them on her lap, and got off the train.

ILLUSTRATION 15

This story tells about someone who took a huge risk for the sake of others willingly. Several years ago in the running of the Indi-500, a driver by the name of Al Unser went into an uncontrollable skid and hit the retaining wall. His car burst into flames, and Al Unser lay slumped in his burning car, not able to get out. Suddenly a second car driven by a man named Gary Bettenhausen, stopped next to the burning car and rushed to the car and pulled Al Unser from the flames.

Completely gone from Bettenhausen's mind was the thought of winning the race, or the money that had been invested or the time that had been given in preparation for him to be in the race—never mind the threat to his own life. All he could think of was trying to save Al Unser.

The key to the spiritual formation "for the sake of others" is the willing, self-giving spirit that limits our wants, our wishes, our dreams, our well-beings, and our desires; all for the betterment of others. This is what taking up our cross is all about. Jesus denied his own safety and security and life by not fleeing from the Garden of Gethsemane. He exemplified the way of sacrifice; the way of compassion; the way of obedience; the way of love for the sake of others.

ILLUSTRATION 16

In the 1985 Madrid marathon, 4000 runners began that great race. At the end, two runners who were very close friends were leading. Near the finish line, one of them was seized with terrible leg cramps and he could not finish the race in his own power. The other runner stopped and picked up his friend and they crossed the finish line together. This is what it means to be a true friend showing mutual affection.

ILLUSTRATION 17

Following is a beautiful dialogue between a young woman dying of AIDS and a caring lay minister in a hospital setting. (This story sermon copy is available from the Rev. James L. Henderschedt, Cedar Lutheran Church in Allentown, PA)

P designates a female patient;
M designates a caring lay minister.

P: "I am hot."

M: "I know. It's the fever. Just lie back while I put this cool cloth on your forehead."

P: "Your hand feels so good on my cheek."

M: "You're crying."

P: "It has been so long since I have felt the touch of someone's hand. Everybody in   the hospital always wear rubber gloves.

M: "People don't understand, and they are always afraid of things they don't understand."

P: "But you are not wearing gloves."

M: "Well, let's just say that if there is a risk, there are some risks that · need to be taken."

P: "You are very kind."

M: "It is nice of you to say so. I try to be. Sometimes, kindness is mis-
interpreted, though. Some people do not recognize when others are
following the whispering of their heart."

P: "It's ironic. Isn't it?"

M: "What is?"

P: "Well, you come to the hospital because you are sick and want
to get well and you leave in worse condition than when you were
admitted."

M: "Is that what happened to you?"

P: "Yes, I needed an operation. During the operation I needed a blood
transfusion. That was before anyone knew anything about AIDS.
Blood wasn't tested as thoroughly in those days. Just one pint, that's
all it took; and now, here I am."

M: "Are you angry?"

P: "No... Yes... I don't know. Whom should I be angry at? It's just that
there's so much I wanted to do. But I won't be able to do it. I'm dying. At least the doctors have been honest with me. It is just a matter
of time, and I don't think there is much of that left any more. I am
so tired. My body is burning, and yet I shiver with chills."

M: "It's the fever from the infection. Do you want more covers? Here,
let me put a fresh towel on your forehead."

P: "No, let it go. I'm okay. Just stay with me and talk to me."

M: "I'm here. I won't go away."

P: "I have a personal question. Do you mind?"

M: "No, not at all. What is it?"

P: "Are you married?"

M: "Yes, I am. I have a wonderful wife and two lovely children."

P: "Do you love your wife?"

M: "Very much."

P: "Does she love you?"

M: "Very much also."

P: "I always wanted to get married and have a couple of children."

M: "You were never married?"

P: "No…almost though. I was going with this guy. We were talking about getting engaged. But then, this happened."

M: "Did you love him?"

P: "Yes. I did. I wanted to be his wife, the mother of his children. But, things didn't work out that way. First, he told me he would be by my side all the way. But then the visits became fewer and fewer. I understand he married someone else last week."

M: "Is there anyone else?"

P: "No, I'm all alone… I am an only child and both parents are dead. I only have you."

M: "I'm very happy I can be here with you."

P: "Is it getting dark?"

M: "Is it getting dark for you?"

P: "Yes. It is. Tell me the truth. Has the sun gone behind some clouds? Is it close to   night?"

M: "No. It is not getting dark."

P: "Is this it? Is this how it is?"

M: "I don't know. What is it like?"

P: "I think I am going to be afraid."

M: "It's okay to be afraid."

P: "I don't even know your name?"

M: "Just call me Josh."

P: "Joshua? I like that name. Josh, Would you…Do you think your wife would mind…hold me?"

M: "I'm sure she would understand. Here, let me sit on the edge of the bed…There.
How's that?"

P: "That's fine. Thank you. Oh Josh. Can you hear that?

M: "What do you hear?"

P: "It's music…Beautiful music…The most beautiful music I have ever heard."

M: "It must be. You are radiant."

P: "You know, Josh… I don't think I'm going to be alone."

M: "No, I don't think you will be."

P: Oh, Josh. I want to go. Do you think it will be alright if I go? They are calling me. There is a light, and a path, and the music. Do you mind, Josh? Do you mind if I leave you?"

M: "No, I won't mind. I will stay here with you until you go."

P: "Will you keep holding me?"

M: "If you want me to."

P: "Please…Josh?"

M: "Yes?"

P: "Do you know what the name Joshua means?"

M: "I do."

P: "What does it mean?"

M: "It means…The Lord saves."

I would like to conclude my book by quoting Dr. Cecil G. Osborne:

"It is my present conviction, subject to change if new evidence is forthcoming, that growth is the meaning of life. We are here to grow. Mistakes are not fatal; they are a part of life and development. Whatever is beyond the curtain of death, it certainly must involve further improvement. For he [God], who brought us as innocent infants into an imperfect world and rejoiced [danced] over our birth, will surely not be content until we are mature and complete. The struggle to be more [like him]: love more, achieve more, and to become totally mature must go on into the infinite reaches of time until, without shame or

333

pride, we shall deem ourselves ready to unite with him
[God], the Pure Source of light and life." (Osborne, The
Art of Becoming a Whole Person, p.32)

As the actively growing disciples of Christ, let's celebrate this life
in the triune God by dancing with the Lord of the Dance in new rhythms
of God's love song (from The UMH, #261):

"I am the life that will never, never die;
I'll live in you, if you'll live in me;
I am the Lord of the Dance, said he.
Dance, then, wherever you may be;
I am the Lord of the Dance, said he.
And I'll <u>lead</u> you all wherever you may be,
And I'll <u>lead</u> you all in the dance, said he."

APPENDIX I

HUMAN RESPONSES TO GOD'S LOVING ACTIONS

HUMAN SYMPTOMS GOD'S ACTIVE VERBS HUMAN'S RESPONSES: ONE ANOTHER (OA)

HUMAN SYMPTOMS	GOD'S ACTIVE VERBS	HUMAN'S RESPONSES: ONE ANOTHER (OA)
Doubt God	assures us.	Live in peace with OA. (2 Corinthians 13:11)
Hoarding	God blesses us.	Be blessings to OA. (Genesis 12:2-3)
Anger/rebelling	God comes to us.	Self-giving love for OA. (John 13:34-35)
Temptation	God delivers us.	Do no harm to OA. (Hebrew 3:13)
Failures/troubles	God encourages us.	Encourage OA. (1 Thess. 4:18, 5:11)
Guilt or Shame	God forgives us.	Forgive OA (Ephesians 4:32)
Hungry/thirsty	God guides us.	Teach OA. (Colossians 3:16)
Crying for help	God hears/answers.	Bear OA's burden. (Ephesians 4:2; James 5:7)
Stressed/weary	God invites us.	Look out for OA. (Philippians 2:4)
Indulging/slothful	God judges fairly.	Not grumble against OA. (James 5:9)
Lonely/excluded	God knocks gently.	Be hospitable to OA. (1 Peter 4:9)
Confused/mixed up	God leads us.	Share experiences of God with OA.(1 Peter 2:19-21)
Brokenness	God makes us whole.	Pray for healing for OA (James 5:16)
Useless/fruitless	God nurtures us	Be kind to OA. (Eph. 4:31-32)
Lost/worthless	God offers salvation.	Accept OA unconditionally. (Rom.15:7; 14:1-4)
Crisis/misfortune	God provides us.	Care for OA. (1 Corinthians 12:24-25)
Bored/indifferent	God quickens us.	Do good works for OA. (2 Timothy 6:17-19)
Sinful/unlovable	God redeems us.	Honor OA. (Romans 12:10)
Ignorant/darkness	God speaks to us.	Speak truthfully to OA. (Ephesians 4:15)
Pretend/masking	God transforms us.	Be transparent to OA. (Colossians 3:9)
Fear/anxiety	God uplifts our souls.	Be devoted to OA. (Romans 12:10)
Criticized/accused	God vindicates us.	Live in harmony with OA. (1 Peter 3:8)
Suffering	God woos us.	Be gentle with OA. (Titus 3:2; James 4:13)
Lie/hypocrite	God X-rays our soul.	Be congruent to OA. (Ephesians 4:25)
Alienation	God yearns to reconcile us.	Be reconciled to OA (2 Corinthians 5:18-20)
Unhappy/insecure	God zips us up.	Joy of living in Christ to OA. (Col. 3:1-4)

APPENDIX II
TWO WORLDVIEWS:
ABUNDANCE VS. SCARCITY

1.	Scarcity in Resource	1 2 3 4 5 6 7 8 9 10	Abundance in Resource
2.	Hording	1 2 3 4 5 6 7 8 9 10	Sharing
3.	Harsh & Hostile	1 2 3 4 5 6 7 8 9 10	Benevolent/kindness
4.	Fearful	1 2 3 4 5 6 7 8 9 10	Confident
5.	Suspicious	1 2 3 4 5 6 7 8 9 10	Trusting
6.	Inadequate or No Risk	1 2 3 4 5 6 7 8 9 10	Adequate Risk Taking
7.	External Support	1 2 3 4 5 6 7 8 9 10	Internal Strength
8.	Dysfunctional Relations	1 2 3 4 5 6 7 8 9 10	Functional Relation
9.	Dependency	1 2 3 4 5 6 7 8 9 10	Inter-dependency
10.	Reactive Rescuer	1 2 3 4 5 6 7 8 9 10	Proactive Helper
11.	Sympathy	1 2 3 4 5 6 7 8 9 10	Empathy
12.	Permeable Boundary	1 2 3 4 5 6 7 8 9 10	Strong Boundary
13.	Judging Self & Others	1 2 3 4 5 6 7 8 9 10	Acceptance/tolerance
14.	Rigid/ Dogmatic	1 2 3 4 5 6 7 8 9 10	Flexible/ Open
15.	Ambiguous Identity	1 2 3 4 5 6 7 8 9 10	Self-esteem
16.	Status Quo/ No Change	1 2 3 4 5 6 7 8 9 10	Growth/ Change
17.	Negative Outlook	1 2 3 4 5 6 7 8 9 10	Positive Outlook
18.	Disconnected	1 2 3 4 5 6 7 8 9 10	Connected
19.	Alienated	1 2 3 4 5 6 7 8 9 10	Reconciled
20.	Broken Communication	1 2 3 4 5 6 7 8 9 10	Excellent Communication
21.	Competition	1 2 3 4 5 6 7 8 9 10	Compassion
22.	Apathy	1 2 3 4 5 6 7 8 9 10	Grace
23.	Vain-glory	1 2 3 4 5 6 7 8 9 10	Ego-less
24.	Pretension	1 2 3 4 5 6 7 8 9 10	Transparency
25.	Indifference	1 2 3 4 5 6 7 8 9 10	Vitality
26.	Bondage	1 2 3 4 5 6 7 8 9 10	Freedom
27.	Anxiety	1 2 3 4 5 6 7 8 9 10	Contentment
28.	Anger/Despair	1 2 3 4 5 6 7 8 9 10	Hope
29.	Doubt	1 2 3 4 5 6 7 8 9 10	Faith
30.	Guilt/Shame	1 2 3 4 5 6 7 8 9 10	Love

Please circle appropriate numbers (from 1 to 10) to find out your worldview.

Add all the numbers you circled. If your score is less than 150 points, this indicates that you have a negative view on life. In order to have a positive outlook on life, ask God to help you as you work on specific areas that were circled at 5 or less.

APPENDIX III
DEGREES OF INTEGRATION

This test is as accurate as you are able to give honest responses to the statements. When you have finished circling your responses, either *True* or *False*, go to page and read scoring instructions. (Osborne, *The Art of Becoming Whole Person*, p. 181)

1.	My mother gave me lots of love when I was small.	*False True*	*False True*
2.	I have a strong religious faith.	*False True*	*False True*
3.	I have no serious physical complaints.	*False True*	*False True*
4.	I have plenty of friends.	*False True*	*False True*
5.	I believe in life after death.	*False True*	*False True*
6.	I feel fulfilled most of the time.	*False True*	*False True*
7.	Most people can be trusted.	*False True*	*False True*
8.	I would like to have the will of God in my life.	*False True*	*False True*
9.	My friends seem to let me down.	*False True*	*False True*
10.	I have little or no difficulty giving compliments.	*False True*	*False True*
11.	Most of the time I am reasonably happy.	*False True*	*False True*
12.	I feel people are usually sincere when they compliment me.	*False True*	*False True*
13.	I felt loved by my father as a child.	*False True*	*False True*
14.	I am basically a very optimistic person.	*False True*	*False True*
21.	I very seldom feel tense and anxious.	*False True*	*False True*
22.	I have never done things, which I think are unforgivable.	*False True*	*False True*
23.	I seldom feel inferior to others.	*False True*	*False True*
24.	People tend to accept me quite readily.	*False True*	*False True*
25.	I don't mind being alone part of the time.	*False True*	*False True*
26.	I find it fairly easy to forgive slights and hurts.	*False True*	*False True*

Attention!

SCORING INSTRUCTION IS LOCATED AT PAGE 170.

APPENDIX IV
THE THREE INTELLIGENCE
CENTERS: THE TRIADS

THINKING CENTER FEELING CENTER INSTINCTIVE CENTER

	THINKING CENTER	FEELING CENTER	INSTINCTIVE CENTER
Body Organ (Function)	The Head (Thinking)	The Heart (Feeling)	The Gut (Doing/Willing)
Getting Information	Seeing & Reading	Tasting & Touching	Hearing & Smelling
Physique	Small	Medium	Large
Face	Cool/Long-Shape	Warm/Egg-shape	Serious/Tough
Focus in Need	Security (Strategy)	Attention (Self-Image)	Autonomy (Environment)
Work Decision (Let's think more.)	Why hurry? (Do I like him/her?)	Who's idea? (Let's do it now.)	I like the idea.
Talking Manner	Simple/Clear	Polite Words/Ask	Direct /Tell
Attitude (Open or Closed)	Passive (Introvert)	Active (Extrovert)	Egotistic (Both Ways)
Basic Desire (Temptation)	Lust (Possession)	Fame (Popularity)	Control (Power)
Facing Crisis solving	Problem Reaction	Emotional (Without Thinking)	Jumping In
Underlying Deep Issues	Insecurity & Anxiety	Identity & Hostility	Aggression & Repression
Blocks to Wellness	Fear/Doubt	Guilt/Shame	Anger/Rage
Remedy for Wellness	Providence of God	God's Uplifting Self-Worth	Receiving/Giving Forgiveness
Essential Quality	Faith	Love	Hope

APPENDIX V.
W.H.O.L.E.N.E.S.S

<u>W</u>ork of Faith: To admit that we are powerless sinners and that we are in need of Lord and Savior: to receive the power to become the children of God through the faith in the salvific work of Jesus Christ; to live in Christ as his beloved disciples.

<u>H</u>ealing (or Wellness): To identify some factors causing brokenness, imbalance, and disharmony; to seek proactive remedies for the identified obstacles; to consider the body-mind-spirit connection to achieve the holistic wellness.

<u>O</u>pening Our Souls to Experience God's Presence: to discipline to experience God in a variety ways in the ordinary as well as mystical encounters; to find the active Presence of God who reveals to us as the Creator, the Redeemer, and Sanctifier.

<u>L</u>abor of Love: To love God for himself alone and love him consistently without being religious; a healthy self-love, not vanity, generates healthy love of others; to give and receive love, with amused, friendly, tolerance; to listen to the problems of others with empathy, and to their good fortune without jealousy and envy.

<u>E</u>go-transcendent Living: to live without turmoil when we are free from ego's dominance; to have a sense of peace (it is called serenity) because our true self (or new self) makes daily decisions of our life, not allowing ego to dominate out life.

<u>N</u>urturing Discipleship: to become a part of the Body of Christ (the church) where believers are called and equipped (trained) to disciples who are empowered with different spiritual gifts for different ministries of the church.

Encouraging Sojourners toward Spiritual Maturity: to have various small
groups to support, sharing, and accountability; to encourage one another in answering God's call of witnessing to the reality of God's grace in
the world and calling all to receive it and live by it.

Steadfastness of hope: to overcome suffering and injustice with the resurrection hope and the eternal life; to face death without regret or fear, believing that the human caterpillar will become liberated butterfly in a
more glorious dimension of time and space.

Servant Ministry: to affirm the priesthood of all believers; to become participants for the coming of the God's Kingdom on earth through the
ministry of reconciliation and compassion for the lost, poor, needy, and
powerless in the hurting world.

SELECTED BIBLIOGRAPHY

Alexander, Donald L. Ed. *Christian Spirituality: Five Views of Sanctification.* Downers Grove, IL: InterVarsity Press, 1988.

Almas, A.H. *Essence: The Diamond Approach to Inner Realization.* York-Beach, Main: Samuel Weiser Co., 1986.

Alston, Wallace M. Jr. *Guides to the Reformed Tradition: The Church.* Atlanta: John Knox Press, 1984.

Arterburn, Stephen and Jack Felton. *Toxic Faith.* Nashville: Oliver-Nelson Books, 1991.

Arthur, Kay. *Learning to Embrace Life's Disappointments as Silver Refined.* ColoradoSprings, CO: Water Book Press, 2000.

Barna, George. *Growing True Disciples.* Ventura, CA: Issachar Resources, 2000.

Brown, Warren S. and Nancy Murphy, and H. Newton Maloney, Eds. *Whatever Happened to the Soul? : Scientific and Theological Portraits of Human Nature.* Minneapolis: Fortress Press, 1998.

Calhoun, Adele Ahlberg. *Spiritual Disciplines Handbook: Practices That Transform Us.* Downers Grove, IL: InterVarsity Press, 2005.

Calian, Carnegie Samuel. *Today's Pastor in Tomorrow's World.* Philadelphia: Westminster Press, 1982.

Chilcote, Wesley. *Recapturing the Wesley's' Vision.* Downers Grove, IL: InterVarsity Press, 2004.

Chilton, Floyd H. *WIN the War WITHIN: The Eating Plan that's Clinically Proven to Fight Inflammation—The Hidden Cause of Weight Gain and Chronic Disease.* New York: Rodale Inc., 2006.

Cho-Kim, Hakyung. *God of Active Verbs, A to Z.* N. Charleston, SC: Create Space 2012.

_____. *A Family Systems Approach to the Small Membership Church,* Pittsburgh: Pittsburgh Seminary Press, 1993.

Cobb, John B. Jr. *Grace and Responsibility: A Wesleyan Theology for Today,* Nashville: Abingdon Press, 1995.

Coleman, Lyman, Ed. *Whol-I-ness: Holy, Wholly, and Holey.* Littleton, CO: Serendipity House, 1994.

Crum, Thomas F. *The Magic of Conflict: Turning a Life of Work into a Work of Art.* New York: Simon Schuster, 1987.

Dulles, Avery. *Models of the Church,* Garden City, NY: Doubleday's & Co., 1974.

Dyer, Wayne W. *Your Sacred Self: Making the Decision to Be Free.* New York: Harper & Row Paperbacks, 1985.

Ellul, Jacque. *Living Faith: Belief and Doubs in a Perilous World.* San Francisco: Harper & Row, 1980.

Foster, Richard J. *Sanctuary of the Soul: Journey into Meditative Prayer.* Downers Grove, IL: InterVarsity Press, 2011.

Gaukroger, Stephen and Nick Mercer. *Sparkling Illustrations.* Grand Rapids, MI: Baker Books, 1997.

Gerkin, Charles V. *The Living Document.* Nashville: Abingdon Press, 1989.

Green, Joel B and Stuart L. Palmer, Eds. *In Search of the Soul: Four Views of the Mind-   Body Problem.* Downers Gove, IL: InterVarsity Press, 2005.

Hagberg, Janet O. and Robert A. Guelich. *The Critical Journey: Stages in the Life of Faith.* Dallas: Word Publishing, 1989.

Hunter, Victor : And Philip Johnson. *The Human Church in the Presence of Christ.* NY: Mercer University Press, 1985

Keating, Thomas. *Open Mind, Open Heart: The Contemplative Dimension of the Gospel.* New York: Continuum Pub., 2000.

Kelly, Tomas R. *A Testament of Devotion.* San Francisco: Harpers & Row, 1992.

Kemp, James W. *The Gospel According to Dr. Seuss.* Valley Forge: Judson Press, 2004.

Ketterman, Grace. *Surviving the Darkness.* Nashville: Thomas Nelson Publishers, 1993.

Knaster, Mirka. *Discovering the Body's Wisdom.* New York: Bantam Books, 1996.

Küng, Hans. *The Church.* New York: Shied and Ward, 1967Leech, Kenneth. *Soul Friend.* New York: Harper & Row, 1977.

Levey, Joel and Michelle Levey. *Living in Balance: A Dynamic Approach for Creating Harmony & Wholeness in a Chaotic World.* Berkeley, CA: Conri Press, 1998.

Lowen, Alexander. *Depression & the Body: The Biological Basis of Faith and Reality.* New York: Penguin Books, 1972.

Lucado, Max. *Just Like Jesus.* Nashville: Word Publishing, 1998.

_____. *Fearless: Imagine Your Life without Fear.* Nashville: Thomas Nelson, 2009.

McGrath, Alistair E. *Spirituality in an Age of Change: Rediscovering the Spirit of the Reformers.* Grand Rapids: Zondervan Pub., 1994.

McMinn, Mark R. and Timothy R. Phillips, Eds. *Care for the Soul: Exploring the Intersection of Psychology and Theology.* Downers, IL: InterVarsity Press. 2001.

May, Gerald G. *Will and the Spirit: A Contemplative Psychology.* New York: Harper & Row, 1983.

Merrell, Woodson and Kathleen Merrell. *Power Up: Unleash Your Natural Energy, Revitalize Your Health, and Feel 10 Years Younger.* New York: Free Press, 2008.

Michael, Chester P. and Marie C. Norrisey. *Prayer and Temperament: Different Prayer Forms for Different Personality Types.* Charlottesville: The Open Door, Inc., 1991.

Moreland, J.P. and Scott B. Rae. *Body & Soul: Human Nature and the Crisis in Ethics.* Downers Grove, IL: InterVarsity Press, 2000.

Moreland, J.P. and Klaus Issler. *In Search of Confident Faith: Overcoming Barriers to Trusting in God.* Downers Grove, IL: IVP Books, 2008.

Mulholland, Jr., M. Robert. *Invitation to a Journey: A Road Map for Spiritual Formation.* Downers Grove, IL: InterVarsity Press, 1993.

_____. *The Deeper Journey: The Spirituality of Discovering Your True Self.* Downers Grove, IL: InterVarsity Press, 2006.

Niebuhr, Reinhold. *Leaves from the Notebook of a Tamed Cynic.* Louisville, KY: John knocks Press, 1957.

Nouwen, Henri J.M. *Life of the Beloved: Spiritual Living in a Secular World.* New York: The Crossroad Publ., 1992.

Oden, Thomas C. *THE LIVING GOD: Systemic Theology, Vol. One.* San Francisco: Harper & Row, 1987.

Ogden, Greg. *Discipleship Essentials: A Guide to Building Your Life in Christ.* Downer Groves, IL: InterVarsity Press, 1998.

_____. *Transforming Discipleship: Making Disciples a Few at a Time.* DownersGroves, IL: Intervarsity Press, 2003.

Osborne, Cecil G. *The Art of Becoming a Whole Person.* Waco, TX: Word Publishing, 1978.

Packer, J.I. and Thomas C. Oden. *One Faith*, Downers Grove, IL: InterVarsity Press, 2004.

Peace, Richard. *Noticing God.* Downers, IL: InterVarsity Press, 2012.

Peck, M. Scott. *The Road Less Traveled.* New York: Simon Schuster, 1978.

Peterson, Eugene H. *The Contemplative Christian: Transparent Lives.* Christian Century: November 29, 2003.

Prichard, Ray. *The Healing Power of Forgiveness.* Eugene, OR: Harvest House Pub., 2005.

Pruyser, Paul W. *The Minister As Diagnostician.* Philadelphia: Westminster Press, 1976.

Purves, Andrew. *The Search for Compassion: spirituality and Ministry*: Louisville: Westminster/John Knox Press, 1989.

Riso, Don Richard. *Enneagram Transformations.* Boston: Houghton Mifflin. 1993.

Riso, Don Richard and Russ Hudson. *The Wisdom of the Enneagram: The Complete Guide to Psychological and Spiritual Growth for the Nine Personality Types.* New York: Bantam Books, 1990.

_____. *Understanding the Enneagram: The Practical Guide to Personality Type.*

Boston: Houghton Mifflin, 2000

Rooney, E. Gene. *Listening with the Mind's Inner Ear: The Value of Metaphors in Forming and developing Belief-Systems and Attitudes.* Reynoldsburg, OH: Lead Consultants, 1991.

_____. *Metaphors for Metamorphosis: The Power of Metaphors and Personal Story.* Reynoldsburg, OH: Lead Consultants, 1992.

_____. *Amphorae: Metaphoric Techniques for Understanding, Enhancing, and Improving Your Self-Image.* Reynoldsburg, OH: Lead Consultants, 1993.

Salmansohn, Karen. *How to Be Happy: A Cynic's Guide to Spiritual Happiness,* Berkeley: Celestial Arts, 2001.

Scanlan, Michael. *Inner Healing: Ministering to the Human Spirit through the Power of Prayer.* New York: Paulist Press, 1974.

Schaeffer, Francis A. *The Mark of the Christian,* Downers Grove, IL: IVP Books, 1970.

Schwarz, Christian A. *Natural Church Development,* St. Charles, IL: Church Smart Resources, 1996.

Stahl, Carolyn. *Opening to God: Guided Imagery Meditation on Scripture*. Nashville:The Upper Room, 1977.

Stevens, Jose. *Transforming Your Dragons: How to Turn Fear Patterns into Personal Power*. Santa Fe, NM: Bear & Company Publishing, 1994.

Tournier, Paul. *The Whole Person in a Broken World*. New York: Harper & Row, 1977

The United Methodist HYMNAL [The UMH]: *Book of United Methodist Worship*. Nashville: The United Methodist Publishing House, 1989.

_____. *The Faith We Sing*. Nashville: Abingdon Press, 2000.

Rick Warren. *The Purpose-Driven Life*. Grand Rapids: MI, Zondervan, 1997.

Watts, Alan. *The Meaning of Happiness: The Quest for Freedom of the Spirit in Modern Psychology and the Wisdom of the East*. New York: Harper & Row, 1979.

Weil, Andrew. *Spontaneous Healing: How to Discover and Enhance Your Body's Natural Ability to Maintain and Heal Itself*. New York: Alfred A. Knopf, Inc., 1995.

Willard, Dallas. *The Spirit of the Disciplines: Understanding How God Changes Lives*. San Francisco, CA: Harper & Row, 2006.

Zodhiates, Spiro. *To Love is to Live*. Grand Rapids: Erdmann Publishing Co. 1967.